CHICAGO STUDIES IN THE HISTORY OF AMERICAN RELIGION

Editors

JERALD C. BRAUER

AND MARTIN E. MARTY

A CARLSON PUBLISHING SERIES

For a complete listing of the titles in this series,
please see the back of this book.

An African-American Exodus

THE SEGREGATION OF THE SOUTHERN CHURCHES

Katharine L. Dvorak

PREFACE BY JERALD C. BRAUER

CARLSON
Publishing Inc

BROOKLYN, NEW YORK, 1991

Please see the end of this volume for a listing of all the titles in the Carlson Publishing Series *Chicago Studies in the History of American Religion*, edited by Jerald C. Brauer and Martin E. Marty, of which this is Volume 4.

Dvorak, Katharine L., 1942-
    An African-American exodus: the segregation of the southern churches / Katharine L. Dvorak; preface by Jerald C. Brauer.
        p.   cm. — (Chicago studies in the history of American religion; 4)
    Includes bibliographical references and index.
    ISBN 0-926019-25-2
    1. Afro-American Methodists—History—19th century—Southern States. 2. Black theology—History of doctrines—19th century. 3. Afro-Americans—Religion. 4. Southern States—Church history—19th century. 5. Segregation—United States—Religious aspects. 6. Methodist Church—History—19th century—Southern States. 7. Methodist Episcopal Church, South—History—19th century. 8. Colored Methodist Episcopal Church—History—19th century. 9. African Methodist Episcopal Church—History—19th century.   I. Title. II. Series
BX8435.D96   1991
287.875′09034—dc20   90-23383

Typographic design: Julian Waters
Typeface: Bitstream ITC Galliard
Case design: Allison Lew
Index prepared by Jonathan M. Butler
Printed on acid-free, 250-year-life paper.
Manufactured in the United States of America.

Contents

An Introduction
to the Series

The Chicago Studies in American Religion is a series of books which deals with topics ranging from the time of Jonathan Edwards to the 1970s. Three or four deal with colonial topics and three or four treat the very recent past. About half of them focus on the decades just before and after 1900. One deals with blacks; two concentrate on women. Revivalists, fundamentalists, theologians, life in the suburbs and life in heaven and hell, the Beecher family of old and a monk of new times, Catholics adapting to America and Protestants fighting each other—all these subjects assure that the series has scope. People of every kind of taste and curiosity about American religion will find some books to suit them. Does anything serve to characterize the series as a whole? What does the stamp of "Chicago studies" mean?

Yale historian Sydney Ahlstrom, in *A Religious History of the American People*, as influential as any 20th century work in its field, pays respect to the "Chicago School" of American religious historians. William Warren Sweet, the pioneer in such studies (beginning in 1927) at Chicago and, in many ways, in America at large represented the culmination of "the Protestant synthesis" in this field. Ahlstrom went on to name two later generations of Chicagoans, including the seminal Sidney E. Mead and major figures like Robert T. Handy and Winthrop Hudson, and ending with the two editors of this series. He saw them as often "openly rebellious" in respect to Sweet and his synthesis.

If, as Ahlstrom says, "a disproportionate number" of historians have some connection with the Chicago School, it must be said that the new generation represented in these twenty-one books carries on both the lineage of Sweet and something of the "openly rebellious" character that scholars at Chicago are encouraged to pursue. This means, for one thing, that the "Protestant synthesis" does not characterize the work. These historians question the canon of historical writing produced in the Protestant era even as many of them continue to pursue themes shaped in a Protestant culture. Few of them concentrate on the old "frontier thesis" that marked the early years of the school. The shift for most has been toward the urban and pluralist scene. They call into question, not in devastating rage but in steady patterns of inquiry, the received wisdom about who matters, and why, in American religion.

So it is that this series of books focuses on blacks, women, dispensationalists, suburbanites, members of "marginal" denominations, "ethnics" and immigrants, as readily as it does on white men of progressive urban bent in mainstream denominations and of long standing in America. The authors relish religious diversity and enjoy discovering the power of people once considered weak, the centrality to the American plot of those once regarded as peripheral, and the potency of losers who were once disdained by winners. Thus this series enhances an understanding of an America overlooked by the people of Sweet's era two thirds of a century ago when it all, or most of it, began.

Rebellion for its own sake would not long hold interest; it might tell more about the psychology of rebels and revisers than about their subject matter. Revision, better than rebellion, characterizes the scholars. Re + vision: that's it. There was an original vision which characterized the Chicago School. This was the contention that in secular America and its universities religion mattered, as a theme in the national past and as a presence in the present. Secondly, it argued that the study of religious history belonged not only in the seminaries and archives of denominations, but in the rough and tumble of the secular university, where no religious meanings were privileged and where each historian had to make a case for the value of his or her story.

Other assumptions from the earliest days pervade the books in this series. They are uncommonly alert to the environment in which expressions of faith occur. That is, they do not take for granted that religion comes protected in self-evidently important and hermetically sealed packages. Churches and denominations are porous, even when they would be sealed off; they cannot be understood apart from the ways the social environs effect them, but their power to effect change in the environment demands equal and truly unapologetic treatment. These writers do not shuffle and mumble and make excuses for their existence or for the choice of apparently arcane subject matter. They try to present their narrative in such ways that they compel attention.

A fourth characteristic which colors these works is a refusal in most cases to be typed in a fashionable slot labeled, variously, "intellectual" or "institutional" history, "cultural" or "social" history, or whatever. While those which concentrate on magisterial thinkers such as Jonathan Edwards are necessarily busy with and devoted to his intellectual achievement, most of the books deal with figures who cannot be understood only as exemplars in a sequence of studies of "the life of the mind." Instead, their biographies and circumstances come very much into play. On the other hand, none of these writers is a reductionist who sees religion as "nothing but" this or that—"nothing but" the working out of believers' Oedipal urges or expressing the economic and class interests of the subjects. Social history becomes in its way intellectual history, even if the intellects are focused on something other than the theologians in the traditions might like to see.

Some years ago *Look* magazine interviewed leaders in various denominations. One was asked if his fellow believers considered that theirs was the only true faith. Yes, he said, but they did not believe that they were the only ones who held it. The editors of this series of studies and the contributors to it do not believe that the "Chicago School," whenever and whatever it was, is the only true approach to American religious history. And, if they did, they would not hold that Chicagoans alone held it. To do so would imply a strange solipsistic or narcissistic impulse which would be the death of collegiality in the historical field. They have welcomed the chance to be in a climate where their inquiries are given such encouragement, where they find a company of fellow scholars in the Divinity School, the History Department, and the Committee on the History of Culture, whence these studies first emerged, and elsewhere in a university which provides a congenial home for massed and massive concentration of a special sort on American religious history.

While the undersigned have been consistently involved, most often together, in all twenty-one books, we want to single out a third name mentioned in so many "Acknowledgment" sections, historian Arthur Mann. He has been a partner in two or three dozen religious history dissertation projects through the years, and has been not only an influential but decisive contributor to the results, and we stand in his debt.

Jerald C. Brauer
Martin E. Marty

Editor's Preface

Probably the most vital and dynamic expression of Christianity in the United States is that exemplified by the black churches. They manage to retain the loyalty and participation of their people to a much higher degree than do their white counterparts. A number of years ago, a distinguished visiting German theologian was asked to preach at and participate in the worship service of a large black church in Chicago. After the service, he was almost ecstatic in praise. He had never before, anywhere in the world, worshipped with a community that exhibited such genuine fervor and commitment. He commented on the tragedy that the white churches had thrown out and excluded their black brethren so that segregation undercut a true Christian community that ought to encompass black and white together.

During the civil rights movement of the 1950s and 1960s, it was discovered that the black churches were a deep reservoir of a drive for justice and equality that embodies the purest principles of the American Constitution. Martin Luther King, Jr. was a symbol of the quality and courage of leadership exemplified by the black Christian community. It was clear that without black Christianity, there would have been no civil rights movement in the United States. Further, it became evident to many that the black churches were calling on Americans to live up to their true nature. In the process of affirming their own rights, black Christians were giving white Americans an opportunity properly to understand and to live out their true rights. A new birth of freedom for *all* Americans is what the black churches were offering.

Much was made of the fact that the hours of 10 A.M. to 12 noon every Sunday were the most segregated period of time in American culture. Even though blacks were segregated in restrooms, in public transportation, and in schools, they mingled in white society at most other points. But on Sunday morning, *all* relations between whites and blacks were severed. That was not always true in American Christianity. In the antebellum South, black and white worshipped together at the same churches. To be sure, they may have sat separately within the church building, but they were under the same roof, sang the same hymns, heard the same word preached, underwent similar conversion experiences, and belonged to the same Christian community. If the whites had not ejected blacks from the churches, the Christian community would not have become segregated. Ecclesiastical segregation was viewed as but one more aspect of the segregation that proceeded apace throughout American life in the post-Civil War period. It was but one more dimension of the Jim Crow laws and customs that marked so much of American society until recent years.

Now this interpretation is being questioned. Katharine Dvorak presents us with overwhelming evidence through a profoundly sympathetic understanding of the black churches that enables us to understand why the black churches voluntarily withdrew from communion with the white churches and established their own organizations. Segregation within the Christian communities is not to be understood as a part of the Jim Crow developments. Nor is it to be understood as an aspect of black racism. Rather, Dvorak convincingly argues that the dynamic for black withdrawal from white churches is rooted and grounded in a deep religious experience that leads to their wholeness or salvation as black human beings.

Dvorak confronts three fundamental problems and deals equitably with each. She is primarily concerned about the process whereby blacks withdrew from white ecclesiastical organizations and developed their own. She then moves on to ask what kind of religious communities the blacks constructed as a result of their withdrawal. Finally, she raises a number of interesting and pertinent questions on the significance of this withdrawal for both the white churches and the black churches. She argues that the question of significance is as important today for our self-understanding as it was when the black churches were founded.

Though this is a historical study, Dvorak draws on sociological theory concerning group boundaries in order to explicate the process of separation. She finds Max Weber and Edward Shils particularly helpful in elucidating this process. If blacks once were a part of white ecclesiastical communities, exactly how did they function as a part? What were the patterns of exclusion and participation present prior to the separation? Were there dynamics of self-separation already at work among black Christians within white Christian communities? In order to answer these questions, Dvorak focuses her attention on the Methodists in the Southern states. In contrast to Baptist polity, which is amorphous and rigorously centered in the independence of each local congregation, Methodism has a distinct, highly organized, and centralized polity and organization. To study how the blacks separated from such an organization enables one correctly to analyze the process of separation. Dvorak thinks that what happened in Southern Methodism provides a paradigm for the larger problem of the separation of blacks from whites in the total Christian community in the South.

A particular strength of her work is the attention paid to the liturgical dimension of religious experience as a means of understanding the social dynamics of a group. By its very nature, liturgical practice is essentially conservative; nevertheless, the way a group expresses its religious experience in worship and sacramental life frequently tells more about it than does theological doctrine. Close attention to the style of preaching developed in the black communities, the use and interpretation of the sacraments, the nature and form of prayers, and the genius of revivalistic black hymnology all help to explain both the push toward black separatism and the consequences for the nature of religion found in the subsequent black communities. Dvorak's study positions us to appreciate the emergence, the nature, and the role of black Protestant Christian groups in American life.

Jerald C. Brauer

Foreword

The problem of the exodus—the segregation of the southern churches—came to my attention on a rainy June afternoon. I pored over the official annual proceedings of the Southern Baptist Convention and puzzled: Why had white Baptists expressed so much hurt and regret over newly separate congregations and denominations for whites and blacks when later they affirmed that such arrangements were most desirable and "natural"? The data contradicted my unexamined assumption that the same forces that led to segregated public accommodations in the South also had influenced the religious separation of blacks and whites. Just how and why had the segregation of the southern churches occurred?

I first attempted to explain the exodus in a study submitted to Martin Marty and Edward Shils. Mr. Shils commented in part, "You must remember that you are discussing religion and not just politics." He reminded me that I was dealing with "above all religious beliefs and institutions with a vitality of their own. Do not forget this."

This volume is a product of my re-examination of the problem with Mr. Shils's admonitions in mind. It has benefited greatly from my work and conversations with him. My studies of revivalism under Jerald Brauer were indispensable for understanding the religious character of the southern churches. Mr. Brauer also helped me shape the case study approach to the problem. Martin Marty has provided unflagging encouragement, beginning with his first bibliographical suggestions and including his wide-ranging criticisms and insights, which have improved both the substance and the style of this work.

John Hope Franklin guided me to crucial historical insights concerning chronology and context, without which this book would not exist. I would not have begun to study religion and society in the American South without the urging of Rosemary Scola and the guidance of Russell Barta; I could not have continued it without the support of family and friends, especially Lynda Byrd and Myra Mattress. I am grateful to these individuals and to many more who contributed to the completion of this project. At the same time I remind myself that my work has only begun.

This volume stresses the indigenous nature of religious development among African-Americans in the South. Such emphasis counters a common assumption that the earlier, northern pattern was normative for and prescriptive of the segregation of the southern churches. I am grateful to John Hope Franklin for pressing, from the start, the issue of northern influence, ensuring continual alertness to that possibility and, in the end, this assessment of the priority of indigenous religious experience and indigenous black religious leadership over northern influence in the segregation of the southern churches.

Due to this work's concern with indigenous southern developments, northern materials are not extensively cited. However, such materials— denominational newspapers, for example—strengthen the case for the thesis by revealing the limited extent of direct northern influence on southern black Methodists' process of self-separation from the Methodist Episcopal Church, South. Northern materials do not support the notion that the southern exodus simply copied the northern pattern of separation in which rejection of discrimination by whites was the driving force in the creation of independent black denominations. A detailed exposition of the evidence in northern documentation, especially the African Methodist Episcopal *Christian Recorder*, will further substantiate the thesis argued here. Because it was not feasible to integrate that discussion into this book, the reader is encouraged to look for it in article form soon.

This volume is being published in a time of great ferment in race relations in the United States. Awareness of how the segregation of the churches came about—in the region where ninety percent of African-Americans lived prior to World War I—brings respect and appreciation for their distinctive appropriation of Christianity. It is my hope that the historical insights presented in the book will contribute to progress toward equality and justice for all Americans.

An African-American Exodus

ONE

Egypt

More than a hundred years after southern black Christians began to worship separately from white Christians in their own denominations, historians have not determined how and why the separation took place. Joint worship was the predominant pattern for Christians in the American South before the Civil War. While slaves and free Negroes generally sat in designated areas and often partook of the Lord's Supper after whites, antebellum Christians shared the same ritual meal and the same denominational structures. Then, suddenly, this pattern of joint worship changed to one of virtually total racial separation in less than ten years after the Civil War.

Historians have devoted surprisingly little attention to this dramatic happening. Discussions subscribe to several combinations of suppositions and conclusions. Among these, three explanations predominate. First, several scholars attribute separation to white pressure on blacks to leave. Yet the evidence shows that whites were ambivalent at first; pressure is apparent only after blacks' initial exodus. Second, many historians explain the exodus by stressing blacks' lack of equal status and opportunities to participate as members in the traditional denominations. However, since both blacks and whites had used religion to control one another in slavery times, one must ask whether status and participation by themselves seemed sufficient compensation for loss of control for either group. Third, a number of historians affirm that blacks wanted their own churches. But their various accounts of black motivation range from simple declaration that blacks desired separation to problematic descriptions of black Christians as reactors to outside initiatives and events.

It is clear that these explanations taken together do not adequately account for what happened. The deficiency is understandable. For one thing, separation occurred during that intensely debated postwar period that included Reconstruction. Historiographical controversy has tended to obscure the evidence. In addition, there is the tendency to superimpose present concerns and perspectives on the past. For example, concern about the phenomenon of racial segregation has tended to obscure the various dimensions and

1

implications of what took place; a white-over-black perspective on power relationships has made difficult an accurate assessment of nineteenth-century black power, inclining scholars to view events as products of white motivation and muscle. However, a fresh look at the data and the documents combined with questions and modes of inquiry generated in sociology promises a more adequate picture of this decisive event in the South's religious history.

Historians Eugene Genovese, Donald Mathews, Milton Sernett, and Albert Raboteau have described the development of the predominant pattern of joint worship over separatist exceptions in the antebellum South.[1] Rufus B. Spain, John Lee Eighmy, H. Shelton Smith, David Reimers, and others have discussed developments in white Prostestanism in the later nineteenth century.[2] But we lack a detailed treatment of the turning point—the exodus of blacks from southern churches between 1861 and 1871. Scholars estimate that two-thirds or more of black church members had left Baptist, Methodist, Presbyterian, and other denominations as early as 1866. With the formation of the Colored Methodist Episcopal Church out of remaining black Methodists in 1871, all but a small fraction of black Christians in the South had separated from now white denominations. Blacks formed churches that were ritually and structurally distinct from white congregations and denominations. The pattern of ritual commensality (table fellowship), with its implications for religious and political ties, was dramatically altered.

It is my thesis that the driving force in the segregation of the southern churches was the black Christians' surge toward self-separation acting on their own distinctive appropriation of Christianity. What they did, said, sang, preached, wrote, and prayed during the period shows that black Christians were not helpless victims of events but rather executors of the religious legacy earned in their forebears' and their own Christian experience. The story of separation shows that in the chaos of ambivalent white pressures, denominational competition, and social confusion of the period, black initiative was decisive in the emergence of a pattern of racial separation in the southern churches.

To prevent distortion caused by present concerns and perspectives, a detailed account of this chosen pattern of separation must make careful note of its proper religious, social, and political context. Right after the Civil War racial separation had a different meaning and different implications in the South from what is suggested by the subsequent Jim Crow laws and segregation strategies fashioned by whites. Establishing the fact of black self-separation from white churches in no way justifies or excuses later injustices.

The pages that follow reflect a combination of historical critical inquiry and narrative with sociological theory. Historical data were drawn from many sources, including those produced by black Christians themselves: letters, narratives, autobiographies, biographies, sermons, songs, and records of black churches and denominations. Other sources gave oblique witness to the initiative of black Christians—for example, denominational records written by whites expressing surprise and either regret or ambivalence at the sudden departure of blacks. These records, accounts in denominational papers and the "secular" press, and other reports by white observers complement data from black sources.

The sociological character and implications of the thesis demand methodological care. One can demonstrate the fact of self-separation best by showing how it took place in a large and representative southern denomination. For this reason, the study focused on the Methodists. Both negative and positive considerations dictated this focus.

Negatively considered, it is unnecessary to tell the story of separation as it occurred in every denomination in every state in the South. Before the Civil War, almost all black Christians with denominational affiliations belonged to the Methodist and Baptist bodies. Documents relating to Baptist Christianity in the South reflect characteristically independent Baptist congregational polity and a less systematic philosophy of record keeping. Moreover, though the story of separation appears the same among Baptists, their polity's fissiparous tendency renders analysis of separation among Baptists alone a less effective demonstration of the thesis.

Positively considered, in the Methodists' connectional polity the separation of black from white Christians stands out in bold relief. Indeed, unlike Southern Baptists, white Methodists in the South reunited with the northern church in 1939, a tardy but still clear indicator of Methodists' historical orientation toward unity. In addition, Methodism's antebellum work among free Negroes and slaves produced a sizable, representative group of black Methodist Christians. Methodism was representative of southern religion by virtue of its size, composition, and revivalistic Protestant character. Moreover, because northern Methodist bodies, black and white, were active during the period, focus on Methodism facilitates a fuller accounting for all of the forces operative in the period. Finally, Methodist documentation tends to be plentiful and more systematic than that of other denominations.

With Methodism selected for case study, new tools were necessary to cut away the obscurities and misinterpretations caused by historiographical

3

controversy and by the imposition of present concerns and perspectives. For this reason, my historical critical inquiry into the sources employed sociological theory about group boundaries—patterns of exclusion and participation. The theory guided inquiry and pointed to conclusions. It is derived from the works of Max Weber, especially *Ancient Judaism* and *The Religion of India*. In these works Weber described the development of distinctive hereditary social groups that lacked autonomous political organization and were bound by prohibitions against commensality and intermarriage. All such groups were self-separating. All understood their boundaries to have religious significance. In the case of India, a social system ("caste" system) of mutually self-separating groups of this type developed. In both cases, the presence or absence of ritual barriers to sharing a meal was important, both sociologically and religiously.[3]

Weber frequently pointed out the role of the ritual meal for early Christianity: Jewish and non-Jewish Christians shared the Eucharist together; commensality forged religious and political ties.[4] In American Christianity, not religious bonds but rather boundaries predominate. Americans view their churches as discrete, often competing organizations rather than as cells in a larger, inclusive body. Boundaries determine one's religious location within or without each denomination. Ordinarily, denominations express patterns of exclusion and participation by admission of persons to the central Christian rite as appropriated in denominational tradition. Historians and analysts of the American South's social structure frequently talk of "caste" as characteristic of post-Civil War southern race relations. But to my knowledge, no one has investigated whether racial boundaries in the South were related to religious separation, especially self-separating groups. Segregation at the Lord's Table existed long before Jim Crow's lunch counter.

Weber's theory directs attention first to the need for rigorous inquiry into the possibility of self-separation. Attention to precisely when separation occurred and specifically whose initiative was the driving force in this change enables one to untangle the segregation of the southern churches from other patterns of exclusion and participation that developed in the post-Civil War South. It also leads to conclusions about the implications of altered religious boundaries for the religious tradition and the social system as well. A discussion of the significance of the new patterns of exclusion and participation for the South in the early 1870s concludes this study, even though the inquiry points beyond itself.

In 1906, when over ninety percent of southern Christians belonged to Baptist and Methodist denominations, an overwhelming majority of southern

Christians worshipped in racially separated congregations.[5] These statistics underline the importance of a detailed accounting for a pattern of racially separated religious fellowship. Analysis of this fundamental event is indispensable for understanding the relationship of religion and society in the American South in every period after the Civil War, including our own time, when racially separate worship is widely practiced but rarely scrutinized.

I have substantiated my thesis by showing in a case study that black Methodists' own self-separation from the parent Methodist Episcopal Church, South, was the driving force in the segregation of southern Methodism, a movement by black Methodists acting on their own distinctive appropriation of Christianity. The story begins amid the patterns of exclusion and participation of the South—Egypt—in the 1850s and amid the pervasive religious atmosphere of southern revivalism.

Southern Revivalism

Revivalism is that mode of becoming and remaining Christian which stresses conversion as the central response both to the human condition and to sacrality itself.[6] Revivalism had dominated southern religiosity at least since the Second Great Awakening at the turn of the nineteenth century. By the 1850s it was entrenched in the traditions of successful southern denominations, influencing everything from the style of sermons to the eschatological expectations of everyday folk. Although this traditional Christian mode was virtually all-pervasive in southern religious experience, not all Christians partook of it in the same way. All shared similarly in some elements, to be sure. But differing appropriations of other elements by blacks on the one hand and by whites on the other revealed the development of two distinctive styles of southern revivalism. The strange combination of shared elements and distinctively appropriated ones made possible the exodus, the black surge toward self-separation that resulted in the segregation of the southern churches.

Of the elements of southern revivalism that blacks and whites shared, six are prominent. Foremost was conversion. Southern Christians believed absolutely that the genuine response to the human predicament was an utter turning about, a being born again. Conversion was the fundamental religious fact not only of belief but especially of experience. Sometimes the experience occurred in solitude, as it did for Morte, a slave whose conversion occurred while he was plowing a field.[7] In September of 1854, Isaac Lane, who would later become a bishop of the Colored Methodist Episcopal Church, also experienced conversion while at work in the field.[8] Religious gatherings provided the context for conversion for many Southerners. Evidence suggests this was frequently the case for whites, who were generally more mobile, financially able, and personally free to attend religious services. But the experiences of Peter Cartwright and Daniel Alexander Payne show that conversion could happen to white and black alike in the group setting. In Cartwright's case,

> To this meeting I repaired, a guilty, wretched sinner. On the Saturday evening of said meeting, I went, with weeping multitudes, and bowed before the stand, and earnestly prayed for mercy. In the midst of a solemn struggle of soul, an impression was made on my mind, as though a voice said to me, "Thy sins are all forgiven thee." Divine light flashed all round me, unspeakable joy sprung up in my soul. I rose to my feet, opened my eyes, and it really seemed as if I was in heaven; the trees, the leaves on them, and everything seemed, and I really thought were, praising God. My mother raised the shout, my Christian friends crowded around me and joined me in praising God; and though I have been since then, in many instances, unfaithful, yet I have never, for one moment, doubted that the Lord did, then and there, forgive my sins and give me religion.[9]

Payne reported:

> My conversion took place in my eighteenth year. Religion among the members of the Cumberland Street Church had waxed very cold, and Brother Holloway called a special meeting of all the classes, and inquired what might be done for the revival of God's work. It was decided to meet every Sunday between the morning and evening service in Mr. Bonneau's schoolroom to pray for a revival. In this place we met Sunday after Sunday. God heard our songs of praise, our prayers of faith, poured out his awakening and converting power upon his waiting children, and many souls were converted and sanctified by it. Of this number I was one. Here I too gave him my whole heart, and instantly felt that peace which passeth all understanding and that joy which is unspeakable and full of glory.[10]

Slave Lucy Skipwith wrote plantation owner John H. Cocke this description:

> I am rejoyced to tell you that we have had a most beautiful revival of religion amongst us. and it is the prettyest revival that I ever saw in my life. we have 11 that has been converted in the last two weeks. There is not a grown person among them. they are all my Sabbath School Schollars. they have all professed

that are large enough but two. and they are crying aloud for mercy and I hope that before this reaches you that those two may be brought to the Knowledge and truth of our Lord and Saviour Jesus Christ. amoung the Converts is my daughter that come home from Mr. Joe Banders. She came home a stranger to god and a stranger to me. but I thank the Lord that she is now able to say that she once was lossed, but now is found, was blind but now she see. the little yellow Boy William also professed. he had a most powerful conversion. you would be happy to see them at this time and hear them talk about the goodness of god. there has none professed at the other place as yet. but some are seeking. it is indeed a great wonder to see so many young people all turn to the Lord in so short a time. I pray that god may dwell with us untill the last sinner may come.[11]

Adherence to conversion as the core Christian belief and experience by white and black alike led to a mutual acceptance of certain physical manifestations by those who were "getting" (or had "gotten") religion. It also led to a rather democratic and laicized view of one's kindred Christians. Historians sometimes have ill understood these two shared elements of southern revivalism.

The physical manifestations that accompanied conversion and enthusiastic religious experience in revivalism included fainting, falling, shouting, sighing, weeping, singing, dancing, and the phenomenon commonly termed "the jerks." The description by Peter Cartwright—whose early years as a Methodist circuit rider were spent in the South—is classic.

A new exercise broke out among us, called the jerks, which was overwhelming in its effects upon the bodies and minds of the people. No matter whether they were saints or sinners, they would be taken under a warm song or sermon, and seized with convulsive jerking all over, which they could not by any possibility avoid, and the more they resisted the more they jerked. If they would not strive against it and pray in good earnest, the jerking would usually abate. I have seen more than five hundred persons jerking at one time in my large congregations. Most usually persons taken with the jerks, to obtain relief, as they said, would rise up and dance. Some would run, but could not get away. Some would resist; on such the jerks were generally very severe.

To see those proud young gentlemen and young ladies, dressed in their silks, jewelry, and prunella, from top to toe, take the *jerks*, would often excite my risibilities. The first jerk or so, you would see their fine bonnets, caps, and combs fly; and so sudden would be the jerking of the head that their long loose hair would crack almost as loud as a wagoner's whip.[12]

Some historians have understood such ecstatic behaviors as a frontier phenomenon. Some white observers of such manifestations by blacks after the

Civil War saw them as savage, barbaric, characteristic of a fundamentally uncivilized (perhaps uncivilizable) people. But in fact, religious lines rather than racial or socioeconomic ones or even geographical or historical ones encompass these physical manifestations. They are simply an irreducible element of Christian revivalism.

Methodism's first historian, Jesse Lee, described the behavior of an eighteenth-century congregation.

> The poor awakened sinners were wrestling with the Lord for mercy in every direction, some on their knees, others lying in the arms of their friends, and others stretched on the floor, not able to stand, and some were convulsed, with every limb as stiff as a stick. In the midst of this work several sleepers of the house broke down at once, which made a very loud noise; and the floor sunk down considerably; but the people paid but little or no attention to it, and many of them knew nothing of it, for no one was hurt.[13]

The prominent early Baptist leader John Leland observed that it was "nothing strange, to see a great part of the congregation fall prostrate upon the floor or ground; many of whom, entirely lose the use of their limbs for a season."[14]

These early examples demonstrate the ubiquity of physical manifestations in revivalism. It is a mistake to base judgments of these manifestations in their southern context on race rather than religion. Yet some postwar reports described such religious behavior by blacks as barbaric, while antebellum reports of such behavior by whites and blacks both—at camp meetings for example—portrayed it as glorious evidence of an outpouring of the Spirit. Some antebellum reports observed that at some camp meetings and other religious services, blacks remained aloof and seemed entertained by physical manifestations exhibited by whites. It has been suggested that these reports constitute evidence that blacks' acceptance of the whites' religion was tentative at best or that conversions of blacks perhaps were motivated by convenience or a need for entertainment and stimulation. The more plausible interpretation is that the blacks behaved as they did because they were "unconverted," not because they were black. They were probably analogous to but less disruptive than the unconverted rowdies who enjoyed plaguing preachers like Peter Cartwright.[15]

If the "unconverted" felt superior to Christians and to the religious behavior Christians manifested, a kind of lay egalitarianism pervaded the ranks of the born again. This egalitarianism in southern revivalism has many implications—sociological, ecclesiological, theological. Here discussion must be limited to how this element was shared by white and black Christians in what was generally a sharing of belief not consistently borne out in practice.

White and black Christians considered all persons who were born again to be equal in God's eyes. They were also equal in denominational wars of statistics. David Benedict, an early nineteenth-century Baptist historian, was proud to announce ingatherings of white and colored in tens, hundreds, and thousands.[16] Though an antebellum congregation might list slave members in the back of its record book, Methodists systematically reported all membership totals together, adding subtotals of white and colored members gathered into the fold.

White and black Christians understood all non-born-again persons to be equally in need of having the Gospel preached to them. Or, if the Christians belonged to a faction that believed God did not need or want missions, others were equally not in need of preaching, since God would work God's will.[17] These egalitarian beliefs about evangelization were commonly held in spite of somewhat contradictory behavior by some white preachers who tended to seek more opportunities to preach to whites than to blacks. Black preachers tended to seek opportunities to preach regardless of setting or congregational composition. In so doing they frequently faced opposition from the slave-holding establishment. Sometimes the difficulty was simple isolation, as in the case of an unnamed, self-appointed missionary who worked as a slave on a Louisiana sugar plantation. In 1857 he and his wife hiked eight miles to seek out sermon and sacrament, and baptism for their baby. The man announced the fruit of his preaching: "Fourteen of our people turned to the Lord last year."[18] "Uncle Jack," a slave brought from Africa to Virginia before the Revolution, preached a Presbyterian message to both blacks and whites until the Virginia General Assembly in 1831-1832 voted to silence Negro preachers.[19] John Jasper began preaching in 1839, but he needed his master's permission and white supervision.[20] Emperor Williams, a slave carpenter in Louisiana, taught himself to read and write; he sometimes carried a pass of his own composition until his master discovered the ruse and declared, "Go preach until you die; I am tired of you and your God bothering me any more."[21] Other slave preachers met much harsher opposition. A Maryland slave was whipped. A slave preacher in Georgia was burned alive for refusing to stop preaching.[22]

Sometimes, however, black preachers received support and assistance. John Charleson was converted in 1780 and emancipated in 1808. After that he traveled extensively as a Methodist preacher for forty years or more.[23] Major

Nelson, a Kentucky slave and overseer, reported that, "While yet a slave, and unable to read a chapter in the Bible, I was allowed to go out on the circuits of white men and preach to their congregations."[24] In 1938, Sarah Fitzpatrick, a former Alabama house servant, recalled, " 'Nigger' preachers in dem times wuz mighty-nigh free, an' we didn't have but er few uv 'em . . . dey preached in de white church to we 'Niggers'."[25] "Uncle Mark," a Methodist preacher on the Washington Circuit in Texas around 1848, traveled extensively and worked with other blacks while neighboring planters paid his master for his time. Then

> the owner of Uncle Mark removed to the West, and the planters, unwilling to lose his labors and influence among their slaves, raised the money among themselves, and purchased him; but as our laws did not allow of emancipation, he was deeded to three Methodist Preachers in trust for the Methodist Episcopal Church, South.[26]

White and black Christians knew that anyone, white or black, could convert anyone else, regardless of race or condition of servitude. Francis Asbury converted Black Punch, who converted his own overseer.[27] God's action in the conversion was variously understood. The Calvinistic view held that God was the author of conversion and that conversion was a sign of election, of God choosing an individual to be saved. The Arminian view held that although God gave salvation, humans had to receive it; that is, an individual had to cooperate with God's action and even strive for it. Many shades of opinion existed concerning the relationship between God's action and human cooperation or self-effort. Nevertheless, southern Christians of all stripes were likely to agree on an egalitarian doctrine of the Holy Spirit. They believed that the same Spirit, blowing where it willed, effected one's being born again; it also issued the call to preach. The Spirit was understood as likely to call any male, black or white, to preach. Any called preacher or exhorter could and did preach to or exhort anyone, black or white. A. C. Ramsey, a white Methodist minister, described a camp meeting in the 1830s:

> The only preachers at this camp meeting were the two circuit preachers myself and Uncle "Levin McRae," a colored man, and slave of Father M, Rae. . . [He] had the privilege of going far and near to preach to his people, where often he would have good congregations of whites. And was often seen in the pulpits of the white congregations. . . I presume there were no preachers in all that Chickasawha, and Pascagoula Country, white or black, that done as much good among the col.[d] people as Uncle Leven.[28]

This lay egalitarian view shared by white and black Christians did not extend to upper-level powers and decision making. While black Christians might be given some authority in certain matters of discipline, and black preachers like Baptists William Lemon and Jacob Bishop of Virginia and Methodists Henry Adams and George Bibb might be called to serve white and mixed congregations, blacks generally were not active in the denominational machinery of, for example, the Baptist Association or the Methodist Quarterly Conference.[29]

Though deprived of upper-level influence, blacks nevertheless shared with whites the associational forms that southern revivalism found most congenial. As Jerald Brauer points out, the associational forms fostered by revivalism pull in opposing directions. Revivalism fosters both division and ecumenism.[30]

Ecumenism draws religionists across denominational lines into an area of shared religious concern. The most conspicuous example of an associational form produced by the ecumenical pull of southern revivalism was the camp meeting. It was born at the turn of the nineteenth century with Presbyterian, Baptist, and Methodist ministers as midwives in the blessed event. The interdenominational cooperation at Cane Ridge in 1801 was typical, though the revival itself was a unique, classic, and cataclysmic event. The more routinized, less spectacular camp meetings of later years also featured interdenominational sharing of religious experience among leaders and layfolk alike. By the 1850s, one could expect a camp meeting to include preachers from more than one denomination, and white speakers as well as black ones. Both blacks and whites attended. Despite certain separatist customs that had developed over the years—such as separate camping areas and the custom of assigning blacks to preach from the "back" of the podium—the word flowed freely in the open air, the Spirit showed no favoritism for either race, and all joined as one in the song festival and marching ceremony that traditionally concluded the gathering.[31]

Less conspicuous examples of the ecumenical tendency of southern revivalism were protracted meetings (revivals) in population centers and interdenominational sharing of a church building when separate buildings were prohibitively expensive or impractical for other reasons. Methodist preacher George W. Moore of South Carolina reported that around 1830:

> I commenced my labors in Beaufort by preaching to the negroes in the old Tabernacle Church, belonging to the Baptists, and holding prayer meetings, with the assistance of a few Christian gentlemen, in the Episcopalian lecture

room. We soon enjoyed as great a revival among the colored people as there had been among the whites. I extended my labors to Paris, Cat, St. Helena, Dathan, Coosa, Lady's, Beaufort, and Big Islands, and on the mainland, where we soon enjoyed much prosperity. I left the converts free to join the Church of their choice. At one time, with my full consent, over two hundred of them were added to the Baptist Church.[32]

Revivalism's opposing pull toward division manifested itself in a tendency toward congregational polity, in intense denominational competition, and in schisms small and large. Whites and blacks suffered and initiated all of these. Prior to the pre-Civil War schisms of the 1830s and 1840s, if race was a causal factor at all in some particular antebellum incident, it was decidedly last——or better, marginal——on the list.[33]

Congregational polity in southern revivalism took various forms. Among Baptists, churches organized themselves as autonomous congregations, fiercely independent in word if less so in deed as the pressures that finally produced greater division——South from North——intensified. Among Methodists, local classes represented the smallest unit of congregational form under the connectional umbrella of efficient organization and hierarchical leadership. While classes tended to be divided by sex and/or race in areas where Methodists were numerous, mixed classes were not unknown. For example, the class book for the Pea Ridge Class for 1845-47 listed as members eleven white males, eighteen white females, twelve black males, and four black females.[34]

Denominational competition was endemic in nineteenth-century southern revivalism. Methodist circuit riders and Baptist preachers competed for members by debating doctrine and attempting to concoct the most convincing arguments and demonstrations. Nor were preachers' fists strangers to the fray for souls. In the final tally, soul count, not skin color, mattered. Methodist preacher J. F. W. Toland was pleased to report that in the slave mission fields of Mississippi in the early 1860s, "we had times of great power among the blacks. The wave of revival spread from the country to the city, and from the city back to the country."[35]

Schism was perhaps the most chronic manifestation of the pull toward division in southern revivalism's associational forms. Outstanding in the region's religious history are the formation of the Cumberland Presbyterian Church and the Stoneites and Campbellites who comprised the Disciples movement, but smaller scale separations took place regularly. Ordinarily a doctrinal issue was a component in the struggle; but the more prominent factor was a conflict of charisma between two (and sometimes more) religious leaders. Such leaders were naturally endowed with extraordinary qualities or powers, but only recognition of their powers by their followers sufficed as proof of their charisma. A confrontation with another charismatic leader occasioned proof for the leader who triumphed. In such schisms, conflicting charismas dominated, a doctrinal difference drew the lines of division, and one racially mixed congregation would become two racially mixed congregations.

Baptist polity, with its congregational autonomy, was more vulnerable to such schisms than Methodism. Methodists' connectional polity helped hold the church together in situations that might split a Baptist congregation. The presence of revivalism's divisive pressures and the connectional tradition of the Methodist Episcopal Church, South, are invoked in the pastoral address of the bishops to the General Conference in May 1858.

> We feel that we have cause for gratitude to God for the general peace which pervades the Connection. In doctrine we believe there is general unity; and in reference to our government and usages, although, as might be reasonably expected, there are diversities of opinion on some points, yet these differences of opinion, cherished no doubt honestly by the different parties, do not interfere with the feelings of mutual brotherly love, nor with feelings of profound respect for the Church and love for her institutions. These feelings of attachment to the Church and her institutions constitute an essential element of success in all our plans. Take away the great connectional principle and our progress to ruin will be certain and rapid. Nor is this devotion to the greatest principles and institutions of Methodism at all inconsistent with honest differences of opinion on many of the minor economical regulations of our fathers. We may never hope that among so many hundreds of thousands all will see exactly alike in all minor details; but we may hope to see all love alike, all equally loyal to the great principles and aims of Methodism, which are to spread scriptural holiness throughout the earth, by raising up and perpetuating a holy ministry and a holy people.

The bishops describe the danger as they see it.

> We are in danger of yielding to personal and local influences, to the destruction of the efficiency of our itinerant system. Local interests tempt us: we yield, and, instead of the ample sweep of vision which took in the interests of the great whole, we take narrow views—we look to our own Conference, our own District, our own Circuit or Station—and we are in great danger of losing that broad and expansive Wesleyan spirit which claims the world as its parish, and of settling down on an easy, comfortable, congregational basis. . . .[36]

Just as the associational forms taken by southern revivalism pulled in the opposing directions of division and ecumenism without respect to race, black and white southern revivalism shared the charismatic style of its leaders.

A religious leader with charisma inspires followers because they believe in the leader's qualities and powers.[37] Religious leaders might possess the charisma and exert the authority flowing from holding a religious office, but in every case, some demonstration of personal charisma was prior and required.

People knew charisma when they saw it. (Indeed, somewhat circularly, genuine charisma requires recognition; without or until recognition, one must doubt that a person has charisma.[38]) In general, race was no barrier to recognition. For example, a black South Carolina preacher born around 1845 reported that "my uncle couldn't read, so Miss X [the owner] just read off a little scripture to him, and he would stand up and preach away for an hour or more." One memorable Christmas, at the owner's request, "I want to tell you he preached. He set that little house on fire. Everybody was shouting and crying. My mistress took her handkerchief and wiped my mother's eyes and nose."[39]

As mentioned, charismatic leaders were hardly collegial in relationship with one another. Charisma faced by charisma forced a showdown. Only one won. The winner then constituted the organizational hub for the congregational associational form. He also served as central local authority, holding sway by virtue of a powerful combination: the extraordinariness of the leader and his ordinariness, which gave him the influencing power of identification. The proportion of ordinary to extraordinary varied, but the combination was a constant. Jesus himself was reported to have the combination: a human being like us in all things (ordinary) save sin (extraordinary).

The most important element of southern revivalism that blacks and whites shared was ritual. Ritual here means the service, whatever the setting—the large and ecumenical camp meeting, the intimate and local love feast, the Sunday worship service. In the 1850s, one could count on the service to include a sermon and, frequently, Lord's Supper or Communion as well. These two components bonded religionists in southern society much as the medieval Mass helped the early cities of western Christendom, where kings, nobles, knights, and peasants all partook of the same Lord's Supper.[40]

Both Lord's Supper and sermon as shared in the South in the 1850s constituted table fellowship. Table fellowship in turn fostered those religious and political ties that commensality encourages. The antebellum ties between blacks and whites flowing from shared Christianity have been explored in nature and extent by such scholars as Winthrop Jordan, Eugene Genovese, Donald Mathews, and Albert Raboteau among others.[41] Here it is important to consider how Lord's Supper and sermon occasioned commensality between black and white.

From its roots, commensality means sharing the same table—*mensa*, in Latin. Together with connubium—the right or privilege of intermarriage exchanged between kinship groups such as families or tribes—commensality is a human practice fundamental to the very possibility of human civilization. How commensality is practiced often reflects or even helps shape a particular society. Thus, in India, caste lines were drawn on the basis of who could eat with whom and—more specifically—who was permitted to exchange food cooked in water and food cooked in melted butter with the Brahmin caste.[42]

Commensality takes many forms. Most familiar to us is the nonceremonial kind. One's relationships with other persons and groups and especially group boundaries are reflected in such facts as whom one will invite to one's home for dinner and whose invitation one will accept for dining out in a commercial establishment. In such cases, social, religious, and political ties are expressed or at least implied. Frequently, bonds are forged in the very act of commensality. The formal, or ceremonial kind of commensal practices outline society's patterns of exclusion and participation more explicitly. Religious sharing of a ritual meal holds great significance for the nature and extent of group boundaries. We will see that the practice of religious commensality has far from simple significance for our period. In its very complexity lie clues to the structure of southern society; in the changes that occurred lay the seeds of later relationships. This study points beyond itself.

However, sociological implications notwithstanding, the sincere mid-nineteenth-century Christian strove to concentrate on religious reflection during the celebration of the Lord's Supper. The ceremony derived from and centered on Jesus' atonement for humanity's sins. Within the Christian, a calling to mind (anamnesis) was to occur. The Christian concentrated on what Jesus did and the theological fact that Jesus' atonement made possible the Christian's salvation. Without sin, there would be no need for conversion; without Jesus' atonement, there would be no possibility of conversion. Therefore, through conversion one was connected to and even participated in Jesus' saving work. In the revivalist Christian's experience, conversion and Lord's Supper were interrelated. Indeed, early in the nineteenth century, one Sunday in mid-July during the administration of the Lord's Supper, several of the more faithful members . . . became strongly moved. Their "loud lamentations and streaming eyes" so affected many of the younger members that they fell to the floor. From this date throughout [presiding elder Stith] Mead's district in central Georgia numbers were "awakened" and fell prostrate on the floor, or laid on the pews, crying, moaning, begging for mercy.[43]

Partaking of the ritual meal held the potential for calling to mind one's conversion together with the other Christians of one's faith community. Both black and white worshippers in a mixed congregation accepted one another into community on the strength of evidence that one had turned, had been born again. As stressed above, Christians believed the converted to be spiritually equal in the eyes of the Lord. Consequently, a Lord's Supper ritual that intended to call conversion and salvation to mind was a celebration of equality and community. It was a powerful affirmation of salvation's transcendence over everyday human affairs.

Understanding these properties of the Southerners' religiosity is indispensable to the correct assessment of certain separatist customs practiced in the ritual setting by antebellum Christians. The most frequently mentioned of these are two: first, the practice of hierarchical seating, which dated back to colonial times, where whites sat according to social status and blacks tended to be relegated to the sides, the back, or even a specially constructed gallery in the church;[44] and the second, the practice of blacks receiving Communion (thus participating in anamnesis) after whites. This latter practice is mentioned with some frequency in contemporary antebellum descriptions of worship services. I have found no explicit report that whites took Communion according to status too, but such a hierarchical procedure would seem more likely than surprising.

What did the separatist customs in the joint worship setting mean? It is certain from contemporary affirmations of faith that they did not mean that the religious significance of the ritual was understood to be any different for blacks than for whites. Nor was taking Communion after whites understood by either blacks or whites to show that blacks came second in the eyes of God. The significance of separatist customs in the view of nineteenth-century Christians was clearly not theological. Thus at a camp meeting, Baptists and Methodists might celebrate the Lord's Supper separately because of profound theological differences in their understanding of salvation. But each of those groups would contain converted members of both races. John B. Boles explains that "even in the midst of their revival support, [the Baptists] never consented to general communion. They would meet, worship, shout, and fall with the Presbyterians and Methodists, but refused to share the sacrament with advocates of infant baptism."[45]

Not theological significance but rather social meaning was expressed by separatist customs. Hierarchical seating reflected a hierarchical society. Socially, blacks belonged in the back (or along the sides, or in a gallery). However, if a black servant was charged with care or oversight of a white worshipper, that black belonged socially at his or her charge's side. Ex-slave Henry Baker described an illuminating reversal of this situation. After his mother died, his mistress took the child to church.

> When we go tuh Church she wouldn't let me set on de seat, made me set down on de floor right by huh feet. So when I went tuh sleep I could jes lay dere 'til a'ter Church . . . en she wuz kerful not tuh let non ub de white folks pull muh years er neder step on muh feet er do nuthin' tuh me.[46]

Besides reflecting a hierarchical society, separatist customs probably also represented (and helped maintain) slavery's function of racial definition and control. Since any human derives social ease (broadly construed) from knowing one's definition in relation to others in a group, both blacks and whites had an interest in knowing their respective places. Methodist Bishop William Capers's sketch of the influential Henry Evans shows that the free black preacher's observance of racial etiquette probably gave him unusual access to slaves, who many whites believed could be corrupted by contact with free blacks.

> He seemed always deeply impressed with the responsibility of his position; and not even our old friend Castile [Selby] was more remarkable for his humble and deferential deportment toward the whites than Evans was. Nor would he allow any partiality of his friends to induce him to vary in the least degree the line of conduct or the bearing which he had prescribed to himself in this respect; never speaking to a white man but with his hat under his arm; never allowing himself to be seated in their houses; and even confining himself to the kind and manner of dress proper for negroes in general, except his plain black coat for the pulpit. "The whites are kind to me, and come to hear me preach," he would say; "but I belong to my own sort, and must not spoil them." And yet Henry Evans was a Boanerges, and in his duty feared not the face of man.[47]

By contrast, control was—at least predominantly—a white interest. From the economic point of view at any rate, it was in whites' interest to maintain a society in which they could control blacks, whether slave or free. But certain considerations lead one to conclude that more than money was at stake.

As Winthrop Jordan shows in an analysis similar to Simone de Beauvoir's analysis of an oppressed group as "other," white Southerners experienced blacks from the first as other. Jordan finds that to whites, blacks had a magical, tabooistic quality with sexual overtones.[48] Blacks' very presence introduced a threat of danger and an anxiety about purity into the previously white society. Blacks represented a possibility of social unraveling (followed by reorganization) analogous to the threat Israelites perceived in their encounter with Babylonian culture in the Exile. The latter encounter inspired detailed legislation about legal and ritual purity among Jews anxious to preserve their own faith, culture, and social organization. It seems likely that white colonists' anti-miscegenation legislation, the separatist customs that developed, and even race-specific chattel slavery itself—a type of slavery unique in history—stemmed partially from anxiety about purity.

It is obvious that economic advantage to those in power played a major role in the development of the peculiar institution. But it was not economic advantage that inspired the white southern Christians in decision-making positions to construct churches with costly galleries. In some cases, the church building had a separate entrance for blacks as well. One can hardly argue that two entrances were cheaper than one. It seems to me that white anxiety about purity in the face of the perceived dangerous otherness of blacks provides more plausible motivation. If, as Mary Douglas argues, concern about purity is concern for order and ideas about purity are meant "to impose system on an inherently untidy experience," whites probably wanted to organize and control their ambiguous—even messy—social, economic, and religious relationships with blacks.[49] Symbolic galleries and separate entrances put each southern Christian in his or her place.

Separatist customs enabled whites to maintain the precarious balance between their anxieties and economic advantages on the one hand and the egalitarian Christian creed of southern revivalism on the other.

In the joint worship setting, despite the separatist customs, the Lord's Supper functioned as a commensal element. Another element of worship also had a commensal function, though less obviously so: the sermon.

It can be argued that the sermon developed into a commensal element in the general history of Christianity.[50] However, there are three more proximate reasons for lifting up the sermon as a commensal element in the worship of southern revivalist Christians.

First of all, sermons were oriented toward conversion. The sermon became a "converting ordinance" whether in the congregational services of a single denomination or in ecumenical or transdenominational mass camp meetings. While theological theories about its role in conversion differed between and even within denominations, the sermon was understood to be important—to some, indispensable— for converting sinners. The sermon aimed to bring the unconverted hearer into the community of the born again. Indeed, the Table of the Lord was "fenced" against the unconverted. Conversion bestowed the right and privilege of ritual commensality.

A second reason for calling sermons commensal also derives from their orientation toward conversion. For the converted hearer, the born again possessor of full commensal right and privileges, the sermon affirmed and celebrated his or her personal conversion by calling it to mind, by anamnesis. Just as the Lord's Supper called to mind Jesus' atonement and one's participation in Jesus' atonement through one's conversion, so the sermon called to mind the same concatenation of faith facts. As inward spiritual or psychological experience, hearing the revivalist's sermon and taking Communion were similar if not identical in content and kind.

The third reason is the most important. Unlike the Lord's Supper, the sermon was received simultaneously by all present regardless of spiritual or social status, race, or condition of servitude. It was an anticipation and an invitation to conversion for some, an anamnesis of conversion for others. In a mixed congregation of believers, conversion was (re)experienced and affirmed in hearers' hearts. At the camp meeting, sermons nourished hearers with the Word in an ecumenical manner impossible at the actual Lord's Supper, due to theological differences about the latter. Some awareness of the simultaneous, biracial sharing of religious experience that revivalist preaching could bring seems apparent in an 1859 report by a white Baptist missionary to blacks in Mississippi.

There is a large scope of country here, populated almost entirely by blacks. Many of them were professors of religion when brought here—many of whom scarcely ever hear preaching—some never. For example: on the fifth Sabbath in August I preached to a congregation of blacks, among whom was an old woman whose owner furnished her with a mule to ride several miles to attend my meeting. On her way she remarked to an overseer that she hoped the Lord would let her hear a white man preach once more, for she had not heard one in thirty years. She was a Baptist when she came into the swamp.[51]

Not all of the elements of southern revivalism were shared by whites and blacks in the same way. Blacks' distinctive appropriation of the Christianity they shared with whites would motivate their dramatic surge toward self-separation after the Civil War. What was distinctive about black Christianity by the 1850s can be described under four headings.

Ritual

Scholars have found that joint worship was the predominant pattern for Christians in the antebellum South. Joint worship entailed ritual commensality, forging religious ties as well as social and political ones. But black Christians' *experience* of joint worship was different from that of whites. Scattered reports of black participation in camp meetings provide one clue to the manner in which differentiation took place. Black preachers and exhorters held forth from the back of the speakers' stand. Apparently, seats for blacks were sometimes provided there, though published diagrams of camp meeting arrangements do not show such a provision.[52] The evidence on the question of where blacks sat during sermons at these meetings is sparse, but some sources record that blacks camped in a section of the grounds separate from whites and often continued singing and praying there late at night after the day's joint services. Johnson asserts that plank partitions came to be erected to separate the sections and that the removal of these for the final day's song festival and marching ceremony contributed to the communal fervor of the summary experience.[53] One concludes from fragmentary reports that in the joint worship of the camp meeting setting, blacks experienced themselves as a special, set aside group—spiritually equal, but other.

The more plentiful descriptions of ordinary worship services reinforce this finding and permit further reflection. Here, too, blacks experienced separateness in the joint setting. Designated seating was separate. Moreover, I find no accounts of hierarchical seating in black sections of the sort Jordan reports was customary among whites from colonial times.[54] That slaves made "class" distinctions in everyday life is well known. For example, they perceived house servants to be in a different category from field hands.[55] But if such distinctions were made in the church gallery, no observer that I know of recorded such a fact. It seems likely that blacks' experience of one another in the joint worship context was less hierarchical than whites' corresponding experience of other whites. Separation in seating would seem to have encouraged a sense of community, of peopleness among black Christians. Being asked to go last—together—to the Lord's Table would reinforce the impression.

In addition to this sense of community, in worship blacks also developed a distinctive style with respect to the sermon. White preachers testified to the greater responsiveness of predominantly black congregations. Reverend George W. Moore reported, "The negroes generally. . . are very apt to give some expression of approbation when pleased with preaching." Reverend A. M. Chreitzberg described a typical 1843 service.

> The service would begin with the rising of the missionary in the pulpit, followed by the simultaneous rising of the entire congregation, who would repeat after him line by line the Apostles' Creed. Then came explanatory questions, which were readily answered. The Commandments would next be repeated, and then the reading of a portion of Scripture, which was always carefully explained. After that a hymn was sung, a prayer offered, and the sermon began, followed all the way through by the closest attention and constantly responded to by a nod of the head, a gentle clapping together of the hands, or a deep "Amen!" according as their religious fervor moved them.[56]

Denominational decision makers noted that in the concrete and centrally important matter of conversion black exhorters and preachers got better results with blacks than white preachers and exhorters did. Some accounts of the interaction between black speakers and black hearers have been preserved. White observers noted a kind of incantational preaching by blacks that drew fervor from congregational response. While the presence of African influence on ritual situations is evident, its role is difficult to assess. To some degree, this was "down-home plain folk preaching" of the sort lower-class whites enjoyed. Moreover, it is possible that the usually illiterate preachers leaned more heavily on repetition as a mnemonic device for their generally illiterate congregations. Such repetitious, almost singsong exchanges between preacher and congregation seem to be the subject of South Carolina black Baptist leader Alexander Bettis's complaint about the "whangdoodle" preachers of the early postwar period.[57] Such incantational-responsorial sermons probably generated charismatic collective religious experience more frequently and systematically for blacks than whites. However, without more plentiful evidence, one must hold this conclusion tentatively and cautiously, remembering Peter Cartwright's boasts about the excitement generated by his sermons before crowds that were probably racially mixed. Cartwright also encouraged congregational participation and predominantly white camp meeting crowds usually obliged enthusiastically.[58] Thus one can say of black sermons on the part of speaker and hearer that they were probably distinctive in incantational-responsorial style and that they probably elicited ecstatic religious feeling among blacks that was experienced communally. Moreover, these characteristics were shaped at least in part by the circumstances of the ritual situation.[59]

More certain than the question of style is the matter of sermon content. It is obvious that in the case of sermons preached to racially mixed congregations, all heard the same words. But closer analysis of both words and hearers' reception and perception of those words uncovers more evidence that blacks appropriated Christianity in a manner different from whites.

The words of a white preacher explicated the Christian myth. By myth is meant a narrative with revelatory power, a story of faith. Though Methodist preachers and exhorters rooted each sermon in a portion of scripture, the primary purpose of the explication of the myth was conversion, winning souls. Along with word pictures of heavenly rewards and the like, moral exhortation was part of good sermon technique. Here the white preacher in a racially mixed setting would set forth the moral obligations incumbent on the Christians before him.[60] That meant stressing that slaves were to be obedient to their masters. All—black and white—were to perform faithfully the duties appropriate to their calling in life. Denominational decision makers knew that the widespread belief that Christianity made better slaves helped them gain access to blacks from otherwise reluctant whites who controlled that access. Since soul-winning (regardless of skin color) held top theological priority, the message of faithfulness to one's calling and in particular of obedience was not neglected. Black preachers and exhorters were trained to stress the same message. Texas slave preacher Anderson Edwards was advised by his master to "tell them niggers iffen they obeys the master they goes to Heaven. . ."[61] The master was to be moved to justice and compassion, the slave to obedience and hard work; all were to be moved to conversion or to call previous conversion to mind.

If the moral message differed, so did its reception. Whites would derive feelings both of moral earnestness and resolve on their own behalf and of reassurance and righteousness on the question of how society was organized. Even the most disadvantaged of whites welcomed this affirmation of the status quo. No matter how disadvantaged, they were white and free. Moreover, whites generally aspired to a bigger slice of the economic and social pie; and in the antebellum South, owning slaves was part of the American dream for most nonslaveholders.[62]

Expressions by slaves of their earnest resolve to obey the master are conspicuously lacking, as are affirmations by them of the righteousness of southern social organization. Such conspicuous lack of data together with accounts of what blacks expressed and affirmed about the Christian message in this period points to the conclusion that in their ears the double moral message was drowned out by the powerful Christian myth and symbols presented in the same sermons by white and black exhorters and preachers.

The joint worship service had different effects on blacks than on whites. One was an affirmation of community—not Christian community (*both* blacks and whites experienced this) but black Christian community. The separatist customs as well as black response to sermon style and content blended blacks into—and gave them a self-perception of being—an *ecclesiola in ecclesia*, a small church community within the larger church. This phenomenon of intense group religious identity within the larger, less intense church body has occurred frequently in the history of Christianity and tended to foster the formation of community—for example, thirteenth-century Franciscans and seventeenth-century Pietists. By the mid-nineteenth century, blacks in the American South had drawn their self-perception of being a church community from their experience of joint worship.

A second effect of ritual on blacks was an affirmation of Christian liberation. Conversion itself was experienced as a liberation. Sermons evoked and affirmed conversion; the Lord's Supper called conversion to mind. When Nora, a young married woman, was converted, she heard a voice say, "Ye are freed and free indeed. My son set you free." Another woman explained that, at the conclusion of her conversion experience, "I came to myself, and it looked like I just wanted to kiss the very ground. I had never felt such a love before." A man explained, "Ever since then, when the Lord freed my soul, I have been rejoicing."[63] For such individuals, ritual recalled and reinforced the experience of liberation that conversion entailed. Significantly, the two effects blended together. Christian liberation—affirmed in a setting that also affirmed a black Christian community—made liberation a communal experience and community a liberating experience. In the light of these outcomes, it is not surprising that in the antebellum period, the *ecclesiola* sought separate—often clandestine—worship services. Secret services definitely took place. However, their clandestine character makes the content and frequency of such gatherings impossible to describe with as much confidence as joint worship. Nevertheless, their significance is clear: Secret religious rituals expressed blacks' self-awareness of their identity as a community as well as their conviction that God was "the God of Freedom who was working out his purposes right here on earth."[64]

Myth and Symbols

Blacks' appropriation of the Christian myth and its symbols was distinctive from whites' appropriation of this aspect of the tradition in three ways: biblical emphases, eschatological vision, and experience of Jesus as Lord.

Most antebellum southern blacks found access to the Bible via oral sources such as songs, sermons, and prayers at religious services, "family" Bible reading by a master or mistress, and Bible stories that entered the oral tradition of the slave community thanks to a literate black person. (Although southern literacy laws were violated with some frequency, they were effective in preventing masses of blacks to read.) The main means of preserving and transmitting biblical materials was human memory. Nevertheless, the original source, the Bible, was prominent in the religiosity of southern blacks. They regarded it with a reverence intensified by their limited access to it.

John W. Blassingame points out that restrictions on education by whites led blacks to invest literacy with "almost magical qualities."[65] Osofsky holds that

> Through the ages, in the most widely divergent cultures, the right to proscribe letters or command a man's name is understood as the power to subordinate—the "word" has quasi-magical, mystical connotations. The right to control it is the power to order reality, to subjugate man himself. Conquerors and conquered have both understood this truth.[66]

It is not surprising that blacks valued highly possession and mastery of biblical materials. Their desire to read the Bible itself would help boost their literacy rate in the postbellum period. It is possible that some slaves regarded the Bible as a fetish or at least as a symbol of religious legitimation, as in the explanation of antebellum marriage customs by Alabama ex-slave Cato: "mostly they just jumped over a broom and that made 'em married. Sometimes the white folks read a little out of the Scriptures to 'em, and they felt more married."[67]

Given the importance of the Bible in antebellum black religiosity, the biblical materials blacks chose to emphasize in songs and sermons are significant indicators of the distinctive appropriation of Christianity by blacks. Despite the fact that, as Blassingame points out, available sources represent only what blacks wanted (or were not afraid) to have whites hear, we can learn a great deal about their religion from what biblical material they used and how they used it.[68]

Black Christians emphasized biblical materials that they could relate to their core Christian experience and to their concrete life situation. Images and figures from the Bible in sermons and letters by blacks and in religious songs they sang at work and at worship tended to express the communal liberation of the conversion and ritual experiences as well as to explore the religious significance of the hardships of daily life. Since blacks generally had less direct access than whites to the Bible itself, it is doubtful that they differentiated sharply between Old Testament and New or among the various books. Nevertheless, they emphasized material from Old Testament books—especially Exodus—and the New Testament book of Revelation. Although other New Testament elements frequently occur—Paul and Silas bound in jail, for example—these elements often are combined with material from Revelation or from the Old Testament. Newman I. White identified this phenomenon as an accumulative tendency—a part of one song was drawn into another, presumably by a process of association.[69]

White believed that black music accumulated images in order to create a feeling.[70] While emotion is an undeniable dimension of religious experience, it is generated in a complex interaction between experience of one's own concrete life situation and one's apprehension of the meaning of a religious image or figure. The resulting cognitive-affective experience was different for blacks than for whites in the antebellum South. White's research convinced him that

> The spiritual songs of the white people prefer much the same sections of the Bible as those of the Negroes; they differ from the regular hymns, just as the Negro spirituals do, in a much greater emphasis upon the Apocalypse, the personal devil, and the narrative parts of the Old Testament.[71]

But if the material emphasized was the same (an assertion needing further study), the cognitive-affective experience of black Christians was not.

In no case is this difference more apparent than the antebellum Southerner's experience of the Exodus narrative—God's deliverance of the chosen people under the leadership of Moses from bondage in Pharaoh's Egypt. A wealthy white planter might indeed apply this narrative to his conversion experience, understanding Egyptian bondage to symbolize his bondage to sin before

Moses (understood perhaps as Jesus? a particularly effective preacher?) led him out of bondage.

It is conceivable that that planter's slaves might understand Egyptian bondage to signify slavery to sin. However, their perception of the situation of servitude would interact with their apprehension of the Exodus narrative and produce additional ideas and emotions. In the ritual setting of joint worship, the story of the Israelites' exodus from Egypt became a vehicle for black expressions of the sense of communal Christian liberation they derived from worship. Antebellum black Southerners recognized a parallel between the Israelites' bondage and their own servitude and the story of God's deliverance inspired hope that God would do the same for them. These concepts and this hope played a part in Gabriel Prosser's plot in 1800 and in the Denmark Vesey conspiracy of 1822 and fired the determination of Nat Turner and his fellow insurrectionists.[72]

Contrary to what some scholars have held, the longing for freedom was not a so-called secular desire, but a religious hope profoundly rooted in biblical traditions.[73] For example, North Carolina slave James Curry reported a rumor from a neighboring plantation before the presidential election that Van Buren would free all the slaves.

> One old man, who was a Christian, came and told us, that now, all we had got to do, was, as Moses commanded the children of Israel on the shore of the Red Sea, "to stand still and see the salvation of God." Mr. Van Buren was elected, but he gave no freedom to the slaves.[74]

Mingo White of Alabama told interviewers that "when de day's wuk was done de slaves would be foun' lock in dere cabins prayin' for de Lawd to free dem lack he did de chillun of Is'ael."[75]

Black religious songs about the exodus gave explicit attention to and developed the meaning of various aspects of the biblical narrative. Best known of these is "Go Down, Moses" with its resounding chorus,

> Go Down, Moses
> Way down in Egyptland
> Tell old Pharaoh
> To let my people go.[76]

Other songs highlighted different aspects of the exodus narrative meaningful in the religious experience of blacks. Three slave songs from an early published collection show interest in various components of the story. "Let God's Saints Come In" employs a recurrent image of God's intervention in the refrain "Come down, angel, and trouble the water"; verses focus on the intimate interaction between God and Moses.

> God did go to Moses' house
> And God did tell him who he was,
> God and Moses walked and talked,
> And God did show him who he was.

Neither God nor Moses appears in "My Army Cross Over." This song portrays the people of bondage as an army crossing the Jordan despite danger—especially peril from Satan. One version juxtaposes the line "My army cross ober" with "O Pharaoh's army drownded." A third song in this collection emphasizes God's choice and advocacy of God's people:

> Come along, Moses, don't get lost,
> Don't get lost, don't get lost,
> Come along, Moses, don't get lost,
> We are the people of God.
>
> We have a just God to plead our cause
> To plead our cause, to plead our cause,
> We have a just God to plead our cause,
> We are the people of God.[77]

Other antebellum black religious songs that draw on biblical material from the exodus story include "Oh Mary, Don't You Weep (Pharaoh's army got drownded)," "Sit Down," "Did Not Old Pharaoh Get Lost," and "When Moses Smote the Water."[78] The exodus narrative was undoubtedly a source for reflection and religious hope for blacks. It was the richest tale of communal liberation in the Bible.

Of course, other instances of God's deliverance provided additional inspiration for the religious aspirations of blacks. "O my Lord delivered Daniel, O why not deliver me too?" could hardly be more explicit.[79] In many a religious song slaves sang, God was active on the side of the powerless. "I bless the Lord I've got my seal . . . To slay Goliath in the field . . ."[80] God empowered Samson against his enemies, helped Joshua fight the battle of Jericho, released Jonah from the belly of the whale, and delivered the Hebrew children from the fiery furnace. The liberating implications of being a people of such a God clearly were more than otherworldly to the slave community.[81] In religious songs about the future, the jubilee—a year specified in the Bible during which slaves were to be freed and agricultural work suspended (Lev. 25)—came to represent deliverance from tribulation. Like many other Old Testament concepts, events, and figures, jubilee was blended by blacks into songs that included material from the New Testament.

White Christians did not neglect the Old Testament, but evidence suggests that they turned frequently to the pages of the gospels and the epistles.

The New Testament contained some favorite texts of slaveholders, including those used in defense of slavery as an institution.[82] It also provided preachers with material for the kind of sermon masters wanted slaves to hear. Whites believed that such preaching made better slaves. Apparently they did not notice that, as Henry Bibb explained, "the slaves, with but few exceptions, have no confidence at all" in this gospel

> because they preach a pro-slavery doctrine. They say, 'Servants be obedient to your masters;—and he that knoweth his master's will and doeth it not, shall be beaten with many stripes;—means that God will send them to hell if they disobey their masters."[83]

For Charley Williams of Louisiana, the gospel of Jesus and the gospel of obedience were evidently two entirely separate matters.

> Course I loves my Lord Jesus same as anybody, but you see I didn't hear much about him until I was grown. . . . Nobody could read the Bible when I was a boy, and they wasn't no white preachers talked to the niggers. We had meetings sometimes, but the nigger preacher just talk about being a good nigger and "doing to please the Master," and I always thought he meant to please Old Master, and I always wanted to do that anyways.[84]

Thomas L. Webber finds that members of the slave community distinguished between the gospel of servitude and God's genuine word. Lewis Clarke explained, "They generally believe there is somewhere a real Bible, that came from God; but they frequently say the Bible now used is master's Bible, the most they hear from it being, 'Servants, obey your masters.' "[85] According to Anthony Burns of Virginia, the truth was that God

> had made of one blood all nations of the earth, that there was no divine ordinance requiring one part of the human family to be in bondage to another,

and that there was no passage of Holy Writ by virtue of which Col. Suttle could claim a right of property in him, any more than he could in Col. Suttle.[86]

Some black preachers may have expressed less egalitarian views. According to Rev. John G. Williams, Brudder Paul Coteny, Gullah slave plantation preacher, warned his hearers about the Last Judgment:

Brudder an sister, one ob dese days de sheep and de goat will sepperate—de goat go to de leff han and de sheep to de rite han. (Here an old sister shouted out: "Bless de Lawd, we nigger know who hab de wool," which idea all the wooly "brudderin an sisterin" were quick to take up, and oh how they did shout, everyone screaming: "We nigger know who hab de wool."

When Brudder Coteny could make himself heard, he admonished, "e ent wool pun de head, but de snowy wite wool ob grace in de haht, dat mek de Lawd's sheep, dat gwine to de right han."[87] Brudder Coteny's apparent orthodoxy notwithstanding, his hearers' explosive reaction suggests they understood goats to signify white people—a meaning found in black folklore.[88] Ironically, Brudder Coteny's probably deliberate anti-white double entendre was faithfully recorded by a white minister interested in preserving examples of Gullah speech.

New Testament references are not as frequent as Old Testament ones in the letters, sermons, narratives, and songs of antebellum blacks, with the exception of references to the book of Revelation. Certain New Testament figures appeared in songs in various settings—Weeping Mary and Mourning Martha were especially popular, as were Paul and Silas bound in jail, yet another case of God's impossible deliverance from unjust bondage.[89] Of course, the story of Jesus' miraculous resurrection was an important narrative of liberation. It was celebrated in such black religious songs as "The Resurrection Morn," "Who Is on the Lord's Side," and "He Rose From the Dead."[90] The last song, as it tells of the crucifixion and resurrection, carries an eschatological line in each verse: "And the Lord shall bear his children home."

For an enslaved people kidnapped from their African homes and too often torn away from "home" slave communities by slave sales, home became an eschatological symbol and the end of time a welcome deliverance. Slaves sang about that home as a new Jerusalem, as Canaan's shore, as promised land. It was gold, from its golden altar to golden streets. One could be carried there in a golden chariot. Once there, one would join the golden band and wear golden slippers. One's robe, however, was the white robe of the book of

Revelation. One might ride a white horse as Jesus would. One might wear a crown as "King Jesus" did.

The new life of freedom at home on the other side of the end time (or the transformation of time) was to be ushered in by terrifying events predicted in the book of Revelation—terrifying, that is, to antebellum whites and (one presumes) any believer at all unsure of God's special providence. Bethany Veney remembered her mistress using Revelation's vision of the end to frighten the young slave into good behavior. The mistress explained that

> *some time* all this world that we saw would be burned up—that the moon would be turned to blood, the stars would fall out of the sky, and everything would melt away with a great heat, and that everybody, *every little child* that had told a lie, would be cast into a lake of fire and brimstone, and would burn for ever and ever, and what was more, though they should burn for ever and ever, they would never be burned up.[91]

Such efforts at intimidation were unavailing because blacks felt Gabriel's trumpet would bring not punishment but final vindication. According to Donald Mathews, such an apocalyptic vision

> reveals the mental framework which made possible the chosen community of love, forbearance, and hope. The anger and judgment of the Apocalypse were necessary to prevent the themes of equality and deliverance from becoming compensation, to prevent the personal achievements within black American religion from becoming mere survival, to prevent love and forebearance from becoming dehumanizing pap.[92]

The mother of Fannie Moore apparently experienced a vision of the slave community's concrete deliverance.

> Every night she pray for the Lord to git her and her children out of the place. One day she plowing in the cotton field. All sudden-like she let out a big yell. Then she start singing and a-shouting and a-whooping and a-hollowing. Then it seem she plow all the harder.

Threatened with a whipping for the outburst, she exclaimed,

> "I's saved! The Lord done tell me I's saved. Now I know the Lord will show me the way. I ain't gwine-a grieve no more. No matter how much you all done beat me and my children, the Lord will show me the way. And some day we never be slaves."[93]

Slaves looked for signs of the end. Their songs, writings, and reminiscences suggest that they expected it to happen soon. Such immediate eschatological expectations are not unusual in Christianity. Disadvantaged groups throughout history have expected, hoped, and prayed for the end time to occur in the near future.[94] An incident, narrated by an ex-slave, shows the readiness of antebellum blacks for the end time.

> I was a young man when the stars fell; and you know that was a long time ago. I seen them; they just fell and went out before they hit the ground. How come me to see it, we had just killed hogs and had the meat hanging upon poles and I had to watch it all night. . .It scared a lot of them. . .Somebody started blowing the horn what you call the dogs with, and they started hollering that Gabriel was blowing his trumpet.[95]

Most antebellum blacks were hopeful rather than frightened at the prospect of the end, and many prayed to hasten the realization of their apocalyptic dreams. Mary Reynolds's family prayed at a forbidden nighttime prayer meeting; Jacob Stroyer's father advised him to pray.[96] Moses Grandy reported that violent thunderstorms could activate eschatological hopes:

> "In violent thunderstorms . . . when the whites have got between the featherbeds to be safe from the lightning, I have often seen negroes, the aged as well as others, go out, and, lifting up their hands, thank God that judgment was coming at last."[97]

Austin Steward remembered hoping Judgment Day had arrived when he saw an eclipse of the sun. "I recollect well thinking, that if indeed all things earthly were coming to an end, I should be free from Robinson's brutal force, and as to meeting my Creator, I felt far less dread of that than of meeting my cross, unmerciful master."[98] Judgment Day would bring freedom and feasting at home in the promised land. The slave song expressed a concrete confidence:

> I'm goin' to eat at the welcome table,
> O yes I'm goin to eat at the welcome table
>   some of these days,
> Hallelujah![99]

Or, as another expression of the same hope went: " 'Gwine to sit down at the welcome table, gwine to feast off milk and honey."[100]

It is significant that the well-known spiritual "Deep River" combines the eschatological imagery of home and feast in promised land with the image of the camp ground. The campground was the locus for Christian religious commensality and—unambiguously—for conversion, that liberating experience that gave the black community a taste of freedom.

> Deep river, my home is over Jordan,
> Deep river, Lord; I want to cross over into camp
> ground.
>
> O don't you want to go to that gospel feast,
> That promised land where all is peace?
>
> Deep river, my home is over Jordan,
> Deep river, Lord; I want to cross over into camp
> ground.[101]

In the light of their distinctive biblical emphases and eschatological vision, it is not surprising that southern black Christians experienced Jesus as an eschatological king and deliverer. This image of Jesus as a powerful, regal figure occurred at least as often in black worship as did the better-known image of Jesus as comforter, friend, and fellow sufferer. What may be surprising is that neither of these aspects of Jesus was stressed by whites in their preaching to blacks and in their training of black preachers and exhorters. Instead whites preached "a meek and submissive Jesus who had urged his followers to become like little children in order to enter the kingdom of heaven."[102] Slaves were to imitate Jesus' obedience to God's will, even when that obedience entailed suffering, as Jesus' had. Ironically, rather than reinforcing obedience, the story of Jesus' suffering gave black Christians confidence that He could understand them in a special way in a kind of kinship of suffering. Moreover, the story of how Jesus bore his suffering inspired blacks' interior resistance to cruelty and injustice. For example, Webber explains, "The spiritual 'they crucified my Lord, and he never said a mumbling word' reflects the admiration slaves felt for Jesus and for those of their own community who were able to bear a whipping without making a sound or begging for mercy."[103]

In the kinship of suffering, Jesus the comforter was "family." Thus, when blacks sang, preached, and prayed about their eschatological expectations they would speak of going home and often of enjoying a friendly, familial feast,

> A-settin' down with Jesus
> Eatin' milk and drinkin' wine[104]

The encounter with Jesus as fellow sufferer, comforter, and friend was compatible in the minds of blacks with their understanding of him as eschatological king and deliverer. King—a title that may have come from the hymns of whites—was the title blacks most frequently applied to Jesus.[105] King Jesus watched over the sinful world from his throne in heaven and heard the prayers of his suffering people.[106] King Jesus was the captain of the Old Ship of Zion (and the conductor of the gospel train), "and he'll carry us all home."[107] This king and deliverer rode on a milk-white horse, as in the book of Revelation. "Ride on King Jesus!" the song exulted. "No man can hinder him!" Callie Williams of Alabama affirmed her faith in the coming deliverer:

> I really believe Christ is comin' again
> He's comin' in de mornin'
> He's comin' in de mornin'
> He's comin' wid a rainbow on his shoulder
> He's comin' again bye and bye.[108]

While blacks' comprehension of the theological meaning of the words they so enthusiastically sang may have been less than full, they clearly understood the central tenets of the Christian myth.[109] When they sang of deliverance, they also sang by implication of exodus, Easter, and apocalypse.

> Jesus Christ, He died for me, Way down in
>   Egyptland:
> Jesus Christ, He set me free, Way down in
>   Egyptland.[110]

With Jesus, their king and friend, the people of God would ride home and feast at the table of the Lord.

Southern whites did not emphasize eschatology as much as blacks did. They stressed the end of one's personal life more than the end of the present order. In their vision, Jesus was first and foremost the divine being who converted sinners. This understanding of Jesus was especially prominent in the camp-meeting religiosity of the plain folk. To yeomen whites or plain-folk—hard-working people who owned few or no slaves—Jesus was the indispensable agent of conversion, the "initiator of grace."[111] He also acted as the saving guide of souls as they picked their way along the perilous path of this world to the next. The danger of backsliding was feared by most religious plainfolk; only after death would the believer be wholly safe and saved.[112] For plainfolk as for planter-class whites, salvation was a highly individualized enterprise undertaken by the solitary soul with the help of Jesus. For them, the promised land was a heavenly hereafter, not an eschatological new order.

It may be that southern whites did not emphasize eschatology and Jesus' role in the end time as much as blacks did because of their more individualized theology of salvation. However, their increasing general commitment to an economy based on slave labor also may have influenced the role of Jesus and eschatology in white religiosity. Especially as northern antislavery voices increased in volume, southern intellectuals developed a countering position that portrayed the South as the perfect society. Insofar as theologizing about a perfect society entered the religious consciousness of the white person in the pew, it would block or at least retard the tendency to hold the concrete, immediate eschatological vision of society that might otherwise appeal to many—especially the disadvantaged and those who dealt daily with the relative chaos of the frontier areas in the expanding South. In a very real sense, the argument that the South was the perfect society probably was postmillenial in its impact on southern white religiosity.

Leadership

Black Christians in the South appropriated religious leadership differently from whites because they compared their experience of actual religious leaders to their experience of the society's authority structure as a whole.

The authority structure of the South was dominated by white males. Preeminent from a socioeconomic point of view were planters. Politicans had authority, too, but they tended to come from the planter class. Other white males participated in authority in several ways. One way was by being white. Any white could question any black's right to be at any place at any time and the black—whether slave or free—was expected to give satisfactory response. Thus a disadvantaged, illiterate white could question and challenge a literate slave who kept his less literate master's books. James Curry of North Carolina reported, "It is the custom, whenever a white man meets a colored man in the road, to call out to him, (no matter what his age may be,) 'hulloa, boy, who do you belong to?' "[113] Another way white males participated in the authority of the planter was by participation in the general economy. Thus, the cotton factor, the shopkeeper, the sheriff, and even the teacher had authority. Finally, many white males held authority directly delegated to them by a planter. Such was the case with white overseers. Such was also the case with white missionaries to plantation blacks. One could not evangelize slaves without the master's leave.

Nevertheless, the church had authority that was not derived from relationship to either the economy or the master class. That authority came from God. Of course, some whites, both believing and nonbelieving, tended to take a pragmatic view of religious authority. They favored religion if they regarded it as helpful in maintaining blacks where they belonged in society. Isaac Throgmorton, a slave barber born in 1809 who worked in Kentucky and Louisiana, described a white overseer who would

> whip a woman with 400 lashes, because she said she was happy. This was to scare religion out of them, because he thought he wouldn't be able to get anything out of them if they were religious. He said he would rather see them stealing and swearing and whoring than be religious.[114]

Fugitive slave William Wells Brown reported a contrasting attitude.

> It was not uncommon in St. Louis to pass by an auction-block, and hear the seller crying out, *"How much is offered for this woman? She is a good cook, good washer, a good obedient servant. She has got religion!"* Why should this man tell the purchasers that she has religion? I answer, because in Missouri, and as far as I have any knowledge of slavery in the other States, the religious teaching consists in teaching the slave that he must never strike a white man; that God made him for a slave; and that, when whipped, he must not find fault—for the Bible says, "He that knoweth his master's will, and doeth it not, shall be beaten with many stripes!" And slaveholders find such religion very profitable to them.[115]

Generally, whites permitted black religious activity within the varied limits of supervision required by local custom and the enforcement of a pass system. Henry Blake reported the limits placed on religion's authority in the Alabama of his slave childhood.

> In slav'ry time black folks go tuh Church en stay dere 'till de meetin' wuz near 'bout ovah ef dey didn't have no pass dey run on home. De patterrollers rode 'round on der horses en mules en dey would come tuh de "Nigger Church" tuh see ef dere wuz eny "niggers" dere dat didn't have no pass en when dey start home dey would come up en ask dem fer de passes en dem what didn't hab no

35

pass, ef dey could outrun dem, dat would free dem but ef de patterrollers kotch 'em dey give dem der 'quired number ub licks en sent 'em home.[116]

Conditions and limits notwithstanding, southern white believers regarded God as supreme authority. Those Christians who were not theologically antimission took the Great Commission with utmost seriousness: "Go ye therefore, and teach all nations, baptizing them in the name of the Father, and of the Son, and of the Holy Ghost, teaching them to observe all things whatsoever I have commanded you. . ." (Matt. 28:19-20). A master of this stripe would not dream of impeding the mandate to preach the Gospel. Thus a planter disturbed by the religious songfest of slaves was stymied when he asked the leader to stop the noise.

> "Now, Dick, I can bear a great deal, but more of this I cannot stand. Now I say, Dick, stop it. . . ." "Yes, massa; but the blessed Gospel is from God, and if He command us to pray, and you command us not to pray, what shall we do, massa?"[117]

As Genovese has shown, antebellum blacks were aware of (and used) the power of religion over those in authority.[118] These blacks saw white religious leaders' authority as twofold: one in relation to white male power structure, the other in relation to the amazingly independent power of the Gospel—thanks to God. The white preacher held some special authority. But holding authority was not unusual for white males. Moreover, many Methodists with religious authority from class leader to bishop held slaves. In many, perhaps most such cases, the religious authority of these men was diluted if not destroyed. Ex-slave J. W. Lindsay told the Freedmen's Inquiry Commission in 1863:

> Clergymen at the South own slaves, and some of them are pretty severe. They don't do much of the barbarous treatment work themselves, but have overseers to do it for them. They sell their slaves, of course. Their biggest text is, "Servants, obey your masters"; and "he that knoweth his master's will & doeth it not, shall be beaten with many stripes", is a favorite text with them. A great many masters call up their servants on a Sunday morning, & give them a slice of meat apiece, after they have fed them all the week on a peck of corn.[119]

Canadian fugitive slave Susan Boggs reported:

> the man that baptized me had a colored woman tied up in his yard to whip when he got home, that very Sunday and her mother belonged to that same

church. We had to sit & hear him preach, and her mother was in church hearing him preach. The daughter was as pretty a young woman as you would ever find in a day's run. He only hired her. She had light skin, & her hair just hung down on her shoulders. And he had her tied up & whipped. That was our preacher! He preached, "You must obey your masters and be good servants." That is the greater part of the sermon, when they preach to colored folks.[120]

John Dixon Long, Methodist author of antislavery bent, argued that even the sincere white preacher unencumbered by other relationships to slaves was hampered by his position in the system itself.

But chattel slavery raises barriers between the pastors and the slave that are seldom, if ever, crossed. If the slaves are maltreated by their masters, they fear to go to their preachers with their trouble. If the masters were to know of their servants making complaints, both preacher and slave would fare badly, for both are in the hands of the master. Slaveholders, united, can starve the preacher and sell the slaves. The whole truth of the matter is, there is no such thing as the pastorate in the South between the white preacher and slaves, and never can be, from the nature of slave society and its consequences.[121]

For blacks, the act of holding authority was less ordinary and more diffuse. The field hand, for example, held no authority. He or she was subject to a hierarchy that could include overseers, suboverseers, drivers, foremen.[122] If any individual in that hierarchy was black, his authority was assigned by the master. (I know of no case of women holding such positions.) If a free black craftsman—a blacksmith, for example—had authority, it derived from his relationship to the agrarian economy dominated by the planters. In general, blacks' authority derived in some way from whites and from a relationship to the economy.

The black religious leader held a unique position in this context. His authority came from the church (an institution generally dominated by whites, but one that did not derive its authority from relationship to the economy), from the Gospel—from God—and from his own people. John Jasper was convinced, as were a great number of his hearers, that he was a "God-made preacher."[123] Isaac Lane struggled against his own sense of call and was discouraged from preaching by a white minister. Unable to resolve his sense of inner urgency, he consulted an old black preacher associated with the Methodists.

He was a pure Christian, and he told me that if God had really called me, he surely knew his own business better than man, and for me not to trouble myself, but to trust in God. I did trust him, and the inspiration soon came to send in to the Southern Methodists my petition to preach. I did so at one of their Conferences. They did not refuse me. Indeed, they held out a hand of help and encouragement.[124]

In fact, denominations fostered the development of black religious leaders because they were more effective with other blacks than white ones.[125] However, as E. Franklin Frazier pointed out, being licensed to preach by the church enhanced the authority these men wielded.[126]

Unlike other southern blacks with authority, the religious leader's work was spiritual—noneconomic or even anti-economic. If black preachers received pay for their labors, it came from a possible donation by whites or—in the case of those who served slaves—from donations by slaves who had the chance to earn money for themselves.[127] An urgent sense of mission, not money, motivated the black preacher. As one explained,

> During the whole number of years I was preaching, I never took any thought of money or how I would fare in life. I have never had anything, but I have never been in want. God knows the needs of them that trust in him.[128]

Black religious leaders were more gifted in the pulpit than whites because effective preaching was the principle by which they were selected and because preaching was the church function to which they generally were limited. In contrast, among whites one could find the extraordinarily charismatic preacher Peter Cartwright as well as the less gifted William Winans, who spent much effort in participating as a presiding elder in the Methodist denominational machinery—an avenue almost wholly closed to blacks.[129]

Perhaps the most decisive factor in blacks' distinctive appropriation of religious leadership was the obvious fact that the white preacher was not black, but the black preacher was "black like me." Therefore, no matter how charismatic in other respects the white preacher might be, he never evoked one response characteristic of charisma—identification. This response, together with the preacher's sense of divine call and his license from the church to exhort or preach, gave the black religious leader a unique power base that successful men protected from the very likely danger of becoming too identified with white interests. Such men continually affirmed—often in clandestine settings—their identification with the slave community.[130]

Of course, the white preacher was not a part of the black community and did not participate in the ritual experience of communal Christian liberation described above. Finally, the factor of identification modified the message itself. When a preacher who was white and participated in the authority structure in several ways said "Jesus saves," it meant one thing to the Christians in the gallery. When a fellow black but God-powered preacher told the community "Jesus saves," the message was re-formed.

Ethics

Southern Christians' outlook on ethics in this period (as even today) was closely related to their concept of salvation. For both Baptists and Methodists, salvation was individual. A Calvinistic Baptist saw salvation as the unilateral gift by God to the individual soul. In the Methodist's Arminian view, some kind of self-effort—from simple consent to strenuous struggle—was required of anyone who would "flee the wrath to come" and receive God's saving grace. This individualistic concept of salvation logically led to the conclusion that the only way to save society was by means of regeneration of the individuals within the society. Ministers stressed the individual's spiritual state.[131]

Ethics were understood just as individualistically. Sin was personal, not societal or systemic. God was interested in the individual.

In His plan of salvation, therefore, God did not expect His children, black or white, to wrangle with each other over right or wrong, justice or mercy. Rather, He desired His people to wrestle with the demons within themselves. The adversary who had to be conquered was not the black man or the white man but the sinful, disorderly, disobedient *self*.[132]

Records of church discipline point to what was regarded as seriously wrong. For example, in 1831 some black members of the Tuskaloosa Methodist Church in Alabama were expelled for "immorality, intemperance, uncleanness, fighting, stealing, lying."[133]

Alongside all the individualism that they expressed in concert with whites, blacks showed a counter tendency as well in their appropriation of Christian ethics. In both the interpersonal and the societal spheres, blacks demonstrated a communal awareness of themselves in decision-and-action situations.

The classic interpersonal case concerns slaves' interpretation of the commandment so often addressed by white preachers' sermons—often at a master's suggestion—"Thou shalt not steal." Whites viewed the taking of one person's property by another person without the owner's consent as morally wrong. To them, a slave who took a chicken from the owner's kitchen was stealing, sinning. (Paradoxically, the law and the society regarded slaves both as persons and as property. In this case, whites regarded the "thief" as a person.) But slaves made a careful ethical distinction between "stealing" and "taking." If a slave took a chicken from the owner's kitchen, since both chicken and slave were property of that owner, not theft but a simple rearrangement of the owner's possessions had occurred. Former house slave Sarah Fitzpatrick of Alabama explained:

> Niggers didn't think dat stealin' wuz so bad in dem times. Fak' is dey didn't call it stealin', dey called it takin'. Dey say, "I ain't takin' fo'm nobody but ma' mistrus an' Marster, an' I'm doin' dat 'cause I'se hongry."[134]

But if one slave took a chicken from another without the other's consent, theft did take place. In both "taking" and "stealing," an awareness of the individual's relationship to the group played a part in judging the deed.

One method slaves used to deal with stealing is particularly revealing of this awareness.

> They believed that if one stole something from a fellow slave, lied about it, and then drank a bottle of water filled with dust from the grave of a recently departed slave, he would die. Most thieves, not wanting to take the risk, preferred to confess when confronted rather than drink from the bottle.[135]

In this case, a kind of "communion of saints"——the dead influencing the living——effected justice in the slave quarters. .

The communal ethic also covered matters of personal and community privacy. Those who betrayed individuals or who revealed group secrets were regarded harshly.[136] Betrayal did occur, as fugitive slaves Henry Bibb and William Wells Brown testified.[137] But betrayal was judged against a communal norm of loyalty and solidarity, values expressed in a variety of everyday situations. Slaves developed a sophisticated standard for weighing truthfulness against the community's welfare. Ambrose Headen, a slave carpenter in North Carolina and Alabama who was born in 1822, wrote in his 1878 autobiography, "We always called 'freedom' 'possum,' so as to keep the white people from knowing what we were talking about. We all understood it."[138] In the interests of the group, blacks told whites what they wanted to hear and developed behavioral masks that guarded their real personalities and attitudes.[139] In many situations, such duplicity constituted a moral obligation. But lying to or otherwise deceiving a community member ordinarily was judged wrong.

The differing socio-ethical attitudes of white and black Christians—like individual interpersonal ethics—were tied to differing views of salvation. The difference is analogous to Buddhism, with its so-called small raft (Hinayana or Theravada) and large raft (Mahayana) traditions. In the first, salvation is an individual matter. One navigates the river of life on a small raft. In the second, salvation is regarded as communal. People navigate on a large raft, and the holy person, or bodhisattva, willingly remains with the rest. As a religious virtuoso, the bodhisattva possesses not only personal virtue, but overwhelming compassion and concern for all humans.

Antebellum black Christians demonstrated a tendency to regard the socioethical enterprise communally. A modern black theologian observes:

> The conversion experience led to different expressions in the religious life of the slave. But underlining these varieties of expression was the experience of the presence of the Almighty Sovereign God wherein the slave was commissioned by the divine for a definite task in the world. Most of the accounts of the conversion experience conclude with God's telling the slave to return to this world.[140]

Blacks thus tended to idealize the holy one who was a "person for others." Many so regarded Baptist Andrew Bryan and Methodist Harriet Tubman. The same vision of a communal socioethical enterprise was reinforced by the heavy symbolic stress by blacks on Moses as prophetic liberator and Jesus as apocalyptic deliverer. Moreover, the evidence suggests that antebellum black Christianity was characterized by an incipient orientation toward action for liberation. Thus the Prosser, Vesey, and Turner episodes were all permeated with religious language and meaning. The informer who betrayed the Gabriel Prosser plot in 1800 reported that a preparatory meeting included a religious service in which "The Israelites were glowingly portrayed as a type of successful resistance to tyranny; and it was argued , that now, as then, God would stretch forth his arm to save, and would strengthen a hundred to overthrow a thousand."[141] A report describing Denmark Vesey, Methodist class leader and leader of an insurrectionary plot in 1822, asserted that

> He rendered himself perfectly familiar with all those parts of the Scriptures which he thought he could pervert to his purpose, and would readily quote

them to prove that slavery was contrary to the laws of God; that slaves were bound to attempt their emancipation, however shocking and bloody might be the consequences; and that such efforts would not only be pleasing to the Almighty, but were absolutely enjoined, and their success predicted in the Scriptures. . . in all his conversations he identified their situation with that of the Israelites."[142]

Nat Turner's religious vision was decidedly apocalyptic. His was an immediate and violent eschatology.

He saw white spirits and black spirits contending in the skies. The sun was darkened, the thunder rolled. "And the Holy Ghost was with me, and said, 'Behold me as I stand in the heavens!' And I looked, and saw the forms of men in different attitudes. And there were lights in the sky, to which the children of darkness gave other names than what they really were; for they were the lights of the Saviour's hands, stretched forth from east to west, even as they were extended on the cross on Calvary, for the redemption of sinners. . . ." On May 12, 1828, the Holy Spirit appeared to him, and proclaimed that the yoke of Jesus must fall on him, and that he must fight against the serpent when the sign appeared.[143]

It has been argued that plots and actual insurrections were atypical and that the religious thought that inspired them did not represent blacks' religious ideas. However, more generally, in the light of blacks' strong if incipient orientation toward liberation in the here and now, white measures to control and monitor black worship look very logical. It was not simple paranoia that induced whites to fear that unmonitored all-black worship might foster revolt. However, as John Lee Eighmy explained, "all states had special slave codes that included prohibitions against the assembling of slaves unsupervised by whites; but these laws, often made more rigid by exaggerated fears of insurrections, were not strictly enforced."[144] In this matter, as with antiliteracy legislation, Southerners honored a tradition of making exceptions.[145]

It must be stressed that this last distinctive characteristic in blacks' appropriation of the Christian tradition was an incipient orientation, not a full-blown development. Although blacks yearned for a social revolution and a new, just social order, there is no evidence that they consciously planned to launch that revolution by forming separate congregations and denominations. Like their white counterparts, the devout sought conversion, the grace to live faithful Christian lives, and salvation. Frequently, southern blacks felt morally superior to whites. But to change one's denomination was something like changing one's nationality.

Methodism in the 1850s

The Methodist Episcopal Church, South (MEC,S), together with the Southern Baptist Convention, comprised the majority of Christians (indeed, of professors of any religion) in the American South. Although nineteenth-century statistics lack reliability, the available figures are indicative. The 1860 census reported a black population of 4,441,830.[146] Of these, 3,632,726 resided in eleven southern states.[147] The MEC,S, counting members from these states and from Kentucky, Missouri, and Kansas, listed a total black membership of 404,430 in 1858. However, in 1866, the bishops of the MEC,S claimed that prewar black membership was notably higher. Available figures indicate that before the war, the racial composition of the MEC,S was aaproximately sixty-three percent white and thirty-seven percent black.[148] But from one local district to another, the ratio of black Methodists to white ones varied, with blacks sometimes in the majority.[149]

Not surprisingly, geographical representation also varied.[150] Methodists were usually neither the richest nor the poorest in wealth or status in the South.[151] Church members ranged in age from the newly converted and admitted (as early as age nine) to ripe old ages. Reliable generalizations about the sexual composition of the MEC,S are difficult to make. However, it is certain that such denominational decision makers and ritual leaders as preachers and exhorters were male, and probably a slight majority of rank-and-file members were female.

In contrast to the variety in the membership of the MEC,S, the denomination possessed a highly organized and unified structure. Individual congregations in connection with relatively nearby congregations comprised a circuit, which was designed so that a man on horseback could reach each congregation in a tour of two to three months. Circuits were served by traveling preachers (circuit riders), who augmented the work of local clergy—local preachers, exhorters, and class leaders. Contiguous circuits comprised districts. Circuit representatives met quarterly at district conferences led by presiding elders—itinerant preachers appointed to this supervisory role by the bishops. The various districts comprised regional conferences, which met annually with at least one bishop in attendance. All districts were represented at the General Conference, a meeting of leaders representing the entire church and ordinarily held every four years with all active bishops in attendance.[152]

This connectional polity, balanced in a nice tension between centralized and congregational powers and responsibilities, was further unified in spirit and purpose by the schism of 1844. That year, accumulating differences and resentment between the northern and southern portions of the denomination broke the church into two autonomous regional churches. At issue was the proper relationship of the church to the social order—most specifically to slavery as a social and economic institution. The northern church continued to call itself the Methodist Episcopal Church, while the southern body adopted the designation of Methodist Episcopal Church, South. In 1846, the southern bishops affirmed their denomination's consecration

> not merely to the common duty of evangelizing the world, but to the performance of a peculiar work—a work as difficult as it is momentous, in connection with the moral and religious wants of millions of the children of Africa, found in our midst, and entrusted to our care."[153]

Both before and after the schism, Methodist worship carried the relatively accurate reputation for moral earnestness and, above all, emotionalism. Five forms were prominent.

1. *Class meetings.* John Wesley intended the class meeting to be, as one southern Methodist leader put it, "a special opportunity for oversight, counsel, and exhortation by one called the leader."[154] The class leader could be black or white, slaveholding or nonslaveholding.[155] The purpose of the class meeting was to foster members' personal moral and spiritual growth. In Wesley's original design,

> The weekly self-examination to which it subjected the member, as well as the instruction, advice, or reproof, as occasion required, which it secured from the leader, would, in the very nature of things, prompt to greater watchfulness and diligence in the performance of duty.[156]

2. *Love feasts.* Love feasts consisted of a commensal sharing of bread and water along with testimonies by believers and some hymn singing. Interested outsiders could attend once or twice; such individuals were likely to be drawn into Methodism by the experience. However, as the nineteenth century progressed, the ritual fell into disuse or was held in modified form. In the postwar period, southern Methodist Bishop George Foster Pierce complained, "I have found love feasts much neglected, and when held greatly impaired in their value by sittings with open doors and letting in a promiscuous crowd."[157]

3. *Circuit rider's services*. The coming of the circuit rider provided many ritual opportunities, including preaching and celebration of the Lord's Supper, special class meetings, and sometimes special meetings for slaves.[158] The circuit rider also provided devotional literature, catechetical instruction, and—by virtue of his itinerancy—a sense of connectedness with other Methodist worshipers.

4. *Revivals*. Revivals occurred sometimes spontaneously, sometimes as a result of planning. They consisted of preaching and hymn singing and were directed toward conversion. Sometimes brief, sometimes long in duration, revivals were local counterparts to more widely attended camp meetings.

5. *Camp meetings*. The ecumenical nature of these worship settings has been discussed above. Here it is important to note Methodist use of camp meetings for evangelizing the South.

Camp meetings receive no space in the Disciplines of the MEC,S. They were always seen as nonofficial but highly effective means for winning souls. From what appear to be spontaneous beginnings in the early 1800s, Methodists adopted, refined, and systematized this form of worship. Indeed, many Methodists felt camp meetings had become artificial by midcentury. But the same complaints about camp meeting developments came from other denominations too. These developments constituted one of several processes of routinization in southern revivalism. In this matter, as in others, southern Methodists were clearly and simply representative of southern religion.

In fact, the MEC,S was representative of religion in the American South in many ways. It was one of the largest denominations in the South. It was resoundingly Protestant and revivalistic in character. Despite its spare hierarchical organization, it possessed a democratic polity. It embraced black and white, rich to poor, male and female. With few exceptions—as with other denominations—white males held all decision making and ritual powers. Its worship centered on conversion and was emotionally demonstrative. It was a forward-looking, frontier church in attitude. Though over the years some theological distinctions from other denominations had grown sharper and others had blurred, Methodists maintained steadfast faith in and dependence on God's grace-full providence.

Methodist religious leaders, whether black or white, exemplified the Methodist spirit and spirituality. They generally viewed one another as brothers in God's service. Ever since Francis Asbury (a founder of American Methodism) inspired the noted Black Punch and traveled and worked with the charismatic black Harry Hosier, white Methodists shared some religious leadership with blacks on the level of preacher, exhorter, class leader. These men shared certain expected characteristics and qualifications.

In general, all antebellum Methodist religious leaders in the South were male. Also, all generally had experienced conversion. Often it was the newly converted who sought to become exhorters or preachers. William, a slave who experienced conversion and the call to preach almost in the same moment, explained:

> Before God can use an man, that man must be hooked in the heart. By this I mean that he has to feel converted. And once God stirs up a man's pure mind and makes him see the folly of his ways, he is wishing for God to take him and use him.[159]

Often, established preachers or presiding elders spotted potential talent and encouraged a young man to serve, as in the case of Peter Cartwright.[160]

All of these men were gifted, some more than others, of course. But Methodist custom and discipline dictated that a man first be admitted "on trial." If he proved effective, responsible, and orthodox, upon examination by established leaders at the local quarterly conference after the designated trial, the preacher was granted official status. As a result, the "office" charisma was a more salient feature of Methodist religious leadership than of Baptist.

Methodists, black and white, were noted for their ardent, enthusiastic preaching style. Preaching was always based on a biblical text and always geared toward conversion. The preachers were dedicated men with strong allegiance to Methodist theology (with its influential Arminian cast) and Methodist worship, known for its enthusiasm and renowned for its stirring hymns.

Paradoxically, Methodist religious leaders were dedicated to education, even though being educated was not a qualification for being admitted on trial and often preachers and exhorters—especially black ones—were illiterate. But the Wesleyan discipline of daily self-improvement transmitted to Americans via Coke, Asbury, and the others, included daily exposure to the Bible and spiritually nourishing treatises.

The major difference between white and black leaders in the MEC,S was not degree of education or literacy, but rather access to leadership opportunity in the denomination. Black access was limited to positions as class leaders, exhorters, and preachers. Moreover, black preachers were local, appointed by quarterly conferences. They were not members of annual conferences, unlike most full-time white ministers. However, a few black preachers and exhorters participated in quarterly conferences such as those on the Hickory Creek Circuit in Tennessee in the 1840s and 1850s.[161] Whites, on the other hand, could aspire to the offices and responsibilities of presiding elder and bishop. Of course, the percentage of whites who became presiding elders was small, and the percentage who became bishops even smaller. More numerically significant and more significant for the developing distinctive traditions of black religious leadership was blacks' limited access to responsibilities that entailed mobility. It was considered dangerous to the social order to appoint a free black circuit rider. Even slave circuit riders were very rare. Slave preachers who traveled generally did so unofficially on the strength of their own charisma and their reputation among whites and blacks. John Jasper's services were much sought after for funeral sermons.[162] But some of the other better-known black preachers encountered great difficulty in obtaining opportunities to preach. For example, Henry Evans, a free black, overcame popular opposition and even a Fayetteville town ordinance in the process of helping establish Methodism in Cumberland County, North Carolina. In a tribute to Evans at his death, Methodist Bishop William Capers pointedly remarked:

> But what shall we say of a system that demanded a prostration of self-respect from a man of the Christly courage of Henry Evans! He did a great work, but might it not have been greater had he been untrammeled by the sense of his subordination?[163]

Indeed, Richard Allen refused to travel in the South with Bishop Francis Asbury and "Black Harry" Hosier because he was keenly aware of his status and of the dangers he would face.[164]

Among Methodist preachers, a tradition of asceticism by circumstances developed. The demands of preaching the gospel in predominantly rural, relatively recently settled areas were rigorous, and financial support from denomination and congregation was usually unpredictable and never abundant. But the ascetical practices dictated by riding circuit differed greatly from those forced on the black who responded to a call to preach. Indeed, only one similarity seems to have prevailed; a tradition of relative poverty within a nonsystematic, anti-economic method of remuneration. For example, according to one report, in 1859 a black preacher might receive some of the denominational funds disbursed by the MEC,S for the maintenance of the missions for blacks. It was possible that he might serve a black church partly supported by whites. "In other cases, where the slaves themselves paid their pastors, they were given the opportunity by their owners to earn the money for themselves."[165] Lucius H. Holsey worked as a circuit preacher for the MEC,S after the Civil War without a fixed salary; he subsisted on occasional contributions. A church member told him, "We are glad you don't preach for money, but for souls."[166]

In general, the white Methodist leader was mobile, devout, perhaps ambitious, often literate, and haphazardly remunerated. The black was greatly hampered in mobility, but just as devout—some might argue more devout in light of obstacles to be overcome and relative paucity of prospects and rewards. He was limited in ambition, not often literate, and haphazardly remunerated if at all. He probably preached in a style that was more incantational and responsorial than that of his white colleagues. On examination, the content of his preaching would betray the developing distinctiveness of black religion.

The patterns of prewar religious relationships of blacks and whites were a mixture of participation and exclusion, with participation decidedly dominant in denominational structures and in ritual. Although blacks were excluded from higher level positions of leadership, a few black preachers participated in local quarterly conferences, and blacks often participated in local disciplinary proceedings. Moreover, the incidence of a pastor or preacher of one race being "called" by a congregation whose majority was made up of the other race was not unknown. In some cases of separate worship services for blacks and whites, sheer numbers and not racial considerations seem to have prompted the initial holding of separate services. But generally, participation was dominant over exclusion in ritual. On the eve of the Civil War, separate denominations were not discussed. But the motivation for separation was present in blacks' religious experience, a distinctive appropriation of Christianity.

TWO

Tell Old Pharaoh, 1861-1865

In the war years between 1861 and Appomattox, black and white Methodists in the eleven states of the Confederacy experienced change, chaos, and confusion. Throughout the South, war affected religious life profoundly yet variously.

It was a time of terrifying emotional and social flux. An elan of confident, almost joyous rage lifted the first wave of whites into the war effort.[1] Males went off to war; females assumed unaccustomed duties. Martha Jane Crossley of Perote, Alabama, "operated every facet of plantation management while her brothers fought in the war. In addition to supervising the planting activities, she cultivated a home garden of vegetables, canned fruits from the orchard, and tended her flower garden of roses and japonicas. A deeply religious woman, Martha had evening sessions of Bible reading for her slaves."[2] But fatigue flattened the certainty of early victory shared by so many southern whites. Events confused and demoralized them. As the fighting failed to produce quick victory and lives and battles were lost, expressions of defeatism began to appear in private diaries and public sources.

Events affected southern blacks variously as well. The absence of so many of the white males who dominated the authority structure of society fostered disorder. Problems with slave discipline were common. As early as 1861, Mary Fitzpatrick of Alabama "admitted that she could not manage the slaves and pleaded with her husband to come home 'right away.' "[3] In 1862, Susanna Clay of Madison county Alabama wrote, "The negroes . . . are ignorant and grasping, as we are, for a happier future. I have a hard time with ours, for they do as they like. I try 'moral suasion' to get them to do their duty. It sometimes succeeds." In 1863 she wrote that "the negroes are worse than free, they say they *are* free. We cannot expect any authority. I beg ours to do what little is done."[4]

Disorder was not limited to black-white relationships. Aggrieved individuals and groups took advantage of the war's confusion to commit violent acts of revenge. White Methodist preacher D. Sullins found himself a member of a band of white and black refugees fleeing Union troops in Tennessee.

> The Federal forces were pressing on all sides, guided and encouraged by Union friends, of whom there were many. The worst elements of society were aroused, and bad men took occasion to vent their spite on such as they did not like, old family feuds broke out afresh, and the land was full of murder and robbery. Bands of the worst men seized the opportunity, and scoured the country by night, calling quiet old farmers to their doors and shooting them down in cold blood. This caused other bands to unite and retaliate. It was the reign of terror—war at every man's door, neighbor against neighbor. Neither property or life was safe by day or night.[5]

Local lawlessness and social disorder and especially incursion by Union troops produced many refugees. As early as 1862, whites and blacks fled Tennessee for the lower South. On 16 February, Nashville's presiding elder A.L.P. Green, his wife, and his youngest daughter "joined the great hegira of fugitives southward—which flight no man has ever described to this day."[6] Union occupation brought not only white flight but also an influx of blacks to Nashville. By June 1863, the Board of Aldermen asked the army to help the city deal with "a large unprecedented collection of runaway slaves, contrabands and free negroes without profitable occupation or place of residence and without means of assistance."[7] Blacks who flocked to population centers tended to settle on the periphery where free blacks already lived in colonies.[8] In 1864, a Union soldier in Nashville stated bluntly, "the negars is as thick as hell here."[9] When Union troops took over New Orleans in May 1862, they attracted runaway slaves. John W. Blassingame asserts that "by March 1863, 29 percent of the slaves on fifteen plantations in Orleans parish were fugitives."[10]

Troop movements in rural areas also resulted in social disorder and produced refugees. As Elizabeth Allen Coxe remembered,

> there was a general look of devastation and pillage, and, worst of all, the absence of many, many black faces, familiar to us from childhood, whom we had cared for in sickness; watched dance at Christmas and sing at prayer meetings; heard delightful Br'er Rabbit stories from, and considered our inseparable

belongings. Except Maumer's family, there were few left but the old and incapacitated, although many of those who followed the troops wandered back by degrees.[11]

Many planters took steps to protect their investments in slaves. "Aunt Adeline," born in 1848 in Hickmon County, Tennessee, reported that

During the Civil War, Mr. Parks took all his slaves and all of his fine stock, horses and cattle and went South to Louisiana following the Southern army for protection. Many slave owners left the county taking with them their slaves and followed the army.[12]

Lewis Mann, who was born in Arkansas, recalled that

Durin' the war my mother's master sent us to Texas; western Texas is whar they stopped me. We stayed there two years and then they brought us back after surrender.
I remember when the war ceasted and remember the soldiers refugeein' through the country.[13]

Some slaveholders took only the more valuable and more mobile male slaves, leaving women and children behind. Such was the case in Louisiana. According to C. Peter Ripley, "The extent to which this situation was common is reflected in the records of contraband camps established by Federal authorities to care for the migrants. At one camp over 70 percent of the adult arrivals in one month were females."[14] Black families who arrived as a unit at contraband colonies underwent further dispersal, often being separated by work assignments.[15] Given all the movement by blacks and whites in this period, it is an understatement to say that throughout the war years, refugeeing aggravated the already unsettled state of Confederate society.

Even before this confusing flux, the South had been a varied region. Some states boasted more population centers than others. (Only after the war would most of these centers grow to merit the name of city.) Though cotton was king, some areas produced other crops, such as rice, sugar, and tobacco.

Demographically, the Confederate South was rural. Although most slave holders (who were ordinarily but not exclusively white) held few slaves, most slaves were held by owners of large plantations. In 1820, thirty-seven percent of southern town dwellers were blacks, but by 1860 the percentage had fallen below seventeen percent.[16] Hence most black religion before, during, and after the war was a rural phenomenon.

Rural demography, social flux, and regional variety, all influential factors, render impossible the drawing of a distinct picture of southern religious history during that period. In addition, military incursions by Union troops varied from place to place in timing, duration, and intensity. Many church records—and many churches—were destroyed. What documents survived provide a picture that is confusing and far from complete. Evidence from some locales shows overall membership growth; elsewhere decline is evident in white membership and black as well. Considered as a whole, the evidence for these war years indicates an incipient trend toward religious separation stemming from blacks' initiative. But the times were too chaotic for the trend to be decisive. After Appomattox, the evidence would tell a surer tale.

War

Chronologically and geographically, the war's progress was uneven. Both Tennessee and Louisiana were occupied by Union forces in 1862. Union troops cut off Texas and Arkansas from the rest of the Confederacy in 1863. In 1864, West Virginia separated from Virginia and set up a government loyal to the Union. In the same year Tennessee and Louisiana also had new Unionist governments and Arkansas produced a new state constitution. Florida felt the first effects of war early in 1861, when Union forces blockaded the coast. Mississippi was the target of intense Union attack from 1863 on. Alabama experienced battles in its northern section beginning in 1862, but central Alabama was not the stage for fighting until July of 1864, the year of Sherman's devastating march through Georgia to the sea. In 1865 his troops scythed upward into the Carolinas and then into Virginia.

By the time of Lee's surrender at Appomattox, the war had affected the Methodist Episcopal Church, South both indirectly and directly. Indirectly, the church was affected on every level, from the denomination as a whole to local members.

As a denomination, the MEC,S was weakened and demoralized. The General Conference scheduled for 1862 was not held due to the occupation by Union troops of New Orleans, where the conference had been scheduled. Instead, Bishop Andrew presided at a meeting in the parlor of an Atlanta home on 10 April 1862. Bishops George F. Pierce and John Early also attended. The meeting dealt with episcopal salaries, consolidation of newspapers, and appeals for support of foreign missions.[17] But no pronouncements and no statements of moral guidance were issued. Moreover, I find no evidence that these denominational decision makers envisioned at this time even the possibility of separate denominations for blacks and whites.

The local organization of the MEC,S was shaken and in some cases completely disrupted. In Georgia, for example, church work at first continued, "but the absence of so many official members, stewards and class leaders especially, led to a sad derangement in the management of church affairs."[18] Later schools were suspended and some church buildings were used as hospitals. The North Georgia Conference met even after invasion; after Atlanta fell, its last wartime conference was held in 1864 in Athens.[19] However, even before invasion, "there was little religious interest. A revival was almost impossible under the existing circumstances of the wild days."[20] In Alabama, the situation was similar. For example, the Socopatoy Circuit apparently did not hold its second quarterly meeting in 1862.[21] Records of the fourth quarterly meeting at the Union Town Station in 1862 describe the spiritual condition of the church as "not very good."[22] In 1864, at the fourth quarterly conference of the Oak Bowery Circuit, nine whites and twelve blacks were admitted on probation and twenty-four whites and thirty-four blacks were received in full connection. However, the Sabbath schools were "all suspended but one and suspended upon account of the receint Yankey Raid." As for the general condition of the church, "the Paster says that he cannot define it."[23]

In general, by the last year of the war, in the judgment of presiding elder A. L. P. Green,

> The Southern Conferences north of the Tennessee River had been for several years in a state of collapse, owing to the presence of large armies and the general demoralization that attends military rule. Even the Conferences in the Gulf States were very much deranged.[24]

Nevertheless, troop incursions and sinking morale notwithstanding, local church life continued in many if not most of the charges of the MEC,S. Ex-slave Felix Haywood, born in 1845 in San Antonio, Texas, recalled that "The ranch went on jus' like it always had before the war. Church went on. Old Mew Johnson, the preacher, seen to it church went on."[25]

Presence or absence of adequate leadership may have made the difference between perseverance in or suspension of local Methodists' religious life. Former Confederate chaplain George G. Smith explained, "Preachers were elected officers of companies and regiments, or they left their charges to go as

53

chaplains of regiments."[26] Many white Methodist clergy served in the Confederate Army. Texas conferences listed preachers who went to war as associates of another preacher assigned to a charge with the footnote "In the C.S. Army" or "Chaplain in C.S. Army."[27] Later in the war, conscription cut away more ministers, especially those assigned to special missions to blacks. The 1864 Conference of the Montgomery (Alabama) Conference of the MEC,S adopted a resolution protesting conscription of licensed ministers by the state of Alabama, pointing out the ministers, especially "local preachers and traveling preachers, who are not ordained, and preachers who served colored missions."[28]

With local organizations disrupted and leaders absent, confusion plagued Methodists. Initially enthusiastic about the Confederate cause, as were the majority of Southerners, white noncombatants expressed progressively less optimistic sentiments. Eliza Frances Andrews made this entry in her journal on 15 January 1865:

> This was the Sunday for Dr Hillyer to preach to the negroes and administer communion to them. They kept awake and looked very much edified while the singing was going on, but most of them slept through the sermon. The women were decked out in all their Sunday finery and looked so picturesque and happy. It is a pity that this glorious old plantation life should ever have to come to an end.[29]

Elizabeth Allen Coxe of South Carolina remembered a church service during the last winter of the war:

> our clergyman in reading the chapters from Jeremiah with the gloomy prophecies, that come in Lent, stopped and said, while we listened to the booming of the far-distant bombs, falling into Charleston: "You will never hear these mournful chapters read again as long as long as you live without recalling these days of suspense and humiliation."[30]

Throughout the wartime period, membership seems to have fluctuated. Conferences that did manage to gather statistics recorded growth here, decline there; but records are not complete, so membership patterns are not clear. A sampling of statistics for the plantation missions alone is indicative. With 1860 figures as a baseline, North Carolina's plantation missions grew in 1861 and 1862 but lost members in 1863 and 1864, for a net gain of about 400. Florida missions lost members in 1861 and 1862, grew in 1863, lost in 1864, for a net loss of about 200. Virginia lost members in all years except 1864, for a net loss of 1,300. Some plantation missions' figures—such as Mississippi's—are incomplete.[31] Overall, there were 112 fewer plantation missions in the MEC,S, in slave states in 1864 than there had been in 1860.[32]

Where the war action directly affected Methodists, the effects were clear. Whites were demoralized—often to the point of defeatism or despair—by the presence of Union troops.

The response of slaves to Union troops varied. Later, nostalgic romantics would recall that slaves had continued loyal, even loving service to their masters and especially to their mistresses. In fact, some slaves did continue to serve. Martha Colquitt, who was born on a Georgia plantation in 1852, worshipped as a slave in the gallery of the Baptist church down the road. She narrated a story of her grandmother's encounter with the Yankees.

> My grandma wuz a powerful Christian 'oman, and she did love to sing and shout. Dat's how come Marse Billie had her locked up in de loom room when de Yankee mens come to our plantation. Grandma would git to shoutin' so loud she would make so much fuss nobody in de church could hear de preacher and she would wander off from de gallery and go downstairs and try to go down de white folkses aisles to git to de altar whar de preacher wuz, and dey wuz always lockin' her up for 'sturbin' worship, but dey never could break her from dat shoutin' and wanderin' 'round de meetin' house, atter she got old.

Religious enthusiasm gave the grandmother exceptional freedom at worship and, afterwards, a private place away from work.

> Dem Yankee sojers rode up in de Big 'Ouse yard and 'gun to ax me questions 'bout whar Marse Billy wuz, and whar everything on de place wuz kept, but I wuz too skeered to say nuthin'. Everything wuz quiet and still as could be, 'cept for Grandma a-singin' and a-shoutin' up in de loom house all by herself. One of dem Yankees tried the door and he axed me how come it wuz locked. I told him it wuz 'cause Grandma had 'sturbed de Baptist meetin' wid her shoutin'. Dem mens grabbed de axe from de woodpile and busted de door down. Dey went in and got grandma. Dey axed her 'bout how come she wuz locked up, and she told 'em de same thing I had told 'em. Dey axed her if she wuz hongry, and she said she wuz. Den dey took dat axe and busted down de smokehouse door and told her she wuz free now and to help herself to anything she wanted, 'cause everything on de plantation wuz to b'long to de slaves dat had worked dar. Dey took grandma to de kitchen and told ma to give her some of de white folkses dinner. Ma said, "But de white folkses ain't et yet." "Go right on," de Yankees said, "and give it to her, de best in de pot, and if dey's anything left when she gets through, maybe us will let de white folkses have some of it."

Mother and grandmother alike apparently obeyed the Union soldiers. Meanwhile, having violated the etiquette governing commensality,

> Dem brash mens strutted on through de kitchen into de house and dey didn't see nobody else down stairs. Upstairs dey didn't even have de manners to knock at Mist'ess' door. Dey just walked right on in whar my sister, Lucy, wuz combin' Mist'ess' long pretty hair. They told Lucy she wuz free now and not to do no more work for Mist'ess. Den all of 'em grabbed dey big old rough hands into Mist'ess hair, and dey made her walk down stairs and out in de yard, and all de time dey wuz a-pullin' and jerkin' at her long hair, tryin' to make her point out to 'em whar Marse Billie had done had his horses and cattle hid out.

As Martha Colquitt told it,

> Us chilluns wuz a-cryin' and takin' on 'cause us loved Mist'ess and us didn't want nobody to bother her. Dey made out like dey wuz goin' to kill her if she didn't tell 'em what dey wanted to know, but atter a while dey let her alone.
> Atter dey had told all de slaves dey could find on de place not to do no more work, and to go help deyselves to anything dey wanted in de smokehouse, and 'bout de Big 'Ouse and plantation, dey rode on off, and us never seed no more of 'em.

The drama over, these slave women helped restore—however temporarily—the customary patterns of living.

> Atter de Yankees wuz done gone off Grandma 'gun to fuss: "Now, dem sojers wuz tellin' us what ain't so, 'cause ain't nobody got no right to take what belongs to Marster and Mist'ess." And Ma jined in: "Sho' it ain't no truf in what dem Yankees wuz a-sayin' '" and us went right on living just like us always done 'til Marse Billie called us together and told us de war wuz over and us wuz free to go whar us wanted to go, and us could charge wages for our work.[33]

More commonly, as soon as the absence of the master and/or the nearness of Union troops was felt, slaves served grudgingly at best. For example, Jane Brasfield of Greene County Alabama wrote Governor Shorter to intercede with President Davis and get her son returned from the army to take over the family plantation. "The negroes . . . are now pretty much at their own will . . . one man has already run away with the intention of going to the Yankee army and . . . doubtlessly he will inspire others to do the same."[34] Mrs. W. D. Chadick, the wife of a Confederate army chaplain, wrote about the "rascality and slothfulness of slaves" when Union troops occupied nearby Huntsville, Alabama.[35]

Very often, slaves simply left their work when Union troops arrived. Some fled outright; others turned to the troops for freedom and in some cases for the chance to fight as Union soldiers.[36] H. E. Sterkx summarized the shift in slaves' attitudes.

> At first the war was viewed as a white man's affair in which they had no direct involvement, but gradually it dawned on them that they did have a vital stake in its outcome. The Emancipation Proclamation of 1863 heightened this realization, and as Union forces widened their control thousands of Negroes deserted to the enemy. According to one Union officer stationed in Huntsville, many became "confident that the rainbow and the bag of gold were in the camps of the federal army. "The mask of loyalty was torn away at last and dismayed mistresses such as Mrs. Chadick rationalized that Negro slaves were duped into leaving 'their real friends' by mischievous soldiers and army chaplains."[37]

More devastated than white Methodists' morale or service by slaves was the property of the MEC,S. Many churches' buildings and records were destroyed. For example, in 1864 the Methodist Episcopal Church, South of Decatur, Alabama, lost a "substantially constructed" brick church building used by the white congregation, a frame church building used by the black congregation, and a frame office building used by the pastor.[38] Single structures in Huntsville and Bellefonte, Alabama, were destroyed.[39] Many churches were occupied as quarters by Union troops. Southern whites expressed outrage and even a sense of desecration at such seizures. By 1865, Susanna Clay of Alabama wrote sorrowfully to her son,

> We have lost all, almost. . . . Your father and myself have the wing of the house. We stay in it as the negroes left long since. . . . Our beautiful town is desolated. Our church injured . . . the Methodist Church was burned; the small *Episcopal Church* is occupied by them.[40]

Worse was the policy pursued by Secretary of War Edwin Stanton with the help of his good friend, Bishop Ames, and the cooperation of the northern Methodists. According to Ralph E. Morrow, northern Methodism saw itself as "the God-appointed church to redeem and possess the South."[41] The War Department evidently saw the northern church as an important potential ally in the war. Late in November of 1863 it issued a directive for the military departments of Missouri, Tennessee, and the Gulf, which gave Ames authority over "all houses of worship belonging to the Methodist Episcopal Church,

South, in which a loyal minister . . . appointed by a loyal bishop of said church does not officiate." Military authorities were to give Ames "all the aid, countenance and support practicable" in carrying out this crusade. Ames's fellow bishops supported the effort and received similar authorizations.

> Ostensibly the permissive authority to hold Southern Methodist Churches was based on the disinterested objectives of "preventing Southern preachers from holding their pulpits as a safe place from which to encourage treason" and curbing "the lapse into semi-barbarism" caused by disordered religious conditions.[42]

While his fellow bishops acted less swiftly elsewhere, Ames took over Methodist churches early in 1864 in Memphis, Little Rock, Pine Bluff, Vicksburg, Jackson, Natchez, Baton Rouge, and New Orleans.[43] Other northern clergymen took over more southern Methodist meeting places, acting sometimes with local military sanction, sometimes with only their own resolve.[44]

The northern church's ambitions embraced southern whites and blacks alike. At its 1864 General Conference, it passed the following resolutions:

> On Colored Pastorates.—It is declared to be the duty of the Church to encourage colored pastorates for colored people, and the bishops are authorized to organize colored Mission Conferences. On Freedmen.—It is recognized as the duty of the Church to assist in relieving the wants of the freedmen. The associations organized for their welfare are endowed and recommended, and Congress is urged to establish a Bureau of Freedmen's Affairs.[45]

Moreover, early in 1864, John Newman assumed direction of Methodist efforts around New Orleans with an inaugural sermon stating "that if the Caucasian should reject the gospel and refuse to fill the churches . . . we turn to the sons of Africa."[46]

Northern Methodist activity during the Civil War was limited for the most part to those areas of the South occupied by Union troops. Nevertheless, it represented a significant disruption of both civil authority and religious life.

Thus, as early as 1862 and probably not later than 1864, the average white southern Methodist noncombatant found both the structure of society and the life of the church in disarray. The local church building was destroyed or occupied by troops or staffed by northern missionaries or manned by overworked southern ministers, either very young or superannuated, trying to hold church life together.

Southern white Methodists' hearts were not hardened as the biblical Pharaoh's had been, but they were just as blind to the message written in the war's events.

Let My People Go

John Hope Franklin points out that Lincoln's September 1862 announcement and January 1863 enactment of the Emancipation Proclamation succeeded in rallying northern political support and in giving hope to blacks. In the South, Lincoln's moves created confusion among Confederate leaders.[47]

Did the Emancipation Proclamation give early impetus to the exodus of black Christians from the MEC,S? Probably not; its influence on the formation of separate black churches, congregations, and denominations was negligible. Many separate black congregations existed before September 1862, the majority of them constituted with the cooperation and supervision of whites. We lack a precise count of how many such churches there were, but the formation of separate ritual situations under the same denominational umbrella occurred more commonly in population centers than in rural areas. For example, as early as 1819 a Savannah preacher reported,

> There was one side of the gallery appropriated for their [blacks'] use, and it was always the most thinly seated part of the church; while there were two respectably large colored churches in the city, with their pastor, and deacons, and sacraments, and discipline, all of their own.[48]

But whites and blacks on many plantations continued to attend common worship. Sometimes the slaves attended separate services either in place of or in addition to joint ritual participation. Some planters continued to provide special meeting places for their slaves. In general, arrangements for worship followed the practical pattern if not the spirit outlined by Holland N. McTyeire (later Methodist bishop and historian) in his well-known 1851 essay on the duties of masters to servants.

> *Provisions for religious instruction*:—In cities and villages, where churches are numerous and convenient, permission for attendance may discharge the master, as far as public ministrations to his servants are concerned. But in rural districts, where they are scarce and distant, permission to go, in many instances, amounts to no gospel privilege at all. To the strong and healthy the walk may be trifling;

but the aged and infirm, who need heavenly consolations as much as any, are entirely deprived unless the means of going be furnished.

McTyeire criticized inadequate accommodations.

Sometimes a portion of the church has been assigned them, roomy and comfortably seated;—sometimes this has been overlooked, and they are left to stroll around, or listen to the sermon at the window, or under the poor shelter of an arbor. They have been invited to the gospel feast, but no places have been provided for them. With hungering, unfed souls they look on—the spectators of others' piety and not partakers of the common grace.

The preferred and dominant pattern was joint worship.

It is desirable that white and colored worship together; one reason among many is, that no distinctions of religion arise between them. Religion appears in its loveliest form where rich and poor, bond and free, meet together, and to a common Father, through a common Saviour, drinking into one Spirit, offer up songs and prayers, and hear what all have an equal interest in . . . . But whenever this is impracticable, the master, either alone or jointly with his nearest neighbors, ought to make special provisions for his servants. A chapel should be built for them, in which he and his own family may be occasionally seen, and a stated supply of religious instruction engaged for.[49]

We lack also a precise count of separate black churches formed during the Civil War itself. Even a reliable estimate is impossible to make. Records of the MEC,S were not everywhere well kept. In addition, more than eighty percent of the South's black population was illiterate.[50] Thus it is difficult to be certain how many additional separate black congregations were formed and still remained under the denominational umbrella of the MEC,S. Finally, reports of separate churches that affiliated with northern denominations were preserved by those denominations with understandable self interest. As a result, these latter separate groups are likely to be proportionately overrepresented in any guess.

Nevertheless, available reports of separate black churches formed in this period indicate that indigenous developments and not the Proclamation or outside interference influenced these groups. For example, the Alabama Conference Journal shows an increase in white membership from 36,985 in 1860 to 38,203 in 1862 and a decrease in black membership from 21,856 to 19,591.[51] These figures suggest an incipient exodus of blacks from the MEC,S. Local records give some support to such a conclusion. For example, records for the Socopatoy Circuit of the Alabama Conference show relatively fewer black members admitted to probationary or full membership at quarterly meetings during the war years. The second quarterly meeting for 1862 was either not held or not recorded. By the second quarterly meeting in 1863, a three-man committee was appointed "to take into consideration the propriety of providing for the supply of the colored congregations within the bounds of Socopatoy circuit by local preachers." Under the question, "What amts have been collected to defray the expenses of the circuit and how applied?" the committee responded that "each local preacher have an appointmt to the colored people at each of their Sabbath appointments until the next quarterly Conference."[52] There was no money to spare, but the need to serve separate black congregations was new and felt with some urgency. In 1863, the Alabama Conference decided to divide into two—the Montgomery Conference and the Mobile Conference. In 1864, the secretary of the Missionary Department of the Mobile Conference noted erosions in black membership, blamed outsiders, and expressed worry about the inadequacy of the Methodist mission to plantation blacks.

> At the beginning of the war, there were some 200,000 colored communicants in the fellowship of the M.E. Church, South. The pseudo friends of the African have sadly diminished that number by their diabolical crusades upon us; but we have still left under our care a vast multitude of this dependent race. It has been, for a long time, a source of pain and anxiety to our Church that there are still in our country many plantations unvisited by the Missionary, unblessed by the means of grace.[53]

Not surprisingly, this incipient trend by blacks to separate from the MEC,S was blamed on outside influence, as had been other black behavior that whites were unable to control. However, if outsiders had influenced these early separations, it is likely that they would have used news of Lincoln's Proclamation to water the seeds of independence they allegedly sowed. Significantly, the Proclamation is not mentioned.

The effect of the Emancipation Proclamation on white Methodists was more pronounced. With other southern whites, they feared that news of the Proclamation would incite slave insurrections. Attempts to suppress the information were common. As Adeline Jackson, born a slave in South Carolina in 1849, explained, in slavery times "we got most our outside news Sunday at church."[54] But during the war, this information network was likely to be monitored carefully or suppressed outright. Anna Miller, a slave in Kentucky, then Missouri, then Texas, stated, "I's don't know much 'bout the war. The white folks don't talk to us 'bout the war, and we-uns don't go to preaching or nothing, so we can't larn much."[55] But if the Proclamation stirred fresh fears of insurrection, religious repression of blacks was not new. As early as 1 December 1860, the quarterly meeting for Union Town Station in Alabama reported a revival that yielded "nearly fourty white persons [who] have been received on probation and fifty-one [who] professed to find peace," but

> Our colored congregation has also shared in the heavenly visitation. There have been no protracted services held for their benefit, owing to the agitation of the political world, yet the work of Regeneration like the Leaven, a woman took and hid in three measures of meal has been going silently yet perceptible onward.[56]

From some whites the Proclamation elicited defenses of the Methodist mission to the slaves. Little effective religious outreach followed, however. Resources were scarce. In Georgia, the missionary collection dropped from almost thirty thousand to seventeen thousand during the war.[57] If white Methodists' spirits were willing, sheer lack of money, energy, and available religious workers put most action out of reach.

Black Methodist preachers and exhorters were affected differently by the war than were their white counterparts. Restrictions on black ministers were lifted in an attempt to relieve the shortage of ministers. Ahlstrom describes this effort as "of little avail."[58] Nevertheless, scattered evidence suggests that at least some of these men stepped into the breach of spiritual leadership created by the volunteering and conscription of white ministers. Where this occurred, the status of black leaders was enhanced in the eyes of their coreligionists, even the whites. Such was probably the case for "Ned the Servant of Dr R Clarke, and Jefferson Servant of Rev L L Fox," both of whom were granted exhorters' licenses at the 25 January 1864 quarterly conference at Union Town, Alabama—the first black religious leadership noted in the Union Town Journal since February 1853.[59] Sometimes, especially when Union troops approached, blacks seemed to have preached a more explicit gospel of Christian freedom to be realized in a concrete future that was near. In an 1872 interview, Thomas Rutling recalled that during the war

> the old slaves told me that something was going on, and I must listen sharp up at the house, and come and tell them what the white folks said. There were about a dozen slaves on the plantation. One was a preacher: he could read a

little. I was table waiter then, and after talking over the news at table, missus would say, "Now Tom, you mustn't repeat a word of this." I would look mighty obedient,—but—well—in less than half an hour, some way, every slave on the plantation would know what had been said up at massa's house. One would see sad faces when the Yankees got whipped, and then the preacher would have prayer meetings. I was too young to know what they prayed for, but heard the old slaves talking about freedom. By and by the rebels kept getting beaten, and then it was sing, sing, all through the slave quarters. Old missus asked what they were singing for, but they would only say, "because we feel so happy."[60]

In 1864, from his Texas prison camp, Union captive A. J. H. Duganne heard "in a jubilant African chorus: Ole massa's runn'd—aha! De darkeys stay—oho! It mus' be now dat de kingdom am a comin', An de year of Jubilo!"[61]

It is difficult to assess the effects of these developments on the relationship between black and white members of the MEC,S. Noncombatant whites (in large part women and males not fit to fight or otherwise exempted from fighting) viewed the outcome of events as uncertain, sometimes with optimism, sometimes with pessimism. According to some reports, blacks were hopeful. William N. Adams of San Jacinto County, Texas, reported that even before the war,

A white preacher he come to us slaves and says: "Do you wan' to keep you homes whar you git all to eat, and raise your chillen, or do you wan' to be free to roam roun' without a home, like de wil' animals? If you wan' to keep you homes you better pray for de South to win. All dey wan's to pray for de South to win, raise the hand." We all raised our hands 'cause we was skeered not to, but we sho' didn' wan' de South to win.

Dat night all de slaves had a meetin' down in de hollow. Ole Uncle Mack, he gits up and says: "One time over in Virginny dere was two ole niggers, Uncle Bob and Uncle Tom. Dey was mad at one 'nuther and one day dey decided to have a dinner and bury de hatchet. So dey sat down, and when Uncle Bob wasn't lookin' Uncle Tom put some poison in Uncle Bob's food, but he saw it and when Uncle Tom wasn't lookin', Uncle Bob he turned de tray roun' on Uncle Tom, and he gits de poison food." Uncle Mack, he says: "Dat's what we slaves is gwine do, jus' turn de tray roun' and pray for de North to win."[62]

Union soldier George Hepworth quoted a southern black:

Massa say dis bery mornin', "De damn Yankees nebber get up to here!" . . . but we knowed better: we all knowed better dan dat. We'se been prayin' too long to de Lord to have him forgit us; and now you'se come, and we all free.[63]

The relationship between white and black Methodists in the South was vulnerable to influence from outside forces, especially the effect of approaching or present Union troops. With these in growing numbers came missionaries and teachers from northern denominations. Among Methodists, struggles over church property multiplied. The relationship between southern and northern white Methodists was exacerbated by the northern church's targeting the black population for recruitment into its fold. The northern church's activity angered southern white Methodists more than the combined efforts of other northern groups such as the Presbyterians, the Congregationalists, and the American Missionary Association. Formerly members of the same denomination, southern Methodists suffered territorial violation by northern Methodists, whose church Lincoln in 1864 praised for sending "more soldiers to the field, more nurses to the hospital, and more prayers to heaven than any."[64] And more missionaries to steal our pulpits and people, the Southerners would add.

But black northern denominations also worked in the South during the war years. AME missionaries were active in a limited number of places, beginning in 1863. In May of that year, AME ministers James Lynch (who would later affiliate with the northern Methodists) and James D. S. Hall went to Charleston, South Carolina, at the invitation of a northern Methodist minister there. Later that year Bishop Daniel Payne, Rev. (later Bishop) Alexander Wayman, and Rev. J. M. Brown traveled to Virginia and took in churches in Norfolk and Portsmouth. In December, Payne was invited to Nashville, where he took in two black congregations affiliated with the MEC,S. In 1864, Rev. Jabez M. Campbell and Rev. M. M. Clark preached in Mobile.[65] The minutes of the Annual Conference that year indicate additional AME activity in the South. New Orleans petitioned for the creation of a new conference; J.M. Brown proposed the formation of a conference comprised of North Carolina, South Carolina, Georgia, and east Florida to border on the Louisiana Conference; and the General Conference called for the creation of a Louisiana Conference. The General Conference also reported that AME ministers had visited Memphis, Vicksburg, Little Rock, Columbia, Natchez, and eight freedmen's schools; however, only South Carolina is characterized in the minutes as a mission.[66] In March 1865, Bishop Alexander Wayman and Rev. Elisha Weaver traveled to Savannah to meet James Lynch, who had been working also in South Carolina. However, it was not until after the surrender that Bishop Campbell organized the Louisiana Conference (including Louisiana, Mississippi, Arkansas, and Texas). On 16 May 1865, Bishop Payne organized the South Carolina Conference (including South Carolina, North

Carolina, and Georgia), which contained 3,000 members.[67] Unfortunately, denominational histories record the reception of members and congregations without describing the dynamics that led to the forming of new affiliations.

The less powerful but no less evangelistic AMEZ organization sent workers South, especially to North Carolina. The small denomination—only 5,000 members at the beginning of the war[68]—had appropriated funds for southern mission work as early as 1858, but its earliest representatives reached North Carolina in 1864.[69]

Expressions of outrage by white Methodists opposing the black missionaries' work during the war years are conspicuously lacking. These missionaries were not as numerous as their white counterparts from the ME Church. Moreover, southern whites tended to view blacks paternalistically, as if blacks were irresponsible children. It is possible that at this early date, they did not take AME and AMEZ activities as seriously as they would after the war. Even then, white Methodists would pay less attention to missionary efforts by the black denominations than to their own resentment of the efforts by the northern church, with the result that the black independents prospered while their white coreligionists feuded.

What was the effect of northern religious workers on the formation of separate black Methodist congregations and denominations during the war? While the kind of evidence and its condition make a summary assessment difficult, northern religious workers' effect was limited significantly by four factors. First, most black Methodists, like the majority of southern blacks, were rural people. However, early northern religious workers came to population centers. Rural black Methodists held their religious life in their own hands as never before.

A second factor was the general disruption of communications. Formal means of communications—newspapers or religious tracts, for example—reached an illiterate people indirectly at best. During the war, many publications missed issues or ceased entirely. More important, informal networks of communication were disrupted. William Mathews, who had been a slave in Franklin Parish, Louisiana, reported, "All kind of war talk floatin' round 'fore de Yankees come. Some say de Yankees fight for freedom and some say dey'll kill all de slaves."[70] Anna Miller explained that in Texas, "De w'ite fo'ks don' ta'k to us 'bout de wah an' we uns don' go to preachin' or nothin', so we can't larn much."[71] Even before northern incursions, rumors could not be confirmed or denied in conventional ways. Thus, religious claims and counterclaims brought by northern missionaries would have to be made

65

in person, and they would have to triumph over the local leader's charisma. Denominational competition was a third factor. The confusion of competing churches and leaders is well represented by the story of a black congregation in New Bern, North Carolina, affiliated with the MEC,S. In January 1864, with Union troops in uncertain charge, this large church had apparently indicated that it wished to change denominational affiliation. The northern Methodists, the Congregational Church, and two AME missionaries from Virginia all were endeavoring to win the church. However, AMEZ missionary James Walker Hood proved the most adept at persuasion, drawing on his own charisma, the "office" charisma of the federal government, and local loyalties. On Easter Sunday, Hood

> preached with "incentive vitality" to an overflowing crowd. At the close of the "highly spiritual" service, he presented a letter from Secretary of War Stanton which he had obtained on a special trip to Washington. It stated, "The congregation of colored Methodists worshipping in Andrews chapel in New Bern, North Carolina, shall have the right to decide their own church relations and select their own pastor." This greatly impressed the people. They took a vote deciding to enter the A.M.E. Zion Church. The people really wanted a church and a preacher of their own race. Also, Christopher Rush, the second General Superintendent of the Zion denomination, was a native of New Bern and was highly regarded.[72]

A fourth limiting factor was disorganization and lack of focus. Northern Methodists divided their efforts unsystematically between evangelizing blacks and trying to absorb the MEC,S, pulpit by pulpit. As early as 1864, the northern church was struggling over the question of separate jurisdictions for whites and blacks in the South. Would they be temporary measures facilitating the religious reclamation of the South or permanent, filled with prejudice, and dangerous to the denomination's mission? The developing pattern itself was confusing: separate conferences along the border where the northern Methodists had been established before the war and mixed conferences farther South.[77]

Disorganization stemmed from inexperience, lack of funds, and lack of sufficient workers to cover the South. The northern independents drew increasingly on indigenous black leaders who, in turn, drew along with them an indigenous following, self-aware and already experienced in at least rudimentary group decision making processes.

Indeed, all of the northern Methodist denominations were structurally inadequate to the task of evangelizing southern blacks during the war years.

There were simply not enough workers to send into the harvest. Thus without hesitation all three northern Methodist bodies adopted the policy of attracting and using indigenous southern black leaders. Many such men would be prominent in "northern" efforts after the war.

THREE

After Apocalypse, Moses

Between April 1965 and August 1866, as never before, blacks decisively acted on their own and their forebears' distinctive appropriation of Christianity. In every state of the now-defeated Confederacy they surged into separate congregations, churches, and denominations. The exodus of black Methodists from the MEC,S from Lee's surrender to the time of blacks' first participation in the political project that historians would later term "Radical Reconstruction" was swift in shaping post-Civil War religious relationships in the American South, yet the interpretation of this decisive event has been problematic. An overview of the period and its historiographical problems provides partial explanation of the difficulties, but an examination of the sociopolitical context is necessary to correct previous descriptions. Only then can one review black Christians' actions in and white Christians' reactions to the exodus and analyze and evaluate the event.

Overview

After defeat, confusion and chaos reigned in the Confederate South. Governments that were formed in confident rage and righteousness only a few years before had to be dismantled. Some southern soldiers returned humiliated. Some Confederate leaders fled the South; others stayed in shame. The United States Secretary of War lost no time in issuing order 77 to effect rapid demobilization of northern troops. By mid-June, demobilization was well on its way. With the withdrawal of troops, refugees and wanderers, both black and white, encountered increasing lawlessness. Gangs, highwaymen, and brigandage in general abounded. It was in this period of enormous social flux that an estimated two-thirds of the black members of the MEC,S set up church communities of their own outside that denomination.[1] The decisiveness with which blacks acted contrasts starkly with the ambivalent words and ambiguous deeds that characterized the other events of the post-Civil War period.

Given such a dramatic event, one would expect early observers and historians alike to have described it clearly. But the contrary is the case. For example, Isaac T. Tichenor, white pastor of the First Baptist Church in Montgomery, Alabama, had a congregation of 300 whites and 600 blacks at war's end. He reported:

> When a separation of the two bodies was deemed desirable, it was done by the colored brethren, in conference assembled, passing a resolution, couched in the kindliest terms, suggesting the wisdom of the division, and asking the concurrence of the white church in such action. The white church cordially approved the movement, and the two bodies united in erecting a suitable house of worship for the colored brethren. Until it was finished they continued to occupy jointly with the white brethren their house of worship, as they had done previous to this action. The new house was paid for in large measure by the white members of the church and individuals in the community. As soon as it was completed the colored church moved into it with its organization all perfected, their pastor, board of deacons, committees of all sorts; and the whole machinery of church life went into action without a jar. Similar things occurred in all the states of the South.[2]

Tichenor's use of passive voice—"When a separation . . . was deemed desirable"—obscures what happened. Whose desire activated separation? The black congregation's initial formal resolution and its eventual organization "all perfected" suggest that black group self-awareness and decision making initiated this separation. However, the white congregation's cordiality and cooperation cause one to wonder whether separation "was deemed desirable" first by whites, who then pressured the blacks to separate. The language of the account masks what actually happened.

Andrew Brown, a black Methodist preacher in Georgia, provided this account of a separation.

> In 1865, I a poor, bare-footed, bare-headed man, had met in Atlanta a man named James Lynch; he told me of the A.M.E. Church. The first of September the M.E. Church, South, held their conference and sent a preacher to preach to the colored people in Dalton. He sent for me and told me he was sent there. I told him we could not comply with his request; we must look for ourselves. He said if I was going to take the people, to take them and leave. I thanked him

and we left. We were in a sad plight, for there was not an ordained minister from Chattanooga to Atlanta.[3]

In this case as in Tichenor's example, the initiative of an unordained black leader with the support of his congregation seems to have been decisive in the group's separation from the parent denomination. But Brown mentions a "request" of the MEC,S preacher. Did that preacher request conditions for continued connection that he was certain the black congregation would feel compelled to reject? Further, Brown encountered then AME missionary James Lynch. Had this outsider been the decisive influence, or had prior indigenous decision making by the congregation inclined Brown to seek out a black Methodist connection, which Lynch then represented? Brown's account raises many questions about the precise nature and sequence of events.

AME historian Wesley J. Gaines gave the following account of the separation of black Methodists in Savannah from the MEC,S.

> At the close of the war the colored Methodists in Savannah, while really under the watch-care of the M.E. Church, South, were under no regular pastor, but were kept together by William Bentley, C.L. Bradwell and William Gaines. When James Lynch visited Savannah at that time, he made secret arrangements with Rev. C.L. Bradwell to take out the church. Through the efforts of the latter, then a local preacher, it was not a difficult matter to bring them into the fold of our church. The affiliation he proposed to them was thoughtfully considered, and after mature deliberation was accepted, and the first African Methodist Episcopal Church in the State of Georgia was organized by Rev. A. L. Stanford.[4]

In this account, an outsider and a local leader seem to have conspired to activate this exodus. But once again, the use of passive voice masks and at the same time hints at what actually happened. The affiliation "was thoughtfully considered" and "was accepted"—by whom? It seems likely that a significant portion of the membership (if not all the black Methodists) engaged in decision making in this case—but only "after mature deliberation." One assumes that the Membership deliberated, that it had the group self-awareness and decision-making processes adequate to produce the outcome Gaines describes. But the language masks precisely what happened.

Precisely who initiated the movements of whole congregations or elements of congregations? Why is the information not more clearly recorded? Analysis of available data supports the following interlocking answers.

Accounts by blacks do not more clearly record the exodus for several reasons. Southern blacks generally lacked training in writing of any kind—including current events or history. At war's end, only about ten percent of the ex-slave population was literate, with the percentage for free blacks only slightly higher. Thanks to whites' repressive attitude toward educating blacks—an attitude exacerbated by Nat Turner's insurrection back in 1831—social pressures with legal teeth had been set against training literate southern black church members, let alone journalists or historians.

Northern blacks were more likely to be educated. But they were also more likely to have vested interests in how events were described and interpreted. This seems to have been the case with the well-known accusation by abolitionist Frederick Douglass that religious revivals in the South actually promoted the peculiar institution.[5] After the war, most northern black observers were also participants in the struggle to win individuals and congregations to a particular denomination. Their accounts are skewed by triumphalism and the human weakness for blowing one's own horn. In such accounts, the leadership of a charismatic but isolated black shepherd in an autonomous congregation of souls—the Baptist pattern—was more likely to go unrecorded than were the activities of black denominational leaders.

Neither lack of training and sophistication nor vested interests marred certain accounts by black eyewitnesses to the exodus. Yet these too tended to mask precise information about what happened. For example, the otherwise lively, colorful narrative of Baptist Harry Cowan becomes flat and blankly factual in its account of the exodus.

> I was born in Davie County [North Carolina], January 20, 1810, was converted in 1825, licensed to preach in 1828, and ordained eighteen months later by Rev. Harry Powers.
>
> In 1830-'31, I organized five churches, three in Rowan and two in Davidson County. Considerable liberty was granted to me by my master, Thomas L. Cowan, to preach the Gospel, but Nat. Turner's insurrection practically suspended the work for thirty years. I was thereafter restricted to hold religious services, as opportunity allowed, within a radius of 40 miles of Salisbury. My subsequent owner, Joel Jenkins, son-in-law of my former master, opposed my preaching, and ordered the patrols to arrest and punish me; but God, on many occasions, brought almost miraculous deliverance to me. My old master, convinced of my divine call to the ministry, gave me a horse, saddle and bridle to be used on my tours. His overseer was hostile to me, mocked my baptizings, clubbed me, and fed me on half rations. He was, however, forced to beg my pardon and dismissed from service. My young master was converted in one of

my meetings, and thereafter frequently attended our services, and related this experience on his death-bed, Wednesday before John Brown was hung at Harpers Ferry.

After the war the colored Baptists rapidly withdrew from white churches and organized independent bodies. I have organized, or assisted in organizing, 37 churches, baptized over 1,500 converts, preached 1,000 funerals, and married an equal number of persons.[6]

This black leader tells only that the exodus happened quickly, a fact evident from statistics alone.

In such cases, it seems that writers were guarding from white eyes what really was being chosen so decisively. They seem to be avoiding almost by reflex a confrontation with whites who were growing increasingly hostile and repressive as the period progressed. This interpretation is congruent with analyses of racial etiquette that find among blacks the custom of communicating to whites only as much as the white community will bear—or, better, as much as is advantageous to black community. Researcher William R. Ferris found that in interviewing

> it was not possible to maintain rapport with both Whites and Blacks in the same community, for the confidence and cooperation of each was based on their belief that I was "with them" in my convictions about racial taboos of Delta society. Thus when I was "presented" to Blacks by a white member of the community, the informants regarded me as a member of the white caste and therefore limited their lore to noncontroversial topics. . . . Blacks rarely speak openly about their society with Whites because of their vulnerability as an oppressed minority. . . . As the group in power, Whites can afford to openly express their thoughts about Blacks, whereas the latter conceal their feelings toward Whites as a means of self-preservation.[7]

Ex-slave Martin Johnson, born in Texas in 1847, stated plainly:

> Lots of old slaves closes the door before they tell the truth about their days of slavery. When the door is open, they tell how kind their master was and how rosy it all was. You can't blame them for this, because they had plenty of early discipline making them cautious about saying anything uncomplimentary about their masters.[8]

Accounts by whites also do not more clearly record the exodus. Initially, at war's end, whites were not so much hostile as hurt—and confused to the point of paralysis. Thus contemporary accounts by whites may mask the story of the exodus partly because of antebellum self-perceptions still operative in their thinking. Whites still thought of themselves as the masters of society, even when they had no slaves. Slaves were their children. How could these creatures, when freed, initiate and carry out the monumental task of institution building? Thus accounts by whites are skewed by mechanisms of apparent denial and projection. Some southern accounts denied the blacks' initiative in the wish to seem more nearly central to what after all did happen. In his *Recollections of an Old Man*, Methodist preacher D. Sullins casts himself in the central role in the exodus of blacks from his congregation. However, his account definitely indicates that these black Methodists had not only group self-awareness but also leadership and an orientation to group activism. It is probable that Sullins simply facilitated a separation toward which his black members were already moving.

> My negro membership was large and a somewhat puzzling factor in our work. Our custom before the war was to have our colored people sit on the rear seats below or in the gallery, and to give them an afternoon service about twice a month. But now they were free and beginning to assert their independence. I told them of the organization of their people in Philadelphia, Pa., the Zion Methodists; and believing they would do better in that church than in ours, I called their leaders together and explained it to them, and advised them to go into that organization. A letter to this effect soon brought a representative of that church to see me. We got the colored folks together, and after a little talk they agreed to go in a body to that church. So I took the church register and transferred them. The work was done, and all were pleased.[9]

Accounts by some southern whites blame the exodus on white outsiders. For Alabama Baptist historian B. F. Riley, whites were wholly responsible for everything—ideas as well as action. After proudly noting gains in black membership between 1845 and 1860, he explains,

> In some instances, in quarters of the South where was massed a large slave population, the colored members exceeded those of the whites. Encouraged by every consideration to persuade the slaves to accept the Christian religion, and rejoicing when they did so in large numbers, the effect of this was not thought of, on the serious side, till the slaves were set free. Then came the question of the possibility of the former slave members, in cases where their membership was more than that of the whites, asserting the right of the majority, under Baptist polity, and of claiming the church buildings. This was not feared from the colored contingent, if left alone by intriguing white demagogues, but the sources of such suggestion were not wanting in the imported white leadership, which had come from other quarters of the country, to take advantage of the

gullibility of the late slaves in the unscrupulous promotion of these miscreant politicians in their greed of self-aggrandizement.[10]

According to Riley, "white adventurers" stirred up in black congregations the notion that they might own their church property. However,

> only one time, in Alabama, was an attempt made to gain by forcible violence, the control of a Baptist church. This occurred at Selma, to the pastorate of which church Rev. J. B. Hawthorne had been called after the close of the war. Learning of the demonstration that was forming in a remote quarter of the town, where the colored people were being incited to action by white politicians, who urged that the church building was theirs, and that they needed only to take possession, Mr. Hawthorne gathered a few friends, all of whom armed themselves, and met the large mob of blacks under white leadership near the church. But when the guns of the small defending party were raised with a threat to kill the first who should come a step further, the mob quickly dispersed, the white leaders being at the head of the retreating crowd. This closed the incident, and was the only instance known. Nor would this have been but for the interference of the white instigators.[11]

Among those who projected blame on foreign influences, many expressed the hope that if the blacks did not die out altogether, they would return to their former ecclesiastical fold. In 1865, one Presbyterian body viewed the exodus as a result of outsiders' plundering their church of its black members and luring them away. In 1867, although the group's tone was more resigned, it stated:

> The Colored membership has melted away from our churches like snow before the rising sun. Very few have adhered to us. They have gone off into organizations of their own, under the influence and control of bodies foreign to us, and all we can do is to wait, until, in the Providence of God, they shall return unto the fold from which they have strayed.[12]

Accounts by northern whites also give southern blacks little credit for their initiative in the exodus. Those that do credit black initiative tend to stress political rather than religious reasons for the move.

Revealing and indeed startling are interpretations by later historians of these contemporary accounts of the exodus. Many read white pressure into the accounts. They believe that whites exerted influence on blacks to leave biracial denominations, some attributing it to political reasons. William Warren Sweet judged that the black man saw "no distinction between his political and

75

religious interests and emotions" and that "unprincipled carpetbaggers" capitalized on this perspective. Sweet concluded that, "It is to be regretted that the independent negro churches should have had their rise in the South in this particular period of our history, but it was seemingly inevitable that independent negro churches should have been formed."[13] Clifton Olmstead asserted that "unscrupulous Carpetbaggers taught the Negro that Christianity and Republicanism were synonymous. . . ."[14] In discussing black Baptists, Sydney Ahlstrom says that they were "encouraged" to form separate churches and associations by southern whites and by federal Reconstruction policies and that "this encouragement had heavy political overtones, for black congregations were often used to strengthen the Republican party. . . ."[15] Other historians hold that whites had social reasons for influencing blacks to leave. Hunter D. Farish explained that

> Though the Negro was cordially urged to remain in the Church, it was expected that he would continue in an inferior and subordinate relation. There was no disposition to concede him any real voice in the management of the affairs of the Church. He was admitted to neither an unrestricted pastoral nor legislative relation. The freedmen, on the other hand, felt that they should enjoy freedom and equality in their Church life.[16]

Robert T. Handy discounts the cordial urging mentioned by Farish. "With few exceptions, the southern white congregations really did not want blacks in their memberships any longer, but preferred them to have their own churches."[17] Winthrop D. Jordan attributes the exodus in part to "the waning social strength of religious principles and the power of deep-set social attitudes." The exodus resulted from a lopsided clash between "Christian equalitarianism" and "American racial mores."[18] August Meier asserts that, "White discriminatory and exclusionist policies were the direct cause of the establishment of segregated institutions such as the Negro Churches. . . ."[19] Joseph R. Washington, Jr., attributes the exodus to "socioeconomic forces" and believes that blacks were "expelled" from white congregations.

> Negro envoys for independent Negro religious organizations were aided by the fever for freedom which they helped impart and when it broke they were able to capitalize upon sentiment, pride, and the opportunity to be in on the ground floor of a seemingly sure-fire organization—as well as identification on the level of race. Without these elements, the sizable number of Negroes in the South who were expelled from the white congregations might have joined all-Negro

congregations of white denominations—the actual response of a minority of Negroes.[20]

Theologian James H. Cone also believes that generally blacks were expelled from the churches, though "many of them left before being expelled." In his view, economic considerations were paramount.

It is important to point out that the new organizations were sometimes directly related to expulsions from white churches. Here it becomes clear that white masters "accepted" black slaves in their churches as a means of keeping the black man regulated as a slave. There was no mutual relationship between equals. Therefore, when whites saw that it was no longer economically advantageous to worship with blacks, they put blacks out of their church as a matter of course. Some whites were gentle in the process, giving the blacks a plot of ground or occasionally a building for a place of worship. (That was a small price for 250 years of slavery!)[21]

Other writers do see black initiative in the exodus, but they interpret the formation of separate congregations, churches, and denominations as evidence that blacks were opting for "freedom" denied them by their white co-Christians. In these interpretations, "freedom" means southern blacks being free to sit where they choose, to vote in church elections, and to fill positions of leadership in the denominational decision-making apparatus. But this view presupposes pressure by whites at least in the form of adherence to antebellum church arrangements that reflected the social status of members of the congregation. For example, Rufus Spain states this position regarding Southern Baptists:

Negroes *did* take the initiative, but white Baptists hastened the separation by openly declaring their intentions of limiting colored members to only those rights and privileges which they had exercised before the war."[22]

I find very little evidence that writers of the religious history of early postwar months and even years at any time considered the black exodus to have religious motivations (later Colored Methodist Episcopal Church accounts are some exception). Winthrop S. Hudson argues that even if the churches had worked for "tangible integration" in governance and worship, most blacks would have left in rejection of the bankruptcy of the gospel of servility preached to them in slavery and of the white ministers' inadequacy in addressing the needs of ex-slaves.[23] Ahlstrom seems to acknowledge that southern blacks had a distinctive appropriation of the Christian faith.[24] These possible exceptions aside, the failure to look at religious reasons is surprising, especially among the historians of church history, a discipline that more customarily overstresses the role of religious motives—especially beliefs. Why would historians who specialize in theology or doctrine or spirituality not ask the religious question or provide religious answers? It is possible that assumptions about blacks implicit in some of the post-Civil War accounts have been accepted unconsciously by later writers. Two assumptions especially, prevalent in contemporary accounts and reports, are expressed or implied later. One is the already mentioned notion that southern blacks were like children, passive at best, gullible and/or irresponsible at worst. Accounts that stress the conscienceless carpetbagger manipulating blacks' religious emotions for base political advantage draw on this assumption. The other notion is that southern blacks were religious primitives. Accounts that stress emotional appeal and blacks' desire for untrammeled expressiveness in worship draw on this assumption.[25] It was particularly deceptive because it relied on the sociological fact of blacks' relative cultural deprivation and was sometimes associated with the racist fantasy that blacks were more sensual, even less human, than whites. Writing in 1924, Henry K. Rowe assessed black churches.

> Negro churches have most needed educated leadership. Millions of negroes belong to colored Baptist and Methodist churches, which attracted them after they withdrew from the churches of their masters, to which in many cases they had belonged. Little educated, they never got rid of all the superstitions of their African ancestry, and their religion expressed itself on the emotional level. Too often negro church members were guilty of moral lapses and they found it difficult to put their religion into life.[26]

The biographer of black Baptist leader Alexander Bettis worked from an assumption of religious primitiveness in his account of the exodus.

> It is a fact, and there seem to be psychological as well as physical reasons for it, "that warm climates are highly conducive of emotionalism. The native African had for countless generations been resident in one of the warmest climates on earth. In his native land he, like all tribes, however ignorant, worshipped a god," but it was a god of his own creation, an image of wood or of stone. His method of worship was to sing, chant, dance, cavort around his god. The African was suddenly seized and brought to America, where, though a slave, he was taught by the earnest Christian white women of the South concerning the true, the living God. Under this helpful instruction, the slave changed the object of his worship, but not the method. In consequence while he was allowed to attend,

and was even encouraged to become a member of, the church which his owners attended, still his religious nature was unsatisfied. There was not enough "spirit" or enough fervor and emotionalism. He attended the church of his master, but it was the plantation prayer meeting, where he could sing loud and shout much, that gave him the greater enjoyment. So when freedom came, that desire for emotional demonstration in his worship was yet one of the negro's dominant characteristics. Even to this day it exists, the graveyard and the school-room being the only effective cure. In consequence, while as a rule the white people did not require or even request the negro to sever his connection with the white church, yet, except in isolated cases, it was one among the first things he chose to do.[27]

If one hopes to assess the role of blacks' religious initiative in the exodus, one must avoid these culturally set historiographical traps. To facilitate a less flawed, more adequate interpretation of the exodus, I propose the following methodological solution. I set down as a case study what black Methodists did and did not do about their religious life in the period, along with what white Methodists did and did not do about their relationship to their black co-Christians in the Methodist Episcopal Church, South. Further, I set all actions and omissions in an appropriate sociopolitical context.

Context

News of the war's end and of emancipation came unevenly to southern blacks, the vast majority of whom lived and worked in rural areas. Many knew as soon as—perhaps sooner than—whites did. Henry Blake of Alabama reported that

> One mawnin' us "Niggers" on de plan'ation wuz gwin down de road en we seed two white men walkin' en dey sed tuh us, "Yuh all come on en go wid us, yuh is jes es free es we is." De news 'bout freedom hadn' got back dere en we didn't pay no 'tention tuh it. A little later on we commence tuh heahin' it all 'round bout "niggers" bein' free den muh ol' grandaddy, he wuz de oldest on de place, he went tuh Marster Harris en he sed, "Marse Harris I heah we is all free." En Marse Harris say, "Yes, Jesse yuh is jes es free es I is en yuh kin go enywhere yuh wanna." En muh grandaddy come back en tole us. . . ."[28]

But in Oketibbeha County, Mississippi, slaveholder John Gay banned all visitors to his plantation and ordered his overseers to maintain the working routine; officials eventually discovered the situation and dispatched a marshall to free the slaves.[29] In Arkansas, Katie Rowe and her coworkers learned of freedom on June 4; for Henry Kirk Miller of Georgia, June 15 was "the day the big freedom came."[30] In the same month, Louis Hughes was still being held as a slave in Alabama. He escaped to Memphis and hired two Union soldiers to help him bring news of freedom to his wife and the other slaves on her plantation in Mississippi. The couple celebrated the fourth of July in Memphis.[31] Jane Montgomery of Louisiana found out about freedom indirectly in July; in Mississippi, Virginia Jackson's mother learned the news from neighboring ex-slaves in August.[32] Not surprisingly, actual emancipation spread very gradually across Texas.

> Freedom arrived officially for black Texans on June 19, 1865, when Federal troops landed at Galveston. Emancipation actually came as Union troops spread out over the state or as individual slaveholders accepted the results of the war and freed their bondsmen. Some East Texas newspaper editors in the summer of 1865 urged slaveholders to maintain control over their slaves and opposed ratification of the Thirteenth Amendment, which abolished slavery, because the editors hoped for gradual emancipation and compulsory labor. Some slaveholders continued to hold their slaves well into the fall of 1865.[33]

Texas ex-slave Susan Merrit reported:

> I hears 'bout freedom in September, and they's picking cotton; and a white man rides up to Massa's house on a big white hoss . . . It a gov'ment man, and he have the big book and a bunch papers and say why ain't Massa turn the niggers loose. . . . Massa make us work several months after that. He say we git 20 acres land and a mule, but we didn't git it.[34]

For preacher Anderson Edwards, it took an entire year for news to arrive.

> One day a bunch of Yankee soldiers come riding up, and Massa and Missy hid out. The soldiers walked into the kitchen, and Mammy was churning and one of them kicks the churn over and say, "Git out, you's just as free as I is."[35]

The unfortunate Toby Jones, born in South Carolina in 1850, was forced by his master to work four years after freedom. Finally Jones stole a horse and escaped with his intended wife—to Texas![36]

The vagaries of rural communications and reluctant slaveholders notwithstanding, word of the war's outcome triggered dramatic developments throughout the South. To many southern blacks, the military defeat of the Confederacy seemed an Apocalypse—a revelation, a discovery. It signified the destruction of the old order and even a judgment upon it. According to Alabama ex-slave Henry Blake,

> Aftuh Surrender, 'Niggers' dey sung, dey prayed, dey preached, yassuh. Ol' man Jesse Wallace wuz a preacher en he 'clared dat God loved his folks en sent his angels down tuh set his folks free en yuh shoulder seen de shoutin'.[37]

Dolly Whiteside explained,

> I was old enough to know when they runned us to Texas so the Yankees couldn't overtaken us. We was in Texas when freedom come. I remember I was sittin on the fence when the soldiers in them blue uniforms with gold buttons come. He said "I come to tell you you is free." I didn't know what it was all about but everybody was sayin' "Thank God." I thought it was the judgment day and I was lookin' for God.[38]

Another ex-slave reported,

> When de war was over de people jus' shouted for joy. . . . 'Twas only because of de prayers of de cullud people, dey was freed, and de Lawd worked through Lincoln.[39]

Blacks' immediate response to the war's end had other religious overtones as well. Many former slaves left their "homes" and began to move about. Howard N. Rabinowitz documented a flow into urban centers he studied, a flow that later seemed to ebb.[40] From private diaries to public papers, whites expressed their concern and consternation about "the wandering." From his home in Aberdeen, Mississippi, Methodist Bishop Robert Paine wrote of his apprehension to Bishop Andrew. "We are threatened with a negro garrison here. And the Freedmans Bureau is to be established here shortly. This will collect thousands of idle thieving negroes and will expose my family in town and property in the country." About his own household, he wrote, "Several negroes gone—the rest waiting to get ready: except the old & useless."[41] Later historians have interpreted this phenomenon variously. But on a practical level, much of the wandering was purposeful searching—for family members sold to distant masters, for work, and for the promise of land. Although this searching—especially for family and land—was religiously important to ex-slaves, it also paralleled the phenomenon of "refugeeing" by whites, a form of mobility motivated by every practical consideration from sheer survival to crass opportunism. Chaotic conditions were pervasive. Ex-slave John Cameron, born in 1842 in Hinds County, Mississippi, gave this insightful description:

> After de war it took a mighty long time to git things goin' on smooth. Folks an' de Gov'ment too seem lak dey was up set an' threatened lak. For a long time it look lak things was gwine bus' loose agin. Mos' everything was tore up an' burned down to de groun'. It took a long time to build back wid-out no money an' den it warnt de grand old place it was de firs' time.[42]

To southern white Christians, the war's end also seemed an Apocalypse. But to them, its revelation was a prophecy of doom without a hopeful promise of a new order. Eliza Frances Andrews recorded her strong feelings in an entry in her journal late in April 1865:

> It is all over with us now, and there is nothing to do but bow our heads in the dust and let the hateful conquerors trample us under their feet. There is a complete revulsion in public feeling. No more talk now about fighting to the last ditch; the last ditch has already been reached . . .[43]

In an 1865 letter, Caroline Merrick expressed exasperation.

> You know I have never locked up anything. Now I am a slave to my keys. I am robbed daily. Spoons, cups and all the utensils from the kitchen have been carried off. I am now paying little black Jake to steal some of them back for me, as he says he knows where they are. I cannot even set the bread to rise without some of it being taken. All this, notwithstanding the servants are paid wages. It is astonishing that those we have considered most reliable are engaged in the universal dishonesty. I understand they call it " 'spilin' de 'Gypshuns!"[44]

Southern whites sorrowed over the realities of their postwar Egypt. Elizabeth Allen Coxe remembered,

> During the war all the privations we had considered only temporary, part of the game, as it were, and so easily borne. The young people all felt that the end of the war would mean wonderful glory and riches and new clothes, but instead we came back to the grim realities of life. The bareness and poverty of everything in our neighborhood was incredible. The first Sunday we went to church the sadness and dreariness of everything was piercing.[45]

Yet it is important to note that despite deep feelings of defeat, both churchgoing and nonchurchgoing whites from the first strove to put their lives back together in a sociopolitical structure as close as possible to the antebellum status quo.

It was the period John Hope Franklin so rightly labels "Confederate Reconstruction," lasting more than a solid year between Appomattox and the beginning of the laborious political struggles between Congress and the southern states.[46] In general, southern whites held the reins of political influence much as before. A few states had benefited from Lincoln's generous plan for reconciliation: Tennessee, Arkansas, and Louisiana had needed to establish only ten percent of the population as loyal to be readmitted to the Union. In fact, whereas Arkansas and Louisiana would later be reconstructed at the insistence and direction of Congress, the government of Andrew Johnson's Tennessee was not "reconstructed" at all. Arkansas, Louisiana, North Carolina, South Carolina, Alabama, and Florida would be admitted to the Union in 1868. The political status of Georgia, Mississippi, Texas, and Virginia *qua* Virginia would not be settled until 1870.

This period was socially and politically uncertain indeed. Provisional governments and armies of occupation often sided with whites' efforts to reassert control, but sometimes opposed them. Swift demobilization spelled dwindling military influence. By November of 1865, the Union army numbered 134,000—900,000 fewer than the previous April. After December, its influence was usually negligible.[47]

The 1865 southern electorate was similar to that of 1860; that is, no blacks voted. From fall 1865 to early 1866 new governments passed legislation meant to effect a social stability similar to that of the antebellum years. They enacted the so-called black codes that enraged the North. Politically speaking, from spring 1865 to spring 1867 "Reconstruction" in the South was controlled mostly by the South, specifically by the white South.

Socially speaking, despite the early postwar growth of urban centers, the South demographically remained predominantly rural. Congruent with the antebellum demographic distribution of slaves, the portion of the black population not "wandering" was overwhelmingly rural. (Indeed, Ahlstrom reports that as late as 1910, when eighty-nine percent of the United States black population lived in the South, two-thirds of them still lived in rural areas.[48])

Communications, always slower in rural areas than urban ones, were further hampered by two factors peculiar to the postwar South. One was lawlessness. Although blacks were not blameless in this period, whites seem to have committed the majority of criminal acts, including purposeful, self-interested crimes like robbery as well as random crimes of terrorism. One ex-slave who had been in the army reported, "I got a discharge all right, but after the War I was met one night out in the woods, and some robbers robbed me of all the money I had, which was $2.00, and took my discharge papers. I never thought much about it then, but I have never been able to get a pension on account of not having them papers." Acts of terrorism often were perpetrated by informal bands of white youths—not surprising in light of postwar anomie and especially of certain southern attitudes toward violence by white males and toward nonofficial enforcement of law and custom by violence.[49] Informal bands began to assume identities as antiblack terrorist vigilantes after 1867 and especially in 1868. Thus it is incorrect to attribute much sociopolitical influence to the presence of such groups as the Ku Klux Klan and the Order of the White Camellias until they became influential, and then only in the counties where they were active.[50]

A second factor slowing communications was the relative lack of rail transportation. Of necessity, religious workers made limited use of the railroads. In this period, a person who wanted to spread any word to non-urban populations resorted to such traditional modes of transportation as traveling by horseback or boat.

Thus both social unrest and the rigor and expense of transportation impeded the flow of evangelization as well as the recruitment of congregations and churches to new alliances. These factors left room—at least in rural areas—for indigenous decision making. It was not unusual for black members of a congregation to seek new alliances after considering among themselves their altered circumstances. Such was probably the case of the black congregation to which Andrew Brown (then a layperson, later a Methodist preacher) belonged. Without an ordained minister of their own, the members nevertheless agreed to separate from the MEC,S and look for another connection.[51]

To assert that the sociopolitical context helped shape religious events perhaps is to assert the obvious. But it is important to note that religious events had sociopolitical significance too. As Max Weber has shown, denied or shared ritual commensality (in this case, sermon and Lord's Supper) reveals group boundaries.[52] Shared ritual commensality forges not just religious but also political ties; denied commensality cuts them. Black Christians generally did not desire to exclude whites from their services and from the Table of the Lord; indeed, some evidence points to early and continued outreach to white co-Christians. But in their surge toward religious self-affirmation, blacks irreversibly modified the antebellum pattern of mutuality and ritual commensality. The two-thirds of the black members of the MEC,S who left the church by 1866 did so while whites held sway sociopolitically and were striving to reestablish antebellum stability and social control. Yet in the antebellum period both blacks and whites used religion sociopolitically to control one another.

Black Methodists: Action

Black Methodists did not differ from other blacks in the South at war's end. Of paramount concern for many was sheer survival. While it is true that an agricultural economy can be rebuilt in great measure in one growing season, the harvest was critical months away in more war-devastated areas. Shelter too was relatively scarce. Many black Methodists found it necessary to expend a large portion of their energies obtaining life's physical necessities. Many sought and some received aid from the federal Bureau of Refugees, Freedmen and Abandoned Land, which had been created as a military measure in March 1865.

An expenditure of energy on survival is hardly surprising. But two other kinds of responses by blacks to the war's end surprised many observers. Blacks tried to situate themselves in what they saw as a new future. In contrast to whites, who were striving to reestablish antebellum social and political stability, blacks made significant strides toward a transformed existence in keeping with the immediacy of their eschatological vision. After Apocalypse, the new order replaced the old at once. Blacks did not wait passively for the new order to happen. They began to create it with determination and optimism.

Families were the first concern of many. Herbert G. Gutman shows that much of the "wandering" was motivated by blacks' desire to reconstruct families torn apart by slave sales. In addition, blacks moved swiftly to legalize marital unions formed during slavery, to assure legitimate status for their children.[53]

Blacks next sought work. However, they were hesitant to enter into labor contracts with former masters. Rumors that land would be given or sold cheaply to former slaves fanned eschatological hopes that blacks' economic relationships to society would be transformed in the new order. The Old Testament promise of land to a people liberated from bondage spoke eloquently to and magnified these hopes. As a result, blacks' reluctance to work under contracts gave them a certain leverage with white employers. Moreover, Dan T. Carter argues that the blacks' reluctance fed whites' fears of retribution by blacks in a rumored insurrection at Christmastime. As 1865 wore on, white dread built to the level of panic as unfounded rumors arose spontaneously and built to apocalyptic proportions.[54] Small events—like the "insolence" of a former slave looking directly at a white during conversation—portended a wrath to come very soon. The governor of Mississippi called out the state militia; South Carolina and other states took similar measures.[55]

In actuality, blacks expended little to no energy on retribution. Education seemed far more rewarding. Both black and white teachers stepped forward to teach the former slaves. When economic necessity—sheer survival—did not prevent them from attending, blacks flocked to classes. Education retained a close relationship with religious hopes in the minds of southern black Christians. Religious leaders often acted as teachers and classes were held in church buildings.[56] Booker T. Washington captured the spirit of the times.

> Few people who were not right in the midst of the scenes can form any exact idea of the intense desire which the people of my race showed for education. It was a whole race trying to go to school. Few were too young, and none too old, to make the attempt to learn. As fast as any kind of teachers could be secured, not only were day-schools filled, but night schools as well. The great ambition of the older people was to try to read the Bible before they died. With this end in view, men and women who were fifty and seventy-five years old would be found in the night-schools.[57]

Charles Hayes's grandmother, Salina Duncan, learned to read with instruction from former owners in Virginia; she taught ex-slaves on an Alabama plantation where they worked on shares after the war.[58] Another literate ex-slave, a Methodist preacher around Murfreesboro, Tennessee, expressed a characteristic reverence for the Bible in an unusual way. According to his daughter Bell Williams, when he died at the age of seventy-seven, "He had read the Bible through seventy-seven times—one time for every year old he was."[59] For many, the desire to read the Bible proved strong motivation for education.

Several historians have declared that the former slaves were "testing their freedom" when they left masters, sought family members, sought jobs, looked to the promise of land, and participated openly in separate worship.[60] I believe that testing freedom is an elusive concept, vaguely put. Another interpretation is more consistent with contemporary evidence and with the blacks' distinctive appropriation of a Christian eschatological vision in immediate and concrete terms. Blacks were fashioning a new order, putting fresh flesh on the dry bones of their traditional hopes.

Nowhere was this creative activity more apparent than in the blacks' surge to create visible structures for the so-called invisible institution, the black church of slavery times. While nineteenth-century Americans recorded statistics with maddening lack of system, we possess enough rough figures to identify the early trends. Methodists reported statistics on all levels from local churches to the General Conferences. Because these figures were not always recorded systematically, they do not tell a consistent, mathematically precise tale. However, at every level they point to the same trends: separations happened immediately, and about two-thirds of the black former members of the MEC,S worshipped in separate congregations by the end of Confederate Reconstruction. Denomination-wide membership figures reported in 1860 listed black Christians in the MEC,S at 207,766. In 1866, that number was only 78,742.[61] A synopsis of Sabbath school statistics for the Montgomery (Alabama) District of the MEC,S listed the black membership at 3,720 in 1864, 1,983 in 1865, and 1,725 in 1866.[62] In April of 1865, the first quarterly conference of the Socopatoy Alabama Methodist Church admitted fifteen white and six black members on probation. But records for the church's succeeding quarterly conferences make no reference at all to black members.[63] In late 1866, the Georgia Conference reported a decrease of 6,353 black members from the previous year's totals; in North Carolina the decrease was 2,014; in South Carolina, 9,844. The Virginia Conference submitted "No Report, in consequence of derangement by the war."[64] The compilers of these figures admitted that they were inaccurate. Nevertheless, they do point unmistakably to black Methodist activity. The evidence is no longer mixed as it was in the war years. Now the predominant antebellum patterns of joint worship and membership in the same denominational structures underwent swift transformation. Moreover, this early exodus of blacks from the MEC,S probably included many more individuals than the statistics suggest. Methodists listed as members only those who had been admitted formally and correctly according to the standards and procedures set down in the Discipline. A Methodist was likely to bring his or her associates in contact with Methodist beliefs and values. Mathews points out that actual antebellum church members were usually over age sixteen. Although "the quality of the relationship between church members and nonmembers is largely a matter of conjecture," it is certain that family members considered themselves associated with

Methodism and it is safe to assume that many others in the black community held unofficial yet heartfelt allegiance to the gospel.[65] To the degree that these considerations were applicable in a given area, the early exodus numbered many more actual departures than records kept at any level can be said to have counted.

How did the first flood of separations take place? Analysis of extant accounts produces only a partial picture. Accounts of these early separations—and later separations as well—were set down for the most part in denominational histories or in autobiographies and biographies of prominent Christians of the period. Thus the story of each separation enters the narrative at the point at which that separation was significant to the denomination or the individual in question. For example, an early AME history includes this biographical sketch:

> [Franklin Kesler Bird] was born December 1, 1856, at Rutherfordton, N.C. He was the only child of his father, William Bird, who died when young Franklin was two years of age. He and his mother, Mary Martha, lived with his grandfather, the "Blacksmith," Wylie Morris, until 1867, when his mother was married to Cain Gross.
>
> By early industry and economy Wylie Morris succeeded in purchasing his freedom for $2,000, and marrying a freeborn woman. All of Franklin's relatives were freeborn, and strict members of the Methodist Episcopal Church, South, until after the close of the war, when they connected themselves with the African Methodist Episcopal Zion Church, which remains the choice of the family. Young Franklin connected himself with the Church of which he is now a member at the age of eleven years, and soon afterward manifested much usefulness and devotion.[66]

Bird eventually became an ordained AME minister. In this account, his family, all of them black members of the MEC,S choose the AME connection. The account does not reveal the circumstances of their choice. It is likely that it was made together with other members of their former connection. But the sketch obscures such events and sheds light only on the career of Rev. Bird and the fortunes of the AME denomination. Another biographical sketch from this denominational history shows the same unsurprising selectivity.

> D. I. Walker was born in Chester County, S.C., in July, 1838. He was married to Matilda McDonald June 1, 1838. He embraced religion and joined the church in early life, and was class leader and exhorter before the war; his father died when he was very young, leaving the mother a widow with twelve children.

The system of slavery which surrounded them was, however, the greatest hindrance to young Walker's progress.

The period at which the war closed found him with a wife and two children and not more than ten dollars. For two years he worked on a farm for part of the crop, during which time he obtained such instruction from Northern teachers as his time permitted. In 1866 Rev. Bird Hampton Taylor, from Charlotte, N.C., went to Chester, S.C, organized the African Methodist Episcopal Zion Church, held a Quarterly Conference, and gave Walker local preacher's license. On the 24th of March, 1867, Bishop J. J. Clinton organized the South Carolina Conference, of which Walker was one of the original members. He was ordained deacon and elder at that Conference, and was given the pastoral charge of the church at Chester and the charge of the county as presiding elder and missionary. He continued to hold the pastoral charge and presiding eldership together for seven years.[67]

Walker obviously was one of the indigenous southern black religious leaders taken up and used with effectiveness by northern denominations. As an established class leader and exhorter, Walker very likely was part of a group or congregation that joined the AME church. But in Hood's account, the story of how such black Methodists came to affiliate themselves with the denomination is passed over. We cannot be certain even that it occurred. Hood's sketch focuses on the individual and on the point of his contact with the denomination's leadership. It is understandable that denominational histories reflect a denominational perspective. However, our dependence on denominational materials is increased by the paucity of materials by literate participants in the exodus.

Some self-separations by black members of biracial denominations were recorded because unusual circumstances surrounded them. The Rev. Matthew H. Moore mentions an attempt to claim an "African Chapel" by blacks who, "under bayonets, came near getting control of it."[68] The action of Richmond black Baptists was decisive enough to be newsworthy. They "seized control of their churches by June 1865, named new pastors, and used church buildings for schools, employment offices, and staging areas for organizing public protests and celebrations." Whites came to resent these churches.

> Incendiaries destroyed the Second African Baptist Church because it housed a freedman's school and because organizers used it to plan a massive celebration of April 3, 1866, the first anniversary of the black liberation and the white defeat.[69]

89

But most of the self-separations lacked such dramatic characteristics as violence. Indeed, the exodus seems usually to have had that kind of ordinariness in the details of its happening that only the fact, but not the process, was memorable to observers and participants. Ex-slaves interviewed in the 1930s sometimes related their life experiences in vivid detail. But this was generally not the case with the exodus. Of those ex-slaves recorded as mentioning it, many referred simply to the change from a pattern of joint worship to one of separate worship. Lizzie Williams, who was born around 1847 in Selma, Alabama, told an interviewer, "All de niggahs have to go to church, jes lik' de white fokes. Dey have a part of de church for demselfs. After de wah we hab a church of our own. All de niggahs love to go to church an' sing."[70] For a number of ex-slaves, the structure in which the new, separate ritual took place stood out in their memories. Milton Marshall, born in 1855 in South Carolina, had attended church and sat in a gallery during slavery. Then, "Atter de war was over de niggers built brush arbors for to hold meetings in. I sho' remember de old brush arbor and de glorious times den, and how de niggers used to sing and pray and shout."[71] While many ex-slaves remembered worshipping in brush arbors (or "harbors"), Jim Allen proudly related that he helped build a still-standing Methodist Church in Needmore, Alabama, in 1865 when he was fifteen.[72] These examples tend to support a picture of self-separation and black activism. A few ex-slaves indicated directly that blacks took the initiative. Ned Walker, born in 1854 on a plantation near Winnsboro, South Carolina, attended a church called Springvale. After a vote, "de members jines up, out of respect to de family, wid de African Methodist 'Piscopalian Church, so as to have as much of de form, widout de substance of them chants, of de master's church."[73] (The master's church had been Episcopalian.) Nicey Kinney remembered:

> Soon atter dey was sot free Niggers started up churches of dey own and it was some sight to see and hear 'em on meetin' days. Dey would go in big crowds and sometimes dey would go to meetin's a fur piece off. Dey was all fixed up in deir Sunday clothes and dey walked barfoots wid deir shoes acrost deir shoulders to keep 'em from gittin' dirty. Jus' 'fore dey got to de church dey stopped and put on deir shoes and den dey was ready to git together to hear de preacher.[74]

Accounts like these imply some earlier activity among the black Christians in each case of separation before the individual or denominational contact was made. A few accounts actually preserve evidence of prior activity. In one instance, a group of black Methodists chose to do without direction from the parent denomination. One of their members—a layman, not even an exhorter or preacher from slavery times—set out to forge Christian connections for his people. It was a classically Methodist move: the layman sought the larger connection at the behest of his co-Christians. (The Baptist solution would have been to "fold by themselves" under a shepherd from their own ranks.)

Case study of black Methodists is both facilitated and complicated by Methodists' connectional propensities: facilitated because the addition of new groups was recorded by the larger connectional body with dutifulness if not mathematical precision; complicated because the several Methodist hierarchies were vying with one another for members. The theologically dictated aim of individual soul-winning had ballooned by circumstances into the ambition to conquer whole congregations.

To identify the predominant factors affecting these early separations, one must begin with the story of any given group of black Methodists as a denominational affiliate of the MEC,S and—more often than not—participants in joint worship with local whites. Between affiliation and exodus into another denomination as (usually) an all-black congregation, each group reached a degree of self-awareness and made preliminary, decisions about how it would situate itself religiously in the new order.

Some historians believe that pressure from whites on blacks to leave was the most powerful influence. But in the case of black Methodists (and probably other black Christians in the South) evidence of white pressure is sparse and relatively late in this dramatic period. Moreover, most of the overt pressure was not motivated by racial animosity in any direct sense.

Indeed, in the early months after the war, influence of any kind by white Methodists on blacks was generally but understandably absent. Many churches had been occupied or destroyed by Union troops. The assertive policies of the northern Methodist Episcopal Church led by Bishop Ames and fostered by Secretary of War Stanton left many church buildings in northern hands. Some congregations continued to worship in these structures as before; many seem to have drifted away. Between 1860 and 1866, the MEC,S reported a decline in total membership from 754,421 to 508,676. Of the total loss of 245,745, white members lost numbered 116,721.[75] Whites who remained in the MEC,S were dispirited both emotionally and religiously. In Alabama, the Union Town Station on its Methodist circuit, having omitted its second quarterly conference, held its third in mid-June of 1865. At least some blacks remained in the connection: someone named Robin was authorized to exhort, "1 colled on probation" was received into the church and "1 Col" was expelled. But

91

conference minutes describe the spiritual condition of the church as, "Demoralized generally but not altogether—this is owing to the Times." After this meeting, quarterly conferences may not have been held; the next entry is for the second quarterly in early June of 1866. No one is recorded as added or dropped from membership. The spiritual condition of the church is "quite low too much conformity to the amusements and varieties of life."[76] On the state conference level, the South Carolina Conference as late as 19-23 December 1866 had the following to report in addition to decreased membership: two churches still in northern Methodist possession, one in the Orangeburg district and one in the Charleston district; one circuit disorganized in the Charleston district; one mission each discontinued in the Marion and Cokesbury districts; one mission not reporting in the Blackville district and two in the Shelby district.[77]

No doubt these reports reflect the prevalent mood in southern society. But low morale among white Methodists was aggravated by the condition of the clergy. Volunteering and conscription cut down the number of clergy available to serve local Methodist bodies. We have seen that conscription had cut especially severely into the already sparse Methodist mission to blacks. When the war ended, returning Methodist clergy as well as those who had not participated in the war showed an unsurprising lethargy and demoralization. In a 7 May 1865 entry in her journal, Eliza Frances Andrews wrote

> the Yankees are denying us not only liberty of speech and of the press, but even of prayer, forcing the ministers in our Church to read the prayer for their old renegade of a president and those other odious persons "in authority" at Washington. Well, as Bishop Elliot says, I don't know anybody who needs it more."[78]

John David Weaver Crook left his assigned circuit at the approach of the Federal army and died in May 1866 at the age of forty-six.[79] An Episcopalian clergyman

> for over thirty years . . . preached the word of God to white and black, master and servant, equal in the sight of God, and so equally under his care. He lived to see the negroes made free and his flock scattered. Then did he write to his two brothers in England to know if a parish could be found for him there, as thirty odd years of his life had been measurably lost in Carolina, the negroes preferring to listen to those of their own colour, who had been reared among them and were as ignorant as themselves.[80]

Meanwhile, in the absence of so many white clergy during the war years, already ordained and licensed black Methodist preachers and exhorters experienced greater demand and many of these grew in influence. In the war's aftermath, these men emerged strengthened in social standing and ministerial skills. Thus after surrender, when twelve-year-old Patsy Mitchner feared capture by the Yankees, she turned to a black preacher, Louis Edwards, who saw to her safety.[81] A black disciple of Baptist John Jasper stated that "it was ekul ter a revival ter se John Jasper moving like a King 'long de street."[82] In contrast with the white clergy, black leaders faced postwar confusion and chaos with the same holy expectation generally held by black Christians, that a new order was at hand. Moreover, the sense of ministerial call to serve must have intensified the resolve of these sons of slavery that God's willed new order was their responsibility to help bring about. A. G. Kesler had been converted in 1857 at age fifteen and had affiliated with a congregation of the MEC,S the following year. According to an AMEZ historian,

> he felt that God had called him to carry the word to the poor and teach all men by the preaching of the Gospel. But in the days of slavery he was not accorded the privilege of his call. He, however, looked forward to and earnestly prayed for the time to come when he could be free to exercise the functions of a Gospel minister, satisfying himself with what he was allowed to do at prayer meetings and class meetings by the permission of his superior, the white pastor. He felt that in the organization of the colored society his prayers had been answered, and he hailed the day with joy and thanksgiving to his God. Accordingly he joined with willing heart the new organization, and began laboring for and serving his Lord as if in a new atmosphere and in a clime more invigorating and pleasant. God signally blessed the new society and it grew rapidly.[83]

After joining the AMEZ denomination in 1865, Kesler obtained a local preacher's license and organized an AMEZ congregation.[84]

In these same early postwar months, many black males experienced calls to religious leadership, adding to the ranks of indigenous southern black religious leaders. Many of these were Baptists; many were Methodists. Among the new southern black Methodist leaders mentioned for the first time was Edward West, who was ordained and assigned to Trinity in the Augusta (Georgia) Conference of the MEC,S. In 1866, newly elected deacons Peter Colquit and Conner Colquit supplied the Newton Colored Circuit in the Bainbridge District of the same Conference.[85] Ex-slave Oscar Carter received his honorable discharge from the Union army in 1865 and joined the northern

Methodists in Vicksburg. He was soon licensed as an exhorter, then as a local preacher.[86]

The behavior of Methodist leaders and laity alike reflects an odd phenomenon in southern revivalism occurring on an unprecedented scale. Revivalism's tradition of ebb and flow, backsliding and ingathering, had never been chronologically and/or geographically uniform. Revivals of religion would break out among certain peoples at certain places and times. Occasionally antebellum histories recorded that revival in an area heavily populated by blacks or by whites was particularly fruitful.[87] But in this period, the evidence suggests that while white religious enthusiasm was at ebb, there was a Southwide revival of religion among blacks.

Parallel with the proliferation of ministerial calls, both black and white observers record the resounding revival of religion apparent in all-black worship services. If antebellum Methodist plainfolk revivals were regarded with disdain by certain observers, the "excesses" of later black services sometimes elicited even stronger negative reactions. In a letter written during the war, Lucy Chase expressed her disapproval.

At one of their prayer meetings, which we attended, last night, we saw a painful exhibition of their barbarism. Their religious feeling is purely emotional; void of principle, and of no practical utility. The Dr says they will rise from prayer and lie or steal if the way opens therefor. The brother who knelt in prayer had the friendly sing-song. His sentences were incoherent, and aimless—"ohuh Lorder! this afternoonugh, hear our prayerer! this afternoonugh! And dontuh let usuh take helluh by stormuh! this afternoonuh! in heavenuh! Save usuh our father in thisuh trying worlduh, and let usuh go upuh to theeuh for Jesus Christ's sakuh amen!"[88]

In February 1865, Eliza Frances Andrews recorded a less negative reaction to a black worship service.

I went over to the quarter after dinner, to the "Praise House," to hear the negroes sing, but most of them had gone to walk on the river bank, so I did not get a full choir. At their "praise meetings" they go through with all sorts of motions in connection with their songs, but they won't give way to their wildest gesticulations or engage in their sacred dances before white people, for fear of being laughed at. They didn't get out of their seats while I was there, but whenever the "sperrit" of the song moved them very much, would pat their feet and flap their arms and go through with a number of motions that reminded me of the game of "Old Dame Wiggins" that we used to play when we were children.[89]

Another white observer recorded a white clergyman's complaint that "after the Civil War, no negroes listened to his preaching but would shout and sing after their own fashion, and surround themselves with their old African superstitions."[90]

But not all black worship met with disapproval from whites. Methodist presiding elder A. L. P. Green attended a camp meeting where he saw

> the encampment of the colored people, situated within one hundred yards of the encampment of the white people, with the services already going on, although it was still early in the morning. I was pleased to learn that they have not been disturbed by divisions, nor misled by designing strangers, but are under the care of Brother Love. . . . They had located their camp-ground close to that of the white people, that they might enjoy the protection and assistance of their old masters, and I was glad to find that they were receiving a full benefit.[91]

The scene confirmed Green's understanding that blacks could be guided into a relationship of sympathy with the MEC,S—more separate than before the war, but in harmony with the parent denomination.[92] Holland N. McTyeire also held a benign view of the revival among blacks.

> A religious sentiment pervaded and dominated the emancipated race, and the chief annoyance white communities pretended to suffer was from endless preaching and protracted meetings. That such a suddenly enforced and universal emancipation did not end in bloody calamity to both races is due mainly to Christian work persistently pursued by Methodists, and also by Baptists, and not wholly neglected by other Churches in the South.[93]

It is doubtful that "bloody calamity" would have been initiated by freedpeople, with or without the work of the churches, since blacks were more interested in the promise of fashioning the new order than in unproductive revenge. But McTyeire's firsthand observation points to a definite revival of religion. Ex-slave William Ballard, born in 1849 near Winnsboro, S.C., proudly confirmed that this was the case in his area:

> I was one of the first trustees that helped build the first colored folks' church in the town of Greenwood. . . . I joined de church when I was 17 years old, because a big preaching was going on after freedom for the colored people.[94]

Nancy Whallen reported that in Hart County, Kentucky, blacks held revivals in the woods, where whites would be unlikely to observe them.[95] Lina Anne

95

Prendergrass gave this vivid description of worship at her grandfather's "prayer-meeting house" on a plantation in South Carolina.

> [Plantation blacks] sot on benches, and den dey would git down on dere knees and pray. I was a little gal, and me and de other gals would fetch water for dem to drink. Us toted pine when it was cole, and us'd take coals 'round fer de ole folks to light dere pipes wid. Atter while, dey git to singin' and shoutin'. Den de Spirit done come down and tuck hole of dem. Dat would be when everybody would get happy. De, ole rafters creak and shake as de Spirit of de Lord sink deeper and deeper in de hearts of the prayin' folks.[96]

The religious revival was not limited to all-black settings. Harry Jarvis of Virginia underwent conversion in solitude, but he had been encouraged in his seeking by a "missionary lady."[97] Members of Benny Dillard's Georgia congregation were served by white preachers "a long time" before they were able to have black ones. Nevertheless, the congregation kept firm control of its affairs. "When somebody wanted to jine our church us 'zamined 'em, and if us didn't think dey was done ready to be tuk in de church, dey was told to wait and pray 'til dey had done seed de light."[98]

It is clear that postwar southern black revivalism retained its core orientation toward conversion and its emotional expressiveness. Indeed, according to black theologian Cecil Wayne Cone, conversion

> created a worshipping community where a "foretaste" of God's eschatological freedom was partially realized in the people's present existence. Here it is important to note the essential characteristic of a black worship service. Black worship is the community celebrating their encounter of freedom which was given in the moment of conversion. . .[99]

The Southwide revival left fields of black Christians—Methodists included—ripe for the harvest. Workers came. The MEC,S found itself faced with denominational competition in its once unchallenged sphere. Scattered wartime representation by rival denominations now became earnest competition. By the time of the Columbus Pastoral address by bishops of the MEC,S in August 1865 on the subject of the black exodus, competing Methodist denominations and other religious groups had made significant progress among southern blacks. The MEC,S was not able to control the situation; blacks were ready to self-separate when contacted by denominations congenial to their distinctive appropriation of Christianity. The denominations most congenial to southern black Methodists proved to be the northern Methodists and the two black Methodist independents.

The northern Methodists were already established in several parts of the South thanks to "missionary" efforts authorized by the bishops, by the General Conference of 1864, and by policy set forth by Secretary of War Stanton. The policy had made available to Methodists abandoned churches, though sometimes these were taken over for military use. In addition, northern ministers were permitted to replace "disloyal" ones in southern pulpits. Takeovers of churches and pulpits inspired great resentment among southern white Methodists.

Where the denomination had been able to contact them, southern black Methodists had been more receptive. No doubt one element in northern Methodist success among blacks was the practice of enlisting indigenous black leaders in the denominational cause. The General Conference of 1864 had encouraged the formation of black pastorates. The policy of "making freedmen the pastors of freedmen" met with evident success. A white missionary wrote,

No one is so well adapted to pastoral labor among . . . the freedmen . . . as these preachers who have arisen among them. . . . [They have] a practical shrewdness and . . . under[stand] better how to manage their . . . race than anyone else.[100]

However, the establishment of the Holston Conference in June 1865 and some border victories, including a transfer of some MEC,S preachers that September in Kentucky, were the most notable accomplishments of the northern denomination in a half-year lull in its missionary activity. Whether reorganizing for peacetime work or simply sorting out policy and strategy, the northern Methodists did not resume vigorous activity until the fall.[101] The period of relative inactivity coincided with numerous congregational decision making processes in the South. Thereafter, when the northern denomination recruited black preachers and exhorters, many groups already had decided to affiliate with a connection other than the MEC,S.

Many southern black leaders chose to work within the northern organization. According to southern Methodist historian Holland N. McTyeire, these men were for the northern church "the most efficient agents for extending their new organization in the Southern field; and some of them have more than once figured creditably in their General Conferences.[102] Though usually lacking in some of the formal qualifications of their northern white counterparts, these indigenous black leaders proved to be "the best instruments we can get" in the northern church's view.[103] Accordingly, the denomination offered black pastors modest but persuasive wages. While low clergy salaries led to a shortage of white ministers and to moonlighting by whites who continued to be active in the denomination, money made answering their ministerial calls possible for many blacks. For one Arkansas leader, northern Methodist wages allowed him to support his family and fulfill his calling at the same time.[104]

I believe that the northern church's decision to employ many a black Moses to lead southern blacks into their denomination was decisive in the success had in missionary work. Morrow estimates that in the end, "Almost four fifths of the members gathered from the region of the former Confederacy were impoverished Negroes."[105] While these new "northern" Methodists constituted a financial drain on the denomination, they also represented eloquently the power of charismatic identification in the self-separations of the exodus. The appeal of a Moses who was "black like me" led many a group into connection with the northern church.

At first, northern Methodists exerted "a strenuous effort" to incorporate both blacks and whites in the same congregation, so that all could sing and shout together—the predominant pattern. Not all northern Methodists agreed with this practice.[106] Nevertheless, many of them worked to make it a reality, in some cases with success, in others with disheartening failure. According to Morrow, considered overall,

> the inclusion of whites and Negroes in the same societies proved a transient phase of the Church North's activity in the South. The mortifying reversal forced upon Timothy Lewis in Charleston exemplified the experience of numerous missionaries. Four months after Lewis had won over a bloc of Negroes with assurances that Northern Methodism knew no color lines, he had to work out with the newly-won converts an agreement which specified that "the blacks worship in their churches and the whites in theirs."[107]

Lewis was forced quite early into the practice of separatism. It was almost a year later that the General Conference provided for a separate black conference that would have its own bishop within the denomination. Nor did this provision represent unambiguous practice in the northern church. Even after 1868, "Along the border, where Northern Methodism had footholds before the war, separate conferences had won canonical sanction, but farther South mixed organizations continued in force."[108]

Despite the importance of the issue of racial separation, the northern church expended much more energy on another issue: property. In the case of churches used (and even built) by black congregations, their titles were held by white trustees. When the black congregations separated from the MEC,S and affiliated with the northern church, the latter tried to obtain the title for itself and trusteeship for a board of the black congregation's members.[109] Disputes over property used by whites engaged even more attention.

The northern church sent teachers and workers to ex-slaves in the South and it finally organized a Freedmen's Aid Society in the summer of 1866.[110] Though significant in their own right, these aspects of denominational outreach did not cause the exodus or influence its direction. In fact, each group's exodus from the MEC,S to another connection ordinarily was preceded by its own process of decision making. However, the direction in which these groups finally went after deciding definitely was influenced by outside factors. For the northern Methodist Episcopal Church, these factors were the enlistment of the indigenous black Moses and the struggle with the MEC,S over property.

Property and leadership also figured in many decisions by southern black Methodists to join the African Methodist Episcopal (AME) Church. The older of the independent black Methodist denominations did not have the financial and human resources of the northern church. Nevertheless, it reaped a hearty share of the immediate postwar harvest.

During the war, the AME Church had sent representatives to various population centers in the South, though only South Carolina was termed a mission in the minutes of the denomination's 1864 General Conference. In May 1865, the South Carolina Conference was created. It included South Carolina, North Carolina, Georgia, Alabama, and Florida;[111] an AME historian states that it had 3,000 members.[112] The Louisiana Conference also was created in 1865; it included Louisiana, Mississippi, Arkansas, and Texas. By June 1866, the denominational newspaper reported the establishment of eight non-urban circuits and of AME churches in eighteen population centers.[113]

Especially in its initial postwar activity, the AME denomination sought to maintain amicable relations with both northern and southern Methodist whites. Northern Methodists lacked the South's rich tradition of shared religious experience and its long-standing pattern of joint worship. Writing in 1857, northern Methodist minister John Dixon Long accused his church of driving away thousands of colored persons by our cold neglect. In all the new congregations established in our church in slave territory, we have made little or no provision for them. As a general rule, they are not desired in our fine churches. And they know the fact as well as we do.

Long did not approve of separate church buildings for blacks,

but I have regarded the arrangement as one of necessity, inasmuch as a half loaf is better than no bread at all; as a little religion is better than none. Our fathers used to shake hands with colored preachers and exhorters; but many of our modern preachers are too dainty for such contact. We have neglected the colored people to please the South . . . and what have we gained by it?[114]

Long wished the black independents success. In 1863, at the invitation of AME missionary J. D. S. Hall, white ministers participated in a communion service in Beaufort, S.C. But after the war, competition rather than cooperation dominated relations between the two Methodist groups. AME policy was to be open to whites and thus allay fears inspired by racial considerations.[115] But northern Methodists viewed the denomination with suspicion, not only because of its aggressive, competitive outreach to southern blacks but also because it seemed too friendly to the MEC,S.

Indeed, odd as it may seem, the increasingly white Church South was more attractive as an ally to AME leaders. They were keenly aware that southern white Methodists held legal title to land and buildings occupied by black congregations. The promise of land lured AME representatives to the 1866 General Conference of the MEC,S, and the southern church's ambiguous behavior led AME diplomats to pursue the cause even after that.[116]

AME success in relationships with the MEC,S was spotty at best. Far more consistent was the message of racial uplift its missionaries brought to southern blacks. They stressed literacy and education and what one might call bourgeois values.[117] Educational needs were undeniably acute. Speaking of his post-Civil War AME organizational work in Georgia, Rev. Andrew Brown observed that

When I was Presiding Elder of the Marietta District, there was but one colored man that could write his name and read the hymn-book. We had to get little white boys and poor white men to act as Secretaries of the Quarterly Conference.[118]

However, the same impulse that emphasized education led AME missionaries to oppose emotionally demonstrative ritual. Although such worship expressed the core southern black religious experience of communal liberation,

> Ministers and members were instructed to approach the altar of God decorously. Loud singing, shouting, gesticulations, the A.M.E. clergy thought, were atavistic practices which did nothing to advance the race. This sort of behavior, they believed, only contributed to the public's negative perception of blacks. Civilized people did not behave this way in church, the racists would say. The black missionaries also opposed such conduct because it kept alive superstitions which, they claimed, were detrimental to the freedmen's uplift. If the ex-slaves were to become model citizens, they would have to be educated to the ways of freedom.[119]

Northern Methodist missionaries permitted and even encouraged uninhibited ritual expressiveness, although their motive was probably competition for new members and not concern for a correspondence between forms of worship and authentic religious experience.

Emphasis on racial uplift, then, including both education and general bourgeois values, hindered as well as fostered the AME mission in the South. Overall, the denomination made undeniable, dramatic gains in membership. As with the northern Methodists, much of the credit for AME postwar growth goes to its use of southern black religious leaders. For example, ex-slave and Methodist preacher Nace Duval had a biracial following in Austin, Texas, and enough influence to promote successfully the building of a separate house of worship for blacks; after the war, he moved to San Antonio, where he organized an AME church. Rev. Edwin G. Cook was once a white elder of a black church in Vicksburg, Mississippi, and his body servant was a preacher; after the war, the servant became a preacher in charge of an AME church.[120] Baltimore-born AME minister David Smith was sent to Kentucky as a missionary in 1865 at the age of eighty-one. "The purpose was to get together all the Churches which belonged to my people, or as many as I possibly could," he explained. He gathered in churches in Lexington, Georgetown, Nicholasville, and Harrodsburg, and apparently also supervised Frankfort, Cynthiana, and Danville. His secret seems to have been delegation of responsibility to indigenous leaders: "The Conference met in Chillicothe in 1866, and I brought my brethren to Conference from Kentucky to be ordained, which was done, and they were sent to enlarge the ministerial ranks of the A.M.E. Church."[121] Thus, in the AME mission to the South after the war, the principle of charismatic identification worked partially for the missionaries—they were "black like me"—but fully for the sons of southern black revivalism who chose the Bethel connection.

The same principle reinforced the efforts of the AMEZ Church. However, the denomination was smaller and missionary manpower was extremely limited. Moreover, the denomination had undergone a split and a reunion between 1853 and 1860, so it was hardly in prime organizational condition as access to black Methodists in the South opened up.[122] The focus of AMEZ activity continued to be its North Carolina Conference, which it had established during the war. Bishop J. J. Clinton organized the Louisiana Conference on 13 March 1865 with fifteen preachers. On 6 June 1866, Bishop Sampson D. Talbot organized a third southern conference, the Kentucky Conference, in Louisville. At its first session, the conference reported 1,841 members.[123] A twentieth-century denominational historian observed that

> In spite of the fact that it did not have closeup supervision, the conference grew so rapidly the first year that the membership reported at the second conference was 3,253. Most of the men of this conference, however, had no experience in itinerant work, and were without knowledge of our church polity. They were sent to their appointments in many places without a church edifice, "nay, without church members, nevertheless they went trusting in God for success."[124]

In fall 1866, the Virginia Conference was organized; it had twelve "pioneer preachers."[125]

Like the northern Methodists and the AME Church, AMEZ leaders augmented what missionary enterprises they were able to undertake by recruiting and using southern black religious leaders. For example, Jeffrey Overton had received from the MEC,S a license to preach in 1831 just before the Nat Turner insurrection, after which the MEC,S would not renew the license. James Walker Hood renewed the license in 1865 and Overton transferred his talents to the AMEZ connection. Isom C. Clinton, an ex-slave from South Carolina, eventually became an AMEZ bishop, as did Thomas Henry Lomax, who had been a class leader in the MEC,S since 1850. Lomax helped erect "the first brick church in the African Methodist Episcopal Zion Connection in the South, at Fayetteville, N.C., named Evans Chapel" for the charismatic black antebellum Methodist hero Henry Evans.[126] Even the smallest of the northern Methodist missionary efforts employed indigenous leadership and organization, preserving and intensifying in the process a continuity with southern black Methodist religious experience in antebellum times.

In summary, one can identify a pattern typical of the way southern black Methodists acted in the first flood of separations. First they developed an at least rudimentary sense of group self-consciousness and process of decision making. Ordinarily this occurred before or during a period when southern white manpower lay dormant—demoralized and confused by the war's outcome. Where there was local black charismatic leadership, it was decisive, though the outcome might be various. Possibly in many unrecorded cases, rural groups gathered independently as local congregations, leaving aside at least temporarily the Methodist tradition of connectionalism. However, the northern Methodist denominational structures were congenial to the oft-noted preference of southern blacks for congregational organization, and denominational strategies generally were congenial to their antebellum religious experience. Denominational competition for black membership often was resolved in contests between charismatic denominational representatives. Each Moses was likely to find some portion of the exodus to lead, for the people were revived and ready to bring about the new order.

Methodist Episcopal Church, South: White Reactions

Before August 1865, white leaders and members of the MEC,S reacted to the black exodus only locally. No annual conference met until September. In general, white Methodists seem to have opposed the exodus. Such is the tenor of continued expressions of loyalty to and responsibility for the spiritual welfare of black co-Christians that persisted into 1866. For example, as late as 15 November 1865, a Montgomery Conference special committee on the relationship of the church and the blacks—chaired by soon-to-be-bishop Holland N. McTyeire—emphasized that

> We cannot recognize as a result of the late revolution any necessity for a change in the relations of our colored members. They are still entitled to our pastoral care and to all their rights and privileges and the means of salvation as heretofore. And the colored people generally, constituting a large portion of our resident population, have special claims upon Christian benevolence and efforts.[127]

The November 1865 Pastoral Address to the South Carolina Conference instructed laypeople to continue accommodating blacks "in all the churches, that, frequenting the schools of catechetical instruction, and occupying their

103

accustomed places in the house of God, they may receive from the lips of a pure and spiritual ministry the messages of the Gospel, and rejoice with you in the participation of the benefits of a common salvation."[128] In December, the Mobile Conference recognized the defections of blacks from the denomination and termed them "unwise," adding, with resignation, "as our spiritual children for whom we have long sacrificed and toiled and prayed in the past, they shall go forth with no bitterness on our part, but rather with blessings."[129] On the local level, white Methodists expressed opposition to the exodus less philosophically and more actively. In Mobile, for example, "several black preachers were accused of inculcating the freedmen with doctrines of murder, arson, violence, and hatred of white people."[130] In Charleston, blacks refused to accept the ministers assigned them by the MEC,S in an effort to regain control over the city's black churches. In Georgia, where the MEC,S sent ministers to black churches, "Several of these congregations refused to hear their ministers designate, and in Marietta, Georgia, the white minister was voted out while he was in the pulpit."[131]

Many white Methodists seem to have viewed early separations as temporary, just as white Southerners in general viewed the freedpeople's "wanderings" as short-lived. It was widely believed—and feared—that freedom would kill the supposedly childlike and helpless race.[132] But many hoped that blacks would recognize that their past relationship with the master race was their true hope for the future. Indeed, one Presbyterian body expressed confidence in 1865 that blacks who they believed had been enticed away from the denomination soon would return:

> turning away from their own blind guides and from wolves in sheep's clothing, that seek not them but *theirs*, and live by plundering, they come back to the old fold and to the old pasture ground, placing themselves under the guidance of their old tried and true friends, content to occupy their old position and desirous of no change in the organization of the church of their choice.[133]

Few whites seemed to look realistically at present circumstances and future possibilities. Those who did saw a danger in continuing prewar patterns of worship. That danger was social equality—a danger so feared by white Southerners that even in the next century a Southern Baptist Convention report would term it "the devil's bugaboo."[134] Thus, in 1865, many whites had mixed feelings about the exodus. An editorial in the Baltimore *Episcopal Methodist* on 2 August 1865 titled "Our Relations to the Colored Population of the South" did not even mention the continuing departure of blacks from the MEC,S. However, ambivalent feelings and an ardent desire for control colored its recommendations. Whites were to "recognize [blacks'] civil freedom as an undoubted fact" and "collect them together and organize as independent congregations" but only "so far as their training will allow." Meanwhile, white southern Methodists should fill blacks' "pulpits with judicious white ministers until such time when native preachers of approved qualifications shall arise among them." In addition, Sabbath schools were imperative:

> the organization of Sabbath schools, no longer upon the system of oral, but of literal instruction, in which the thousands of ignorant children shall be taught to read the word of God. This we believe to be a solemn debt which the South owes to the African race. It ought to have been paid long since. She ought to claim the privilege of paying it now, and, no doubt, will rejoice to cancel it at once.

The editorial also recommended a limited kind and quantity of secular education. After all these measures were taken, the editorial recommended "finally, when, in the course of events, they [blacks] shall be fitted for it, to furnish them with ministers of every grade, of their own color, to perfect the idea of their ecclesiastical, as well as their civil independence."[135] The evident ambivalence in such a tightly controlled, gradual plan for independent churches (which probably would remain under denominational authority) is hardly an example of whites wanting blacks to leave biracial churches and denominations. In fact, one question must be addressed baldly and boldly: Was there any pressure by white Methodists on blacks to get out of the MEC,S? The evidence supports the conclusion that there was no pressure on blacks *qua* blacks. But this conclusion does not rule out all influence by the leaders and members of the MEC,S on the outcome of the period's struggles.

To assess the role played in the black exodus by white influence, it is necessary to set the exodus once again in the sociopolitical context of the times. From the summer of 1865 on, "Confederate Reconstruction" governments were institutionalizing the negative response of whites to black independence. Actions like the passing of the black codes provide an unmistakable measure of southern whites' attitudes toward the freedpeople. Moreover, beginning in late spring and through the summer of 1865, a good deal of white guerrilla-type terrorist activity was directed against blacks exercising their freedom. Control, stability, and the restoration of black labor to its customary relationship with the economy—these were the social, political, and economic goals of the white South. Likewise, in the churches, whites hoped for a return of the status quo. But here a complex mixture of motives and emotions were at play. Scholars widely believe that whites feared that free blacks might rightfully demand an equal role in church affairs and an elimination of separatist practices in ritual.[136] This view is plausible, though I find no explicit discussion of such worries early in 1865. Given more time—or, more precisely, given no black initiative toward self-separation—it is equally plausible that whites would have found a satisfactory theological formulation to permit retaining freedpeople in a (perhaps slightly modified) status similar to slavery times. Certainly the question of whether or not slaves should be baptized had been resolved by such theologizing in colonial times.

Whites feared "social equality"; their concern included psychological and sexual elements as well as social, economic, and political ones. Slavery had provided protective mechanisms of location and definition for everyone in society; thus it is not surprising that white Methodists worked to retain blacks in a church informed by its traditional antebellum ecclesiological vision. Furthermore, in the first half of the nineteenth century, Southerners increasingly favored a static view of theirs as the perfect (or near perfect) society. Thus, it is probable that insistence on antebellum ecclesiastical practices was motivated by old fears and old social and ecclesiological visions along with a failure of imagination and an inability to adjust or to innovate. At least early in 1865, demoralized Methodists were clinging desperately to the departed past rather than fashioning a new order. They neither pushed the blacks out nor strove aggressively to retain them, despite Christianity's proven potential for forging political and religious ties in the antebellum period. For white Methodists, the central religious issue was to remain faithful to their historic and sometimes admirably executed commitment to evangelization and Christian nurture of southern blacks. The central political issue was to retain control.

The presence of workers from northern denominations and parareligious organizations greatly complicated the southern whites' mixed motives and emotions. Especially influential were the vigorous and varied efforts of the northern Methodist Episcopal Church. As mentioned, its takeovers of church property and pulpits justified by allegations of disloyalty inspired deep resentment in southern Methodists as did its energetic efforts to evangelize both whites and blacks.

Thus by 1865, the northern church was a villain in southern eyes on three distinct counts: it had forced the North-South schism in 1844 over the issue of slaveholding by Bishop Andrew; it had unlawfully and un-Christianly seized churches and properties that rightfully belonged to the MEC,S; and it now brazenly was gathering black congregations into affiliation and in some locales even was permitting worship practices that smacked bitterly of social equality.

> A declining enrollment and a recognition of the problems involved adjusting the relations between whites and blacks under the new order of things quickly convinced Southern Methodists that the most workable plan was to cut loose the Negro communicants. *Without official sanction*, Southern Methodist preachers encouraged the freedmen to enter one of the African denominations and, to reduce the likelihood of their lately-freed parishioners wandering into the Northern fold, white clergymen often went to elaborate lengths to transfer their Negro membership *in toto* to an African Church.[137]

Cases in which white ministers of the MEC,S appear to take initiative seem at first glance to constitute proof that they influenced, pressured, or arranged outright the transfer of blacks from the MEC,S to one of the northern independent black denominations. But the gritty grain of truth in this interpretation lies on a beach of resentment toward the northern church. Blacks were about to leave, and the northern black independents were lesser evils than the northern church with its criminal maneuvering and subversive meddling.

Such was the situation and such the mentality of the men who formulated the 17 August 1865 Columbus Pastoral Address. Bishops Andrew, Paine, and Pierce issued the first denomination-wide pronouncement on policy pertaining to the separating blacks. At what was perhaps the crest of the first flood of separation, the bishops of the MEC,S set down a statement that would be so widely published that the bishops considered it common knowledge among Methodists—at least among the clergy—by April 1866.[138] Significantly, the address dealt most substantively and at great length with two topics: colored people and the northern Methodist Church.

The bishops credited Christianity in general and the MEC,S work among blacks in particular because "it has materially contributed to their subordination and inoffensive behaviour through the late defenseless and excited times" and because "their safe though sudden passage from a state of bondage to liberty, a transition accompanied by no violence or tumult on their part, is largely due to the same cause." But the bishops went on to acknowledge that a large-scale exodus was under way and to set down guidelines for the southern church's response.

Our numerous membership among them of over two hundred and forty thousand, exclusive of the congregations and catechumens who receive instruction from our pastors and missionaries, has been much reduced by recent changes and casualties. If it should be still further reduced, we need not be surprised. Defections, doubtless, will take place from their ranks to churches offering greater social inducements for their adhesion. If they elect to leave us, let them go, with the assurance that as heretofore we have been, so we continue to be, their friends, and in every suitable way aid their moral development and religious welfare. We must still keep up a place and a service for those who remain with us and for others, who after a brief experiment elsewhere, may wish to return. While no factious opposition, on the one hand, should be offered to the exercise of their fullest liberty in choosing their ecclesiastical associations; on the other, no desire of being rid of a responsibility should incline you to treat their action, in so grave a matter, with indifference or to let them take their way in ignorance of all the issues involved. Give them exact information and patient explanation. Act faithfully and kindly in all things toward them, and as becomes those who truly care for their souls.[139]

This address makes clear that the black exodus was a continuing and unstoppable occurrence only four months after Appomattox. The number of blacks likely to be affected was high——240,000. The bishops were certain that the exodus would continue, though they were careful to take pains to provide for those blacks who might not leave and those who might leave and then return. The bishops' interpretation of the motivation of blacks became very popular with many——regardless of race or historical frame of reference——who have viewed the event. "Greater social inducements," not black religious experience, supposedly activated the exodus. This interpretation understandably appealed to southern white religious leaders who believed that Methodist work with blacks had been "a great work" done "under divine blessing."[140] How could the bishops believe that any denomination but their own offered the most authentic option? Perhaps most important for correct historical interpretation is, "Give them exact information and patient explanation." It follows admonitions not to offer "factious opposition" to blacks who chose to leave, yet not to be irresponsible by permitting blacks to make uninformed decisions. What "exact information" would a white minister of the MEC,S volunteer on the relative merits of the parent church, the northern church, and the northern black independents?

The bishops did not mention the African denominations. However, they discussed at some length the behavior of their northern denominational counterpart. The bishops accused the northern church of violations of the original plan of separation. They charged that northern Methodists preached human rather than divine doctrines and laws, and that they "incorporated social dogmas and political tests into their church creeds." The bishops held that the wartime takeover of houses of worship and the retention of those churches were opportunistic and wrong. Finally, they claimed that northern Methodist leaders had met and "resolved to send preachers and plant societies in our midst wherever there is an opening. Their policy is evidently our division, and ecclesiastical devastation."[141] Whatever "exact information" the bishops wanted blacks to receive would certainly be informed by their allegations about the northern church, especially the charge that it had set as a matter of policy the destruction of the MEC,S. It is probable that the recommended "patient explanation" to blacks would take the form of persuasion. In the southern bishops' eyes, the northern church was a hated aggressor; they saw the African independents as less powerful, less threatening, and by their very race-specific makeup, less likely to "spoil" southern blacks by encouraging social equality. The diplomatic language of the address does not hide the bishops' concern to influence the unstoppable exodus in the directions most desirable under the circumstances. They accepted the inevitability of losing the majority of their black membership. They interpreted the times more accurately than most other whites in the spring and summer of 1865.

In the open market of denominational competition, "exact information and patient explanation" degenerated into ugly polemics. Many ministers—regardless of denomination—did not scruple to introduce "racial" arguments in the months that followed. In their evangelizing, northern Methodists alleged that their church was the only one that accorded the same privileges to blacks and whites alike. Farish argues that northern missionaries

aroused the Negro to a bristling sense of race consciousness. They continually appealed to the blacks on the basis of the "equality of relations" enjoyed in the Northern Church, denouncing the separation of the races in the Southern Church as a most wicked manifestation of caste spirit. Even the exclusively colored organizations were condemned as fostering the spirit of caste.[142]

Morrow reports that when northern evangelist Timothy Lewis persuaded Charleston freedpeople to affiliate with his denomination, he countered

the pleas of Southern Methodist clergymen "to stay with us in your old places in the galleries" with the declaration that "there will be no galleries in heaven [and] those who are willing to go with a church that makes no distinction as to race or color, follow me." Lewis' valiant effort won him the field.[143]

Of the northern independents, the AME Church representatives were the most visible and aggressive in using persuasion based on racial considerations.[144] However, both African denominations were targets of criticism by polemicist L. M. Hagood.

> The African and African Zion Churches whispered continually, and sometimes preached, that the colored membership in the Methodist Episcopal Church was a burden to the white folks. These organizations . . . saw there were but two ways in which they could induce the colored element in the Methodist Episcopal Church to join them,—by loud professions of "race pride," and appeals to their ignorance and prejudice. This they attempted by appeals to the dignity of our colored local preachers; by telling the more ignorant that they were being imposed upon by "white folks." They told the local preachers, class-leaders, etc., among our members, that it was a shame for them to have white masters during the week and white masters on the Sabbath-day also; that they were as well qualified literarily to have charge of congregations with white members as some of the white pastors; that they possessed intelligence enough to do business for themselves. Then, again, they would say: There will never come a time when the Methodist Episcopal Church will allow one of you colored members to preside as their presiding elder or pastor; that all the property you buy belongs to "white folks," and not to you.[145]

Racial persuasion tended to create a climate of animosity. Yet, as Morrow tartly observes, "Certain it is that neither African nor white Methodism, by its choice of argumentative weapons, did anything to alleviate a condition both professed to deplore."[146] For ex-slave Will Long, however, racial considerations were just one part of his religious memories. Born in Maury County, Tennessee, and later moved to Texas, Long learned to read scripture from his white mistress and attended log churches in both states. He reported that, "Sometimes er w'ite preacher an' sometimes er nigger 'ud preach ter us." He explained his membership in an African Methodist Church this way: "De preachers allers say de Baptist Cherch fer de w'ite folkses, de Catholic fer Mexicans an' Indians and de Mefodist fer de nigger."[147]

Every denomination in the fray used education to induce self-separating black groups to choose that denomination. White Methodists seem to have employed education more frequently than black Methodists, although black efforts also were significant given the limitations of denominational resources. Robert C. Morris uncovered an early (January 1865) example of an AME minister trying to convince a black Baton Rouge congregation to choose black teachers and preachers instead of their current white ones.[148] According to

Walker, the AME Church held that it was better for blacks to be educated by other blacks.[149] Northern Methodists believed that Methodists were better educated by Methodists; their denominational teachers in the South cared about conversion as well as academic progress.[150] Not surprisingly, southern whites believed that other southern whites were the most (if not the only) suitable teachers for the freedpeople. In this case, region was probably more important than denomination. However, southern denominations did attempt to use education to retain black members. As early as 1865, Southern Baptists favored education and especially Sunday schools for freedpeople, so that, as the 1866 Convention put it, "they should become able to read for themselves the blessed Word of salvation."[151] The issue of educating blacks is eloquent testimony to the intensity of denominational and regional competition and of the powerful appeal education held for most southern blacks.

Southern white Methodists' education of freedpeople merits special comment here. Their actions in this area reveal their true state of mind.

Southern Methodists were financially and emotionally devastated by the war. Their mission was crippled by the incursion of the northern church into every area of endeavor and even into the house of worship. In spite of these disadvantages, members of the Church South affirmed a commitment to educating freedpeople and sometimes managed to act on that affirmation. For example, a white southern minister served as teacher in a Freedmen's Bureau school in Russell County, Alabama, for two years.[152] (Blacks then asked for a southern black teacher or a northern teacher.) To favor teaching blacks to read—and especially to read the Bible—represented a dramatic reversal of opinion. The insurrection led by the Bible-reading, quote-wielding Nat Turner had inspired laws against black literacy throughout the South. These had been more or less enforced since 1831. Why would white Methodists advocate education in the summer and fall of 1865 when fear of a Christmas insurrection by blacks (one more fearsome than Nat Turner's revolt) was building to a panic? It is difficult to interpret this fact as anything but an attempt to keep black Methodists from leaving the southern church. In fact, as late as April 1866, Methodists in Union Springs, Alabama, apparently were using education to attract departed blacks back into their previous biracial connection. According to a local paper,

> Reverend Mr. Motley, Pastor of the Methodist church here, aided by Rev. George Stewart, has organized a colored Sunday School in connection with that church. Their plan embraces scholastic, education to a limited extent, and as accessory to

religious training. This is a move in the right direction, and we hope to see it followed up throughout the country. The education of the negro, moral and secular, should be attended to by the Southern people. Of all people, they are most deeply interested in its being well and properly done. This Sunday School presents a most inviting field for those who desire to do good, and at the same time keep from among us an element that would result only in mischief. Care and watchful interest bestowed in this field now, will bind these confiding and needy people to the altars around which they have hitherto worshipped, with ties of love and gratitude.[153]

White Southern Methodists who advocated education to stop the exodus were illogical if not utterly blind. On the one hand they espoused innovation in educational practices while on the other they refused to consider permitting blacks better status in church decision-making and devotional practices. In light of their change in policy on the education of blacks, white Methodists' adamant adherence to past customs in the case of participation in polity and worship is more adequately explained as white paralysis than as an oblique white pressure on blacks to leave.

Christmas 1865 passed peacefully. The early months of 1866 showed that the MEC,S was ineffectual in its efforts to retain black members but effective in facilitating the transfer of many black congregations to the northern independents. The congregation of black Methodists who built Collins Chapel in Memphis, Tennessee, around 1865 provides an instructive example of developments in "urban" areas in early 1866. The congregation previously had been affiliated with the biracial Wesley Chapel and had come to hold separate worship services in the basement of the chapel. In late 1863 or early 1864, some federal chaplains representing Bishop Ames took possession of Wesley for the northern church. According to the Memphis *Christian Advocate*, some of the black members "became uneasy in regard to their Church relations. They believed the Methodist Episcopal Church, South, was gone." Apparently, Collins Chapel was constructed in this "uneasy" period and the congregation incurred "an indebtedness of a few hundred dollars." But their white coreligionists rejected a proposal to pay the debt in exchange for the black congregation's transfer to the northern Methodists.

> We advised them, if they wished any change in their Church relations, to go to the African Methodist Episcopal Church. This met their views much better. We gave them the use of the church, and turned them over to Brother Woolfolk, an experienced minister of that Church.

However, in this case,

> In a few weeks they saw the error they had committed—came to Brother
> Plummer, who was their pastor, asked pardon for their folly, and we received
> them back. We believe they are as truly loyal to the Methodist Episcopal
> Church, South, as any in the country. They have been blessed with fine revivals
> of religion, and are now in a very prosperous condition. Brother Collins has
> charge of them, aided by the colored preachers of the charge. He reported to
> the recent Quarterly Conference forty additions to the membership during the
> last quarter.[154]

Perhaps the Memphis AME ministers were unequal to the task of serving such
a congregation, with its long-standing sense of group identity and autonomous
decision making. The African denominations struggled to keep up with the
demand for their presence in the South, drawing for manpower on small
numbers of missionaries along with newly recruited indigenous leaders of
varying kinds and degrees of training and talent. Meanwhile, as noted above,
four-fifths of the northern church's harvest in the South was black.[155]

By the summer of 1866, the hopes of southern blacks for a new economic
order were replaced by labor contracts with white planters. Congress intended
the Homestead Act of June 1866 to provide land for freedpeople and loyal
southern whites, but few blacks found the biblical promise of land fulfilled by
this or any other means. Blacks discovered that the Union generals who
discharged their black troops the year before had been correct: they would
have to "earn" equality. As Eugene Genovese explains,

> when some of President Andrew Johnson's Reconstruction governors and
> military officers addressed the freedmen right after the war, they blithely
> informed even the veterans of the black regiments that blacks had had no part
> in the struggle for their own freedom, that the war had been a white man's
> affair, that equality remained something to be earned by future effort, and that
> blacks had to prove their worth by staying on the land and calling their old
> master, master, and their old mistress, mistress. The freedmen everywhere heard
> this splendid oration in one form or another from Yankee officers.[156]

Bringing about the new order would take more time and more work.
Adversity grew. Race riots broke out in Memphis in May 1866 and in New
Orleans in midsummer. At the same time, politics became more promising for
blacks, more threatening to the men in political control of "Confederate
Reconstruction." In the spring of 1866, Congress passed the Civil Rights Bill
and in summer the second Freedmen's Bureau Bill, both over President

Andrew Johnson's veto. In June 1866, Congress passed the resolution that would become the Fourteenth Amendment. The signs of the times pointed to politics as the tool of promise for working out the new order after Apocalypse. Given blacks' communal appropriation of Christianity, the visible institution they had so swiftly formed became the natural base for further fulfilling the scriptural promise of liberation from bondage.

Analysis and Evaluation

The fact that an estimated two-thirds of the black members of the MEC,S separated themselves into other churches, congregations, and denominations during "Confederate Reconstruction" effectively refutes various contentions that the new black churches were the result of "purely political" historical forces. The flood of self-separations had crested before federal legislation made black participation in politics possible. When black Methodists separated themselves from the MEC,S, they were acting on their distinctive appropriation of Christianity. Careful analysis and in-depth evaluation of six important issues support this thesis.

1. *Initiative*. Underneath the masking effect of denominational and personal accounts of the early separations, it is clear that southern black Methodists took the initiative in separating themselves from the MEC,S. The overall pattern began with group self-awareness and at least rudimentary indigenous decision making. The decision to leave generally preceded the choice of new denominational connections.

It is fallacious to argue that other denominations created the separate churches by aggressively evangelizing and eagerly accepting these self-separating groups. That argument miscasts outcome as cause and portrays southern blacks as passive. Black Methodists were, on the contrary, very active right after the war, initiating searches for family members and new jobs as well as separating themselves from the MEC,S.

Perhaps southern black Methodist religious initiative would have been recognized more readily had they then constituted a separate denomination of their own. However, there was little if any reason for them to do so, and there were many reasons for affiliating with existing denominations.

Each of the existing organizations offered a setting in which the distinctive religiosity of blacks could flourish. For example, they accepted and fostered black religious leadership, and they affirmed in polity and ethical stance blacks'

114

religious experience of communal liberation. In 1866, a convention of freedmen claimed "the right to unite in brotherhood with any christian body that may, in its teachings and sympathies, accord with our feelings."[157] As a young man, ex-slave Joseph Holmes thought that "nobody wuz a Christian 'ceptin' us Baptists"; ex-slave Annie Hill referred to her mother as "a full-blood Baptist."[158] North Carolina ex-slave Nathan Best explained

> I b'long to de Methodis' church, I jined in 1866. We went to our marster's church in slavery time. He was a Methodis' an all his cullud folkses was Methodis', all dem dat b'longed to church."[159]

Clearly, a denominational preference was usually part of blacks' appropriation of Christianity. For Methodists, as W. E. B. DuBois pointed out, episcopal polity fostered the early formation of new affiliations.[160]

Complaints about rival denominations by spokesmen for the MEC,S must not distract attention from the limitations and weaknesses of the denominations southern black Methodists chose. The energies of the northern Methodist Church were divided between evangelizing the South and property struggles with the MEC,S, and also by trying to win both whites and blacks away from the southern church. In addition, the northern church suffered from many of the limitations that also hampered the African independents even more.

The role of northern black denominations among southern blacks was limited to the locales they could reach with their sparse manpower. Often population centers were the most convenient locus for recruiting efforts, while the majority of blacks lived in rural areas. Heroic efforts by individual missionaries and newly recruited indigenous leaders and the charisma of these men provided some compensation for disorganization, inefficiency, and frequent inability to offer educational opportunities.

If the northern denominations were limited in their access and capacity to recruit southern blacks, the blacks faced options that were limited by their circumstances. The general condition of freedpeople right after the war was undeniable poverty. For black Methodists this circumstance was significant. The existing denominations made financially feasible adherence to a characteristically Methodist connectional organization with spare hierarchical leadership structure.

Finally, all the denominations that black Methodists chose offered some promise of education, a pursuit the twentieth century mind is likely to view as purely secular. But nineteenth-century blacks valued education because black religiosity was biblical. Many blacks' prime motivation for learning to read was the desire to read the Bible.

Beyond personal access to Scripture, blacks sought education as a means of communal uplift. Many a black Moses—himself often illiterate—favored education. It was a way of bringing about the new order. Education drew real religious value from the concreteness, immediacy, and communality of blacks' distinctive appropriation of Christian soteriology.

There is little evidence of anti-intellectual sentiments expressed by black Christians in this period. Respect for learning underscores the power of the black religious experience of communal liberation, the importance of which outweighed the anti-intellectual heritage not only of the blacks' religious traditions but also of the very South itself as a region. Booker T. Washington's non-religious philosophy of education for racial uplift had a distinguished religious predecessor.

2. *Religious legitimation.* The drive for religious legitimation of status provides important evidence of black initiative. By legitimation I do not mean finding an excuse or a rationalization or a boost in social standing, though in many instances in the history of Christianity, legitimation has at least one of those meanings. But in the black Christians' decisive striving for it, religious legitimation was sought precisely for its religious character. Religious legitimation affirmed one's belonging to God's people and one's title to the hopes such belonging implied. The church represented God's independent power to antebellum blacks; it was an authority separate from and possessing leverage against the otherwise all-pervasive, oppressive, white male socioeconomic authority structure of the South. No wonder, then, that blacks sought marriages and baptism and the separate churches themselves.

Some suggest that legitimation of a crasser sort was what led every black Moses of this period, who in turn led sheeplike southern blacks out of, for example, the MEC,S into other folds. Besides being unwilling to attribute sheeplike religious behavior to such an active and purposeful people, I am unconvinced that such motivation would be sufficient to support the heroic labors of missionaries or of indigenous black religious leaders. Although human greed and ambition were of course present in this period, power, status, and economic advantage were more likely and apparent inducements to ministerial service in periods later than this one. During "Confederate Reconstruction," leading a movement for black independence of any kind was a generally thankless and often dangerous task. Moreover, many indigenous preachers were plunged into the movement by the circumstance of the ministerial status they had established in slavery times.

3. *Congregational polity.* The groups that separated early from the MEC,S affiliated with denominations receptive to their preference for congregational organization. This fact may reflect a desire by black Methodists for a sense of belonging and a refuge in an increasingly hostile society. However, the MEC,S offered a less palatable refuge that nevertheless had potential for soothing white hostility. In slavery, the joint church gave slaves a certain amount of shelter from which to prick white consciences and manipulate white behavior. To leave this shelter was dramatic expression of the desire for communal religious self-affirmation and self-determination.

4. *A revival of religion.* The postwar ritual behavior of southern black worshippers received harsh criticism from outsiders, both black and white. Anna Julia Cooper, an educated black Episcopalian, labeled "rank exuberance and often ludicrous demonstrativeness" as "faults of worship."[161] Black Baptist preacher Alexander Bettis denounced men who tried to evoke emotional demonstrations with the cadence of their voices.[162] Methodist Henry M. Turner found the worship of some freedpeople characterized by crude religious concepts and frenzied, extravagant expressions of emotion.[163] The AME denominational paper stated that primitive ideas of worship were leftovers from bondage to be discarded, especially the "ignorance," "clownishness," and "incorrect speech" of black preachers.[164]

In the immediate postwar period, blacks did engage in enthusiastic worship services, some of notable duration. Some of these services did include dancing and other ritual elements rooted in African religious heritage. However, so many of the surviving accounts come from observers outside of the traditions of southern revivalism, which was always replete with emotional and physical manifestations in worship. African influence on various postwar black ritual behaviors notwithstanding, they fit somewhere on a predictable continuum for southern revivalism. It is inaccurate to generalize that,

> In many, if not most, of the separate Negro churches, the established forms and dogmas of Protestant worship degenerated into primitive, near orgiastic rites, day-and-night-long travesties of the backwoods revivals of the early nineteenth century, sometimes even a partial reversion to voodooism.[165]

What seemed so alien and disordered was actually governed by what Morrow aptly terms "the missal of habit."[166] Uninhibited group worship fittingly expressed for blacks the core religious experience of communal liberation. But even a New York journalist knew that it was not "heathenish" or "barbaric." He recorded the following observations in 1874.

> As to churches, in the cotton country the colored people . . . have their own churches and preachers of their own color. The meeting is a curiosity. The preacher is almost always so far illiterate that he uses large words in a wrong sense; but he freely denounces the sins of the congregation. Then come screams, violent contortions, jumping, dancing, and shouting—but not more violent or ghastly than I have seen in Western camp-meetings among white people, in my younger days, I must own.[167]

Black services were part of the revival of religion that swept through southern black religious communities. Observers singled out the services partly because black Methodists were now more visible: they were separate from and independent of white supervision. These factors magnified the traditionally high visibility blacks have in perspectives of white Americans. To most whites, especially those sensitized to racial considerations, a group of ten or twelve blacks seems like more people than ten or twelve whites.

However, such considerations notwithstanding, the black worship services seem to have been more enthusiastic and spirit-full than before. This evidence suggests that blacks' religious initiative drew strength from a uniquely occurring but characteristic spurt of revivalistic ardor.

5. *Politics.* Some historians have condemned politics, especially the alleged manipulation of black religiosity, especially by northern and Republican politicians. In addition, some have explained separate black church formation as at least partially a northern political scheme. This etiological myth ignores the fact that the so-called invisible institution had been in some senses political long before blacks gave it visible form. Antebellum blacks had a social sense of salvation as communal; they possessed incipient social ethics; their decisions about personal ethics had a group referent factor, due to their status as other even when free. These same elements were at work during the period of "Confederate Reconstruction."

Finally, the MEC,S, the northern church, and other white-led denominations were not exactly apolitical in their activities. Moreover, during the Civil War itself, patriotic maunderings in official denominational documents provide abundant evidence that for all Americans, religion and politics pertained to each other. Indeed, one can argue that all religions in all periods possessed the tendency to become civil religions. In Christianity in particular, shared table community was the crucial religio-political issue. It related to the Jewish tradition of sacred law as well as to the gospel of freedom in Christ. In the Pauline epistles, the notion of freedom—which had Jewish, Greek, and Roman roots—was religious and theological but also political and social.[168] It was related to the image of Christians as one body—an essentially political analogy.[169] In early Christianity as in this period, shared table community meant new freedom, new community, and new social and political alliances.

6. *Separation and Segregation.* Southern black Christians, then, separated themselves from white churches and denominations. This action was initiated by blacks acting on their own religious experience. If not understood in historical context, the argument is bound to elicit undue rejection or inappropriate glee. But one must understand the context in which blacks acted as they did. There were no Jim Crow lunch counters, no separate railroad waiting rooms, no double drinking fountains side-by-side. Slavery as a system had bound black to white with an interrelatedness that was familylike in intensity. Worship in slavery times expressed this interrelationship in its predominant pattern of shared worship, of ritual commensality.

To a black woman or man in 1865, segregation as a concept was value-neutral. Not separation but relationship—master to slave—had negative meaning. Separation then could mean liberation. To show that black churches so formed themselves is to affirm the liberating power of southern blacks' Christian experience. It in no way justifies the wrongs wrought on all Americans by segregation.

In this chaotic time, churches offered both blacks and whites a sense of social location with religious meaning. As a culture, the South was accustomed to seeing itself as explicitly religiously meaningful. Now white Christians saw the mighty arm of God's judgment; black Christians followed each God-made Moses and strove for the promise of land.

FOUR

The Red Sea, 1866-1868

Black Methodists already were separating from the Methodist Episcopal Church, South in the early months of the war; by the end of 1866 their exodus involved at least two-thirds of the denomination's black members. But the self-separating Christians discovered that legal freedom did not buy the promised land. So they strove for citizenship, suffrage, and justice, sometimes bending their new religious bonds to these tasks, without making artificial distinctions between politics and religion. The earth was the Lord's and the Lord's liberation was whole.

Pharaoh's chariots were in pursuit. Southern whites had recovered some poise and perspective. Andrew Johnson's ineptitude polarized national politics. As a result, southern whites could indulge again in self-righteous wrath. Many men turned to their southern tradition of violence as well.

The bed of the Red Sea was far from dry. Though black Christians continued to come out of the MEC,S, denominational competition muddied their marching. Sectional, political, and race conscious arguments obscured an event of great significance in American religious history. But words would not halt the exodus. In 1866, the MEC,S counted 78,742 black members still in the old fold; in 1869, only 19,686 remained.[1]

Religious Separation and Southern Politics

The questions of citizenship and suffrage for blacks were the central political issues. Although President Johnson favored resident alien status for blacks, a majority of Northerners as well as the dominant party in Congress came to support citizenship. Indeed, in practice Southerners had accorded blacks the status of resident aliens from the first. Blacks had long sojourned in the South as what Max Weber termed a guest tribe. Bereft of their ancestral lands and homes, blacks had "belonged" in America by living in designated areas and providing types of work not otherwise available to the community. They had been occupied completely in meeting the demands of the South's economy.[2] Developments during "Confederate Reconstuction"—the Black Codes, for example—convinced many in the North that protected status was not enough for southern blacks. The sojourners would become citizens—males and females, the whole "tribe." Southerners resisted the Fourteenth Amendment, but it was ratified and went into effect finally in 1868. The longest amendment to the constitution, it defined citizenship, set forth the principles of equal protection under the law and of due process, and specified elimination of the three-fifths ratio—in the Constitution since 1807—thereby raising blacks to equal rights, including (many hoped) suffrage.

Citizenship created political ties between blacks and whites: suffrage tightened them. However, the Fourteenth Amendment did not provide enough pressure to guarantee suffrage (that would be the concern of the Fifteenth Amendment two years later). Meanwhile, in March 1867, Congress jolted the South with its Reconstruction Bill, which would have extensive consequences for political, social, economic, and religious life.

Provisions of this bill profoundly affected the relationship between blacks and whites. Military rule was reestablished in every state of the former Confederacy except Tennessee, where the Fourteenth Amendment already had been ratified. The actual force deployed numbered only about 20,000 men in 1867, with the largest contingent under General Sheridan in Louisiana and Texas. But Congress effectively interrupted the reassertion of the supremacy of southern white males that had characterized "Confederate Reconstruction." Five U.S. Army generals in five southern districts supervised such matters as voting qualifications and delegate apportionment for constitutional conventions, whose work Congress had to approve before a state—having also ratified the Fourteenth Amendment—would be "reconstructed" and readmitted to the Union.[3]

The South experienced further dislocation of its white male authority structure in the bill's provisions that, in order to vote, whites must take the so-called Ironclad Oath to assert loyalty and that the franchise included all males twenty-one years of age and older, regardless of race, color, or previous condition of servitude. Throughout the spring and summer of 1867, Southerners registered to vote for delegates to their respective state constitutional conventions. Thus, in a year when religious ties continued to loosen or be cut, the potential for political ties between white and black tightened. Tension tightened, too.

Resulting political strife took on predictable trappings. Given the cultural deprivations of slavery and the present struggles for family, work, land, and sometimes survival itself, blacks showed unusual energy and sophistication in political affairs; they did not use violence as a political tool.[4] Whites employed both violent and nonviolent means. Democrats and Republicans alike used persuasion and economic pressures to influence the black vote. Republicans formed secret political Union League groups with fraternal and parareligious practices that attracted activist black men. In addition, bands of southern white men, often costumed in disguises sewn by their womenfolk, increasingly engaged in acts of terrorism that ranged from psychological intimidation to murder. Parareligious and paramilitary practices characterized such developing groups as the Knights of the White Camellia and the Ku Klux Klan.

It is true that both strong religious identity and a cult of the military were traits of antebellum southern culture. However, the adoption of parareligious and paramilitary practices by white terrorist groups points to a felt presence of both the military and religious groups. Moreover, it draws attention to the fact that the planter aristocracy no longer dominated the authority structure. Northern intruders and white Southerners from lower social strata and blacks all jostled with the aristocracy over control of the new order.

I find no evidence of a direct causal relationship between struggles over citizenship, suffrage, and the states' constitutions on the one hand and the continuing segregation of the southern churches on the other. In particular, where black political activists like James Lynch and Henry McNeal Turner had clear-cut religious identities, those identities were wed to groups already separate from the MEC,S. Political groups belonging to the Union League—a patriotic association that came to support the Republican Party in the South—sometimes met in Methodist churches. However, they did not create the separate churches and in fact did not always even include blacks.[5] At most, membership in a Union League group may have indirectly drawn some blacks to fellowship in an already existing separate church. Recorded acts of terrorism by Klan-like groups against separate churches and black religious leaders reveal a pattern of political rather than religious intimidation.[6] For example, in April 1868, three freedpeople's churches were burned by terrorists probably seeking to punish blacks for their participation in a recent election.[7] That same year, shortly before the presidential election, Klan members in St. Helena Parish, Louisiana, burned two churches and a school that belonged to blacks.[8] Lee Pierce told of a Klan attack on a black Methodist church in Texas; the target of the attack, however, was a colored militia organized to protect blacks from the Klan.[9] "Disguised men" forced the destruction of a church built by a family of prospering freedpeople in North Carolina because the men believed blacks held Union League or jayhawking meetings in the building.[10] Apparently, groups of white terrorists did not care particularly whether blacks worshipped separately. According to one self-confessed North Carolina member of the "Invisible Empire," opinion was mixed on the subject of blacks meeting and preaching.

> They did not have much objection to it, only they said they did not believe that the black people ought to be allowed to preach. Some of them thought that; and some of them said they ought to be allowed to have a preacher of their own, and that the whites ought not to be allowed to preach to them. Some of them thought they ought not be allowed to preach at all.[11]

But the men who participated in white terrorist groups clearly cared very much about who voted and how.

After "Confederate Reconstruction," an indirect causal relationship between political struggles and religious separations may have developed out of the climate of instability introduced into the South when Congress wrested the program of Reconstruction from the hands of the president (formerly Lincoln, now Johnson) and the states. At best, however, new sociopolitical instability increased existing instability of other sorts, perhaps fostering further separations, probably not hampering them in any way.

Competing denominations strove to use political ammunition made available by contemporary struggles. It is difficult to assess how effective political arguments were in themselves. For example, in some areas the northern church was called "Massa Linkum's Church," a characterization that with its connotations of liberation may have attracted freedpeople or may have repelled them because its association with politics and the North invited the resentment of so many southern whites. Even where a denomination's political associations did not arouse such ambivalent responses, it is difficult to argue that political persuasion effected authentic religious commitment, since each denomination was a religious institution, regardless of the political label with which it was charged. Between 1866 and 1872, charges and countercharges of political influence on religious choices certainly flew; however, they seem to have influenced historiography far more than they influenced actual events.

Certainly the course of the exodus from 1866 to 1868 cannot be reduced simply to a political explanation.

By 1868, blacks were recognized as citizens and had voted and participated in varying degrees in constitutional conventions in Arkansas, North Carolina, South Carolina, Louisiana, Alabama, and Florida, with Georgia first recognizing, then expelling blacks from the political process. Tennessee had its "reconstructed" government and had ratified the Fourteenth Amendment in 1867; white terrorists attempted to nullify such measures.[12] Georgia, Mississippi, Texas, and Virginia had yet to resolve crucial citizenship, suffrage, and constitutional issues. Yet in all of these diverse states, the formation of separate black congregations, churches, and denominations proceeded. Its steady progress indicated continuing religious motivation.

Black Methodists: Action

Following the established pattern of prior local initiative and indigenous decision making, black Methodist groups continued to seek new connections that were at the same time harmonious with their own distinctive appropriation of Christianity. In 1867, Simpson Memorial Methodist Church in Charlotte, North Carolina, organized as a northern Methodist congregation; previously it had been meeting for Bible study under the leadership of ex-slaves.[13] In April of that year, black members of the Union Springs, Alabama, Methodist Church voted unanimously to break with the white Methodists and to affiliate with the AME denomination, which was represented by Henry Stubbs, an elderly AME missionary from Georgia.[14] In 1868, AME minister Theophilus G. Steward took up pastoral duties at a Macon AME Church, which had recently separated from the MEC,S and was involved with the parent denomination in a legal dispute over church property.[15] These separations easily could have taken place in the first year after Appomattox. The characteristic elements are still evident: apparent indigenous group self-awareness and decision making; black leadership, probably charismatic; an available alternative Methodist connection with which to affiliate; and, possibly, encouragement from white interest groups, which could be northern or southern, Republican or Democrat. However, in the established pattern, new elements budded, then bloomed. The most notable of these occurred in two areas: leadership and ecclesiology.

The long-standing tradition of charismatic leadership showed signs of yielding gradually to routinization, inspiration and revelation giving way to forms of everyday authority. Charismatic leaders came to be surrounded by or even replaced with other leadership that was more routine, whether in the traditional or bureaucratic sense.[16] Thus, Theophilus Steward was assigned his pastorate; he succeeded whoever helped to galvanize its earlier separation from the MEC,S. The denominational organizations with which southern black Methodists were affiliating were more tightly structured than Baptist groups. As a result, the tendency toward routinization appeared earlier and more clearly than was possible given Baptist polity and congregational autonomy. Each Methodist body struggled hard to set standards of education for its ministers. Not just orthodoxy but "racial uplift" was the earnest concern of black bishops, most of whom seem to have reached office on the strength of personal charisma, not education. AME bishop Daniel Alexander Payne was the most prominent advocate of ministerial training, and his denomination maintained a literacy requirement for ministers.[17] In fact, the northern independents promoted education more strongly than their northern or southern Methodist competitors. In this period, the MEC,S had no black bishops and a tradition of relative neglect in educating black clergy. Black religious leaders who remained within the Church South were generally less able and even less likely to advocate education.[18] They were also, as the exodus continued, less numerous.

In addition to education now being desired of new black Methodist preachers, official recognition of their vocations by the denomination itself became as or more important than popular recognition of a preacher's charisma. For example, James Bartlett Johnson, who was born in Kentucky in 1830, as a slave had organized a church, preached a revival, and converted many persons. After serving in the Union army, he moved to Louisville with his family and joined the AMEZ Church, hiding his past as a preacher. Then, in 1867, Bishop W. Haywood Bishop ordained him a deacon and he was appointed to a congregation in Springfield, Kentucky, where he began his postwar ministry.[19] Lucius Cooper's former owner was a Methodist preacher of notable piety. In Texas after the war, the ex-slave reported, "he made me a speaker in the Church and they licensed me to preach."[20]

Some evidence and several charges by contemporary whites suggest that individual black leaders sought to find social status as well as to flee the wrath to come. It is difficult to assess to what extent status-seeking motivated black leaders and thereby affected the exodus. For example, Graham Bell was born a slave in Mississippi and moved to Louisiana in 1852. He was not converted until 1868, whereupon he became active in Wesley Chapel in New Orleans. His was rather a "late vocation" by some southern standards, and he also got an education and later participated both in government and in his denomination. Without additional information, one can interpret Bell's career variously but not conclusively.[21] However, it is clear from many sources that the ministry remained a dangerous occupation. As a result, a status-seeking minister's personal courage would have to be equal to his ambition.

One of the most ambitious men who participated in the exodus was also one of the most dedicated to the Methodist gospel and to his people: Henry McNeal Turner. Born in 1834 in South Carolina of free parents, Turner joined the MEC,S in 1848 and in 1853 was licensed to preach. He worked as a missionary for the MEC,S in South Carolina, Georgia, Alabama, Louisiana, and Missouri, preaching to both blacks and whites. In 1858 he discovered the AME Church and joined at once—"partly," says one interpreter, "as an act of defiance against whites, and partly from attraction to an autonomous black organization in which he could realize his ambition for status and power."[22] Turner did achieve status within the church: he became a presiding elder and later a bishop. However, his political efforts in Reconstruction-era Georgia left him frustrated and disillusioned, not at all the epitome of the powerful man of high status. Nevertheless, in political and ecclesiastical endeavors, he was unfailingly faithful to the goal of betterment for his people. In this commitment he represented the communal self-awareness and communal ethic characteristic of the Christianity of blacks as appropriated in antebellum times. Therefore, Turner's forceful drive and his attempts to obtain and use power were perhaps symptomatic of ambitious statusseeking, but they were also subservient to and expressive of his black Christian identity.[23] It is likely that the same could be said—on a less heroic scale—of each black Moses in this period.

With routinization stabilizing the charisma of southern black religious leadership and status seeking becoming a realistic possibility, ministerial involvement in politics grew more prominent. Turner, for example, was a delegate to the Georgia constitutional convention and a representative in the Georgia legislature: other men held less highly visible but decidedly public posts. It was inevitable that current national political events would interact with the traditional here-and-now immediacy of blacks' eschatological vision. As a result, what some observers saw as nonreligious maneuvering was surely to at least some black leaders a holy striving to bring about God's justice and the new order. Turner offered in the Georgia state legislature resolutions designed to stabilize economic life.[24] He also engaged in early efforts to promote black-white harmony and to form political alliances with whites in the legislature.[25] Georgia Baptist preacher William J. White is a less well-known exemplar of the immediacy and practicality of southern black Christian eschatology. AME Bishop William H. Heard remembered that in 1867, when Heard was seventeen, White

> came to Elberton, my home, as an agent of the Freedmens Bureau, and made a political speech. He was the first colored man I had ever seen who was well educated, and who could use the King's English readily, accurately and convincingly. He very much influenced me and I determined from that night to be a MAN, and to fill an important place in life's arena.
> It was just the dawn of political awakening for the Negro. The Democrats that night tarred his horse all over with pitch, but the next morning he was up, had his horse attended to, hitched him to his buggy and went on his errand. I knew him for many years afterwards . . . He was always outspoken for Orthodox Religion and for the Republican Party.[26]

The courageous leadership of such men preserved the eschatological traditions of blacks in the face of a growing number of hostile forces. A black Baptist preacher who had been whipped for allegedly political sermons told Congress's Joint Select Committee that he preached "love universal" and "scriptural salvation." He charged that whites were "determined to keep us [blacks] from using any influence for republicanism, which we believe is God's will. I believe it comes nearer to God's will and universal love and friendship in this world than any other." For this preacher, "republican" included both the government and the party. He declared, "I believe the republican party advocates what is nearer the laws of God than any other party." As for his preaching: "I preach the Gospel, repentance toward God, and faith in our Lord Jesus Christ."[27]

The way men like Turner and White combined religious and political careers was more likely to raise the eyebrows of white observers than of black Methodists. For blacks, new developments in the area of ecclesiology reinforced rather than opposed this fusion of sacred with mundane calling. Two developments exerted most specific influence.

First, the church extended its nurture role. Slavery had permitted religious nurture by controlled word and by supervised worship. The continuing disruption of the South's authority structure opened opportunities for ecclesiastical outreach in the traditional areas of evangelization and ritual. Blacks preached and celebrated and taught the word more freely than before.

In the process, Bible study—by necessity—was also reading instruction. Moreover, the worshipping community's Christian understanding motivated it to provide both ritual bread and everyday material assistance as well. At least for this period, the modern differentiation between secular and sacred is a bankrupt notion. Feeding and clothing needy freedpeople probably advanced their economic fortunes, but these deeds followed Gospel injunctions as well—as did education and offering instruction in civic matters such as voting and labor contracts.

A second ecclesiological development influential between 1866 and 1868 was a growing awareness of and concern for tradition. Competition between rival denominations raised the issue of blacks' authentic religious tradition for the audiences it touched. For Methodists, tradition included episcopacy. AMEZ historian (and bishop) James Walker Hood reported that some AME controversialists told unsophisticated hearers, "Zion has no bishops."[28] This issue and the general concern for tradition would be even more important in the final act of the exodus—the completed formation of the Colored Methodist Episcopal Church by the separation of the last remnant of black Methodists in the MEC,S.

Meanwhile, the northern Methodists and the northern black independents moved to consolidate their gains. They created new denominational structures. Among northern Methodists, structural change proceeded at a gradual and uneven rate. The General Conference of 1864 had encouraged the formation of "colored pastorates for colored people" where practical. Further, it had authorized the bishops to form black mission conferences "where in their godly judgment the exigencies of the work may demand it" with the conditions that the rights of black members not be impaired and that transfer of white ministers to such conferences not be forbidden.[29] In April 1865, the northern church's New England Conference deplored the formation of two black conferences. Northern Methodist minister Gilbert Haven vigorously opposed separatism, charging that if blacks did prefer separate conferences, it was only because whites did not treat them as equals.[30] In its 8 November 1866 issue, the New York *Christian Advocate* admitted that the church had been remiss in practicing separatism in the North. It editorialized that instead, especially in the South,

> Our official action should be distinct and outspoken on this subject; the theory of "color blindness" should be clearly enunciated and at once reduced to practice. Colored ministers should be invited to membership in our Annual

Conferences, and introduced into our pulpits. Colored families should be welcomed to our Churches, not to sit on separate seats assigned to them as a distinct caste; but in free churches to sit where they please, and in pewed churches, in such pews as they may choose to pay for. . . . With this theory and practice our Church should go forward with her mission in the South.[31]

The two separate conferences created in 1864 were Washington and Delaware; they probably represent the context of racial attitudes that fostered the formation of the AME Church in Philadelphia early in the nineteenth century. In more characteristically southern areas of northern Methodist activities, conferences remained mixed until the 1868 General Conference. That conference responded to petitions for separate conferences by white and black clergy from Kentucky by authorizing the bishops to form such conferences if the black ministers so requested. Morrow observes, "Already aware of the tastes of Negro parsons, the performance of episcopal duty in the Bluegrass state was merely perfunctory."[32] The Kentucky impulse toward separatism was then another instance of self-separation, this time within a denomination. Indeed, the black clergy petitioning to constitute a separate conference may have led congregations that already had undergone the process of self-separation from the MEC,S. In this case, one reason for further separation may be read between the lines of representation: at the 1868 General Conference, white delegates represented the nine mixed conferences; the two black conferences sent black delegates, who were duly seated at the meeting.[33]

The AME Church experienced considerable structural development between 1866 and 1868. In 1867, the mission conference of South Carolina became three regular conferences—North Carolina, Georgia, and Florida. In 1868, the AME conference structure in the South was completed with the formation of the Alabama, Mississippi, and Texas conferences and of Kentucky, Tennessee, and Arkansas conferences, which had been the mission responsibility of the Missouri Conference.[34] The AME denomination now had a national structure, with at least one church in every state but four, none of which was a southern state.[35]

The smaller AMEZ Church also underwent structural development, beginning in 1866. At that time the church had three conferences that could be considered southern: the Southern Conference (redesignated the Baltimore Conference in 1868); the North Carolina Conference, which was strongest and most influential; and the Louisiana Conference, which included the whole lower South. In 1866, the church created the Kentucky Conference and organized the Virginia Conference out of the existing North Carolina jurisdiction. In 1867, though it was technically part of the Louisiana Conference, the South Carolina Conference received help in organizing from North Carolina. The same year, the Alabama Conference—which would achieve influence and power second only to North Carolina—came into existence, followed by the Georgia Conference, which had a promising beginning but was drastically weakened by the loss of Augusta. Also in 1867, the Alabama and Georgia Conferences were formed out of the old Louisiana Conference; the Florida Conference would take shape in 1869. The year 1868 saw the organization of the Tennessee Conference; the West Tennessee-Mississippi Conference would be created in 1869.[36]

Despite such notable structural development, the AMEZ Church remained relatively weak, partly due to simple lack of manpower, possibly also due to top-heavy organization. A historian and observer remarked, "As in 1860, likewise in 1868, more bishops were made than could be used to advantage. Some of us contended that four bishops were all we needed, but the majority would have six; only five, however, were employed to any advantage at any one time during the four years."[37] The denomination showed definite willingness to unite with other Methodist groups. The AME Church apparently rebuffed AMEZ attempts to unite in 1868, after which the smaller northern independent received and took seriously overtures from the northern Methodists—especially attractive due to the prospect of episcopal equality. However, the conservative element within the northern church effectively blocked any merger.[38]

Thus, some black Methodist leaders strove to consolidate gains by working out agreements and even proposing denominational mergers. However, in general, poor communications and a general atmosphere of polarization among religious groups in the South effectively hindered ecumenical efforts, even though they were intra-Methodist and, in the case of the northern independents, intraracial. As a result, in the year most of the former Confederate states were readmitted by Congress to the Union, Methodist strength in the South was divided. The northern Methodists were strongest north of Atlanta.[39] The AME Church was best represented in urban centers. AMEZ efforts placed that denomination most firmly in its North Carolina and Alabama Conferences. Finally, even the MEC,S still claimed some black members, but these seem to have been located more generally in rural areas, and their number was decreasing steadily. The conceptual world of this group of black Methodists may be represented by later CME bishop Lucius Holsey, who wrote in his autobiography, "After I was licensed to preach in 1868, I belonged to the M.E. Church, South, as all colored people did who were Methodists in the slave states."[40] There were no statisticians to tell such Southerners that by 1868, most of the black members of the MEC,S had left the denomination.

Methodist Episcopal Church, South: White Reactions

Morale among southern whites took an upward turn in this period, despite political complications developing in Washington. Records kept by white Methodists of the Church South had a more positive tone. For the first time after the war's disruption, in 1866 all of the annual conferences met and compiled and submitted reports for publication.[41] In 1867, after missing or not recording its first and second quarterly meetings, Alabama's Socopatoy Circuit recorded eleven added members at the third quarterly in June and twenty-five additional members at the fourth quarterly at September's end.[42] Even fund-raising resumed its more customary place in church life as the South's economic recovery continued. On the last Sunday of May, 1868, Ellen Blue Jones recorded in her diary that a Sunday school agent named Atkins from the Holston Conference had preached "a good *begging* sermon."[43]

Small-scale revivals—conspicuously lacking immediately following the war—broke out here and there. For example, in 1866 the third quarterly conference of Union Town Station in Alabama summed up the state of the church there with the phrase "much formality but little vitality." It added no new members or preachers until its fourth quarterly conference in November 1867, when it reported "a glorious revival of religion, during which forty-nine souls have been added to the Church."[44] To be sure, such happenings were sporadic and by no means constituted a widespread awakening among southern whites. However, they indicated that among white Methodists, southern revivalism had returned to its customary rhythm of breaking out and subsiding, over and over.

In another mutation of morale among white Methodists, the overwhelming postwar sense of confusion and keen hurt subsided. Expressions of regret and anxiety regarding the exodus did continue to appear in denominational and private sources. In 1867, the Missionary Board of the South Carolina Conference resolved firmly that "we will continue to serve, as heretofore, the colored people who have remained under our care, and those who may return to their former Church relations." However, the board further resolved to serve blacks separately if they desired, to license black preachers, and to "render them [blacks] any service, even in their new Church relations, which may be desired, and which may be consistent with other claims upon us."[45] More and more, white Methodists—especially the clergy—reacted to the continuing exodus with resignation and pragmatic concern to control the outcome of this religious realignment. In July 1866, an Alabama newspaper summed up the new attitude.

> ministers of the M.E. Church South were at first disposed to object to the loss of so large a portion of their flocks, but finding that their opposition was useless, they now co-operate with the colored congregations; turn over the colored members of their colored congregations; help them to erect churches, and, in short, generally manifest a liberal Christian spirit in their dealings with them.[46]

Kolchin judges that, in Alabama, "By 1867 most white church bodies were actively advocating the secession of blacks."[47] However, if whites were advocating secession, it was in the interests, ultimately, of control. Where possible, MEC,S conferences provided "colored charges" for blacks within existing denominational structures.[48] Conferences elevated black preachers to higher ranks. In December 1866, the Montgomery Conference elected seven preachers to deacon's orders. In 1867, the Mobile Conference ordained five black preachers and the Montgomery Conference elected five and ordained two to deacon's orders.[49]

Leaders of the MEC,S adopted two strategies for dealing with self-separating black groups. First, they actually facilitated some separations by donating money occasionally and more commonly by giving advice, and especially by providing buildings and land. For example, North Carolina's Elias Bryan built two combination church-schoolhouse buildings for his former slaves.[50] Concrete forms of assistance, when provided by church leaders, were meant not only to control the manner in which separation occurred, but also to block the northern Methodists from further encroachment on the southern church's land. Both aims probably figured in the case of the sale of lot and building of Montgomery's Old Ship Methodist Church by whites to the black congregation for one dollar. The congregation then affiliated with the AMEZ Church.[51]

The second strategy adopted by leaders of the MEC,S consisted of arrangements for reciprocal relationships between the parent body and the self-separating group, such as exchanges of ministers, especially between urban pulpits. Not all such exchanges were initiated by whites seeking control, however. Rabinowitz records that blacks extended invitations to whites to attend church services and benefits.[52] It is not surprising that whites responded feebly or not at all to such outreach. Whites' fear of social equality rendered such Christian sharing highly unlikely.

Those black members of the MEC,S who showed little or no inclination to separate from the parent church comprised a special problem for the denomination's white leaders. Given time and the depredations of the northern missionaries, these blacks might separate eventually into connection with the rival northern church. Equally undesirable was the possibility that these blacks might remain as a small but embarrassing element in the life of the southern church. They already had raised the issue of leadership, and they were receiving more recognition from and legitimation by the denomination in the form of elections and ordinations, although black leaders ordinarily were assigned only to black missions and congregations. But the issue of black presiding elders and—even more—black bishops would inevitably become critical as long as blacks continued to be members in full connection with the MEC,S.

The actual number of black members still involved was small—only 78,742 in 1866, down from the prewar 240,000 estimated by bishops Andrew, Paine, and Pierce in their 1865 Columbus Pastoral Address. However, the problem these members posed called for diplomacy. How they were handled would be scrutinized closely by rival denominations, black and white, by the press, northern and southern, by the white members of the MEC,S and by the faithful remnant of blacks themselves. Although southern white Methodists were generally myopic when it came to the issue of freedpeople's participation in denominational structures and services, some were farsighted when it came to assessing the impact on opinion that the denomination's treatment of its remaining black members might have. For example, as early as November 1865, a Georgia Conference committee pointed out that neglect of the freedpeople

> would signalize ours as a Christianity so low, that it gave the gospel to the negro, because he was our slave yet would deny it to him as a freedman, though he no less has a soul to save. This would leave our church under the imputation that self interest rather than Christian principle lay at the foundation of all those efforts for the negro's religious instruction, for which the world has commended us, and on which we sometimes plumed ourselves.[53]

Such insight no doubt informed the attitudes of some delegates to the General Conference of 1866, which began on 4 April 1866 in New Orleans.

However, delegates also brought with them a number of other notions. Most retained a nostalgic commitment to the way things were in slavery times. They were unwilling to change customary separatist practices in ritual and reluctant to accord black religious leaders more status and denominational legitimation than they already possessed. Many delegates, including theologian Thomas O. Summers, were bewildered by the exodus. Shortly before Christmas 1865, he wrote,

> We once fondly thought that speaking after the manner of men, Providence was making a grand experiment on the African race of this country, having ulterior bearing upon the fifty millions on the African continent. That experiment seemed, moreover, to be in a state of successful development, and that too very largely through the instrumentality of our communion. . . . But a violent and sudden check has been given to this great undertaking, and it is impossible to divine what the developments of the future will be.[54]

Besides bewilderment, some southern white Methodists brought to the conference feelings of anger and betrayal. Surveying the increase in separate worship in Charleston the previous August, George W. Williams concluded caustically, "I am not sure but Methodism will be improved by the separation."[55] A denominational editor pointed to "much irritation against the blacks, for their ungrateful behaviour towards those who had always been their best friends."[56] Those who shared this sentiment either wanted to win back the blacks or adopted an attitude of "good riddance."

This confused mixture of emotions and ideas evidently influenced the conference's actions regarding blacks. Later historical interpretation frequently has read the reports of its Committee on the Religious Interests of the Colored People, especially Report No. 2, as a clear blueprint for the eventual exclusion of the faithful remnant of blacks from the MEC,S. That interpretation is erroneous.

Question.
What shall be done to promote the Religious Interests of the Colored People?
Answer
1. Let our colored members be organized as separate pastoral charges, wherever they prefer it, and their numbers may justify it.
2. Let each pastoral charge of colored members have its own Quarterly Conference, composed of official members, as provided for in the Discipline.
3. Let colored persons be licensed to preach, and ordained deacons and elders, according to the Discipline, when, in the judgment of the

Conference having jurisdiction in the case, they are deemed suitable persons for said office and order in the ministry.

4. The Bishop may form a District of colored charges, and appoint to it a colored Presiding Elder, when in his judgment the religious interests of the colored people require it.

5. When it is judged advisable by the College of Bishops, Annual Conferences of colored preachers may be organized, to be presided over by our Bishops.

6. When two or more Annual Conferences shall be formed, let our Bishops advise and assist them in organizing a separate General Conference jurisdiction for themselves, if they so desire, and the Bishops deem it expedient, in accordance with the Doctrines and Discipline of our Church, and bearing the same relation to the General Conference as the Annual Conferences bear to each other.

7. Let special attention be given to Sunday-schools among the colored people.[57]

In the hindsight of history, the report seems to describe in advance the process by which the Colored Methodist Episcopal (CME) Church came into existence. However, when the report was issued on 18 April 1866, it was understood variously by delegates. Gravely points out that white Methodists disagreed whether the organization of "separate pastoral charges" could take place without dividing the southern church or whether it would result in the formation of a new black denomination. Soon-to-be bishop David S. Doggett was a major proponent of the plan to organize blacks separately; he argued that the proposal actually would prevent separation. Doggett believed that blacks' "idea of their ecclesiastical liberty and status is associated with their political liberty and status." He argued

> We can do nothing by restriction. We must convince them that we are as much interested in them and in their work, as their pretended friends are. If we do not acknowledge that, what will be the result? Let it go forth from this body that we do not appreciate their position, it will react upon us and large numbers of the colored people, who belong to us, will detach themselves from us.[58]

Doggett's continued interest in retaining blacks in the denomination was dominant at the conference. An earlier version of the report advised formation of a "separate general conference jurisdiction" of blacks that would retain a relationship of "fraternal union" with the MEC,S. The delegates amended that to call for a relationship that would be the same "as the Annual Conferences bear to each other." It was as inclusive a plan as possible under the circumstances of the continuing exodus of blacks from the MEC,S.[59]

The other two reports of the Committee on the Religious Interests of the Colored People provide further evidence that southern white Methodists wanted to retain blacks in the church. Report No. 1 urged the establishment of day schools for black children—obviously a proposal to combat the divisive influence of northern teachers.[60] Report No. 3 politely but firmly rejected an AME appeal for transfer to the northern independent of church property held for black congregations by whites of the MEC,S. This report based its refusal on the fact that the conference had—no doubt in Report No. 2—"provided for the full development of a Church organization, for the colored people, up to a General Conference, in connection with the M.E. Church, South."[61]

The conference did agree to begin talks on union with the AME Church and to work out agreements for *use* (not transfer) of local church property where occupied by black congregations now affiliated with the northern independent. These actions and indeed the whole package of provisions made for blacks created confusion reflective of the mixed opinions and feelings of whites in the MEC,S.

The implementation of provisions made at the conference created further confusion. A local dispute between AME and MEC,S leadership that summer elicited some clarification from J. E. Evans of Columbus, Georgia, a white minister who had helped make policy at the conference.

The General Conference provided for both kinds of black Methodists . . . those who preferred "the new order of things" which could be most easily implemented in an alliance with the A.M.E. Church, and those who preferred "the old order of things" within the M.E. Church, South. The black denomination had agreed not to "seek to divide our Churches, or to induce them to leave us," Evans continued, and white Methodists had consented not to prevent any members or churches who wished, from joining the A.M.E. Church. Furthermore, Evans declared, the white churchmen "expected and understood" that the A.M.E. ministers would "give themselves to the one work of preaching the Gospel . . . avoiding all questions that may stir up strife between the whites and the Colored People."[62]

If AME leaders understood Evans's explication as an accurate representation of an AME-MEC,S concord, intradenominational AME conflict and interdenom-inational competition among Methodists in the South effectively blocked the cooperative element detailed by Evans.[63]

Thus in the period between 1866 and 1868, the MEC,S gradually was pushed by circumstances into relinquishing even more black members to other

Methodist bodies and reconciling itself to a less inclusive interpretation of the 1866 Conference's recommendation of separate black pastorates. But at the same time, the southern church recovered some of its poise and at times managed to demonstrate a diplomatic self-interest in dealing with the exodus. Eventually, most white Methodists came to recognize the futility of pursuing the self-separating groups of blacks and the impossibility of reabsorbing them in a church life patterned on antebellum practices. Moreover, it remained unthinkable that whites would permit social equality. District by district, in state after state, the MEC,S lost self-separating groups—to the preferred northern independents wherever MEC,S influence prevailed—and at the same time began implementing the more exclusive interpretation of the 1866 plan for what would become the Colored Methodist Episcopal Church.[64]

Denominational Competition

The contestants were many. Methodist groups included the native MEC,S, the Northern Methodists, the AME and AMEZ churches—also from the North—and even the southern Methodist Protestant Church. Also competing in the fray for souls were Baptists in great numbers, Congregationalists and Presbyterians from both North and South, and other groups, such as the Episcopalians. In 1867, MEC,S Bishop Pierce wrote about the danger his church faced from denominational competition.

> Much of our labor is bestowed upon fields unfenced, left open, and the devil and the world, to say nothing of better folks, forage upon our plantation, and we are left to glean where we ought to have reaped. . . . We need [more spiritual life] to save the Church from the schismatic plans of Northern Methodists and the subtle proselytism of the Episcopalians. These last, despairing of building up their own sect by conversions from the world, are beguiling some of our people by shallow talk about succession, confirmation, mother church, our beautiful liturgy. Our young people they are bribing with an assurance of larger liberty in worldly amusements, fasting in Lent purchasing the privilege of dancing the rest of the year.[65]

The issues raised in the competition were several and complex. Six were especially prominent and revealing of the religious concerns of both the people of the exodus and the denominations they chose.

Evangelization. A kind of territorial imperative had organized evangelization before the denominational schisms of the late 1830s to mid-1840s.

Southerners, not Northerners, evangelized in the South. After that, denominational documents record some encroachment on previously undisputed fields for home mission work. In 1844, the Alabama Baptist state convention viewed even monetary cooperation with the North as suspect. It asked, "Is it proper for us in the South to send any more money to our brethren at the North for missionary and other benevolent purposes before the subject of slavery be rightly understood by both parties?"[66] After the war, northern denominations acted on the notion that southern denominations had lost the right to evangelize in their own territory due to their dual sins of secession and slavery. Northern denominations asserted the right to evangelize as corollary to the duty to reconstruct the South religiously. The northern church held especially explicit convictions about God's will in this matter. God had chosen the North to punish, cleanse, pacify, and bring God's justice to the South by means of war.

> Once heresies of secession, states' rights, and slavery were extirpated, a new moral and religious social system would follow. Ministers of the M.E. Church, North believed that they were the agents of southern reeducation and redemption and that other religious organizations were incapable of doing the job."[67]

Needless to say, southern Christians believed that God had mandated them to evangelize the South and regarded northern missionaries as outrageously presumptuous at best, politically and socially subversive at worst. But, as later CME bishop Lucius Holsey observed, "after emancipation the Negroes held themselves aloof from the Southern people to such extent that no proposition made by the latter could reach the former. Consequently, the margin for evangelistic labors among Negroes by Southern white people was narrow."[68]

Religious identity, experience, and meaning. Each competing denomination offered a clearly labeled (if less clearly defined) version of Christianity along with its characteristic doctrines, discipline, rituals, and interpretations of current events. Among Methodists, each competitor tried to argue that it was the most authentically Methodist denomination and that God authorized or at least blessed its efforts to win black souls in the South. The MEC,S saw itself as the rightful, indigenous church with a true spiritual gospel. It held that the northern church's commitments to antislavery and other social concerns had made it a political organization, not a religious one. The northern church maintained that it was the MEC,S that was guilty of heresy and politicization.

Such sniping was not limited to the predominantly white churches. For

139

example, a white northern Methodist warned a black congregation about considering James Lynch's urging that it affiliate with the AME Church, since "it was dangerous to come out of the Methodist family."[69] Only the northern church was truly Methodist. The northern independents adopted similar arguments. An AMEZ missionary told an unsophisticated Augusta, Georgia, audience of ex-slaves that the AME Church was purely local and not even known outside the state. Another AMEZ missionary called into question the validity of AME founder Richard Allen's ordination.[70] Such charges attempted to counter the AME argument that the AMEZ Church was not truly Methodist because it lacked an episcopacy, having superintendents rather than bishops. Indeed, it is hard to see as coincidental the 1868 AMEZ abolition of the office of superintendent in favor of having bishops. At least one scholar of this period hesitates to draw a causal relationship between the AME polemic and the AMEZ action.[71] However, it is clear at least from the very raising of the issues of AMEZ episcopacy and AME valid ordination that such matters of Methodist legitimacy were extremely important to southern blacks and that the northern independents knew it.

Northern independents drew on another, nondenominational title to legitimacy: color. Some white missionaries tried to turn black charismatic identification into a negative argument about color consciousness in the African churches, but the northern church's shifting racial policies made this argument unstable ammunition indeed and likely to backfire.[72] However unscrupulous and even dishonest the arguments about religious identity and meaning may have become, each denominational polemicist sincerely believed his to be the best church for southern blacks as indicated by the Will of God, his church to be the best interpreter of the experience of the war and its aftermath.

Church property. The debate over who rightfully should hold a particular structure built on a certain plot of land had a triple significance. It was a dollars-and-cents issue. It was a bitter point of contention for all involved, especially the MEC,S and the northern church, from whose maneuverings the northern independents sometimes benefited, sometimes did not, especially later in the formation of the CME Church. But it also touched on religious concerns about sacred space and holy land. At stake were the loci of decades of baptizings, marryings, and buryings. And in the case of self-separating blacks, a church of their own on land of their own had the potential to represent a symbolic fulfillment of the biblical promise of land at a time when hopes for real agricultural acres grew dimmer daily.[73]

Social control. Although this issue was rarely articulated except in veiled terms, it was very important to Southerners, both black and white. Without slavery, the society needed reorganization into a new system with new mechanisms for effecting social location and meaning. Blacks were understandably more concerned about social location and meaning; whites were most anxious to establish control. One white minister of the MEC,S may have felt he had met both concerns when his black congregation affiliated with the AME Church. He told them that "the redemption and the elevation of the colored race was to a greater extent than ever before placed in [their] hands."[74] But as Bethel's agenda of racial uplift led to increasing "political" activity outside of the control of white Southerners, they tended to oppose the northern independent as the answer to the problem of social control. Missionaries were not unaware of this issue or its significance for both whites and blacks. As a result, they tried to articulate a definite if unspoken outline of the advantages for social control that affiliation with their particular denomination might offer.

Social equality. Social equality between the races was feared by southern whites. Blacks professed little interest in social equality and often disclaimed it in favor of economic equality. In fact, blacks desired social equality very much, but they knew that to express that desire was dangerous. Southern whites interpreted the desire for equality as including a desire for sexual intimacy and physical proximity that blacks could hardly have wanted given the plenitude and negative quality of those experiences under the coercion of slavery.

Northern Methodists and the black independents well appreciated what social equality meant to southern blacks. An AMEZ minister told a Louisville congregation that the AME Discipline supported slavery.[75] AME spokesmen charged the northern Methodists with racial discrimination; northern Methodists ordained blacks and sent them South to win souls. Not surprisingly, the northern independents used the issue of social equality with greatest effect. Writing in 1890, Reverend L. M. Hagood provided this account of the independents' approach:

> They told the local preachers, class-leaders, etc., among our [Southern Methodist] members, that it was a shame for them to have white masters during the week and white masters on the Sabbath-day also; that they were as well qualified literarily to have charge of congregations with white members as some of the white pastors; that they possessed intelligence enough to do business for themselves. Then, again, they would say: There will never come a time when the Methodist Episcopal Church will allow one of you colored members to preside

as their presiding elder or pastor; that all the property you buy belongs to "white folks," and not to you.[76]

While whites worried about miscegenation, the black independents provided a persuasive message directed at the heart of southern black Christian religious experience. Communal liberation and the liberated community obviously were incompatible with ecclesiastical subordination and inequality. The issue of social equality was decisive in the relative success of the black independents and of the separate jurisdictions proposed by the Church South.

Autonomy. The pioneers' frontier experience had fostered a southern tradition of individualism. Ecclesiastically, Southerners expressed this tradition in their preference for congregational polity and congregational self-determination. This issue, generally understood as a given rather than articulated in the debates, influenced the outcome of many a competition. Indeed, some have blamed Presbyterian insistence on an educated ministry for contributing to the failure of the denomination's energetic postbellum work among blacks. But it is likely that self-separating black groups perceived Presbyterian polity as antithetical to their preference for congregational autonomy. Methodists, on the other hand, retained an emphasis on the local group, their spare, hierarchical denominational structure notwithstanding. Baptists' congregational polity facilitated the "mushroom growth" of the postwar years.[77]

These six issues animated denominational debates. One can recognize them at stake in surviving accounts, even when detail is sketchy and denominational interest strong, as in this narrative of competition between the AMEZ Church and the northern Methodists. Note especially that evangelization, religious identity, and church property were important in this case.

> The desire to unite with some other branch of the Methodist Church was so strong in some that they were ready to unite on any terms, or even to make an unconditional surrender . . . In some cases the contemplated union was used against us, and our people were told that we were going soon to be all one anyway, and those who went first might fare best. The result was that thousands of our members went to that Church. Rev. G.W. Price, Presiding Elder of the Lumberton (N.C.) District, attempted to take his whole district and the church at Wilmington, N.C. He took several churches and about one thousand members. We got the church at Lumberton back, but it took us seven years to do it, and the Methodist Episcopal Church had the advantage of possession and the use of our property all those years, while our people were without a place of worship.[78]

Although arguments inspired by racial animosities added little of positive value to the discussion, none of the Methodist denominations was impervious to the temptation of appealing to sentiments concerning race. This temptation would grow as denominational competition continued. MEC,S spokesmen stepped up attacks on northern Methodists for "spoiling" blacks with social equality. Northern Methodists accused the black independents of racial exclusivity. The African denominations drew starker contrasts between racial pride and subservience to whites—especially as they experienced disappointment on issues of property and ecumenical outreach.

But denominational competitions employed more than words for weapons. Missionaries also offered aid to the indigent, some political organization and guidance (less than southern whites imagined), and above all in the case of southern blacks, education. As noted, even the MEC,S used education to retain groups or influence them in desirable directions. However, denominational competition ultimately seems to have hampered the cause of education itself. In June 1867, a Radical politician gave recognition to the fact that literacy had become less a problem for blacks, except in "remote country districts." But in 1868, Freedmen's Bureau officials began to note a decline in blacks' zeal for education, and in 1869 sectarian or denominational jealousies were described as a hindrance to work in bureau schools.[79]

By 1868, interdenominational struggles were far from over, but religious forces in the South had established some spheres of influence. While somewhat less visible than the several Methodist denominations, Baptists had undergone considerable development with northern competition of their own.[80] Among Methodists, the southern church continued to lose members to its northern rivals, despite the provisions for black annual conferences made at the 1866 General Conference. Of the three major northern competitors, the Methodists had more money and workers, but the African Methodist independents were stronger in charismatic appeal. Not to be forgotten in this institutional picture was the individual black Methodist and the individual black Methodist congregation. A decreasing number of these remained within the MEC,S. Many had separated and formed new and lasting affiliations with the other Methodist denominations. Some groups shifted allegiances under combined pressures of denominational competition, charismatic leadership, and each group's own sense of religious identity. These seemingly unstable groups and the congregations that remained in the MEC,S would be central players in the denouement of the exodus drama.

Summary and Concluding Observations

From 1866 to 1868, the South seethed with political activity of unprecedented character and scale. Every state of the former Confederacy was involved. Congress's Reconstruction Bill introduced suffrage to all males, excluding only those who could not—or, better, would not—take the Ironclad Oath. Freedmen voted for the first time in every state except Georgia and Mississippi. The writing of new state constitutions required fundamental rethinking of social and political relationships with extensive if unforeseen consequences. In education, for example, Louisiana's and South Carolina's new constitutions provided for integrated schools while other state constitutions did not specify integrated or separate schools for black and whites. Black and white political leaders worked together fairly effectively in South Carolina and Florida; but political conflict rather than cooperation characterized political activity in Georgia and Mississippi.

The depth, scope, and variety of political change notwithstanding, effects on the exodus were negligible. The momentum of separations was neither accelerated nor slowed by political activity. Politicians of every stripe did not scruple to solicit support among religious groups. They did not hesitate to form political cadres within congregations where feasible. Occasional association between Union League or Loyal League groups and certain black churches illustrates the potential of ritual commensality to facilitate not just religious but also political ties. Nevertheless, if politicians used the separate churches for political ends, they did not create the churches. Indeed, it is important to remember that at least two-thirds of the black Methodists who separated from the MEC,S had done so before a single southern black was enfranchised by Congress.

Terrorist activity by white members of parareligious, paramilitary bands likewise had little if any effect on the formation of separate black Methodist congregations with their altered denominational affiliations. Klan-type activity peaked at the height of political struggles because of the political issues at stake.

It is impossible to separate Klan activities and purposes into exclusive categories or to measure accurately their respective importance. But the Klan movement reached its fullest dimensions only with the advent of Negro suffrage, first in Tennessee and then in the South at large. Moreover, the testimony of its victims points to the intimidation and punishment of Republican voters and officeholders as its central purpose.[81]

As a rule, the Klan did not care about religious commensality. Recorded attacks on black church members or their buildings by groups of white terrorists were in most cases clearly politically motivated.[82] For example, Jane Wilson of South Carolina reported that the Klan sought to kill her father for praying and preaching over the body of a man they had slain at the courthouse.[83] The political activities of northern Methodist missionary A. S. Lakin drew Klan attention. A northern Methodist preacher named Sullivan, who worked in Alabama and was associated with Lakin, reported that he had been whipped, warned that the presiding elder would be killed, and told to preach for the MEC,S, which his attackers declared should be the only church south of the Mason-Dixon line.[84]

Occasionally, white terrorists targeted churches and church members for other than political reasons. Racial etiquette concerned many Klan groups. George Washington Miller of South Carolina remembered that poorly disguised raiders came to his church and told blacks "to behave and settle down, and believe in their own White folks."[85] Hattie Anne Nettles described a Klan raid on a black prayer meeting: "De Klansmen beat up lots of dem . . . If a nigger didn't behave, dey'd nigh 'bout kill him."[86] Pauline Fakes reported that a man had been killed in a Klan attack on a log cabin church used by blacks. She guessed that the man "may have acted 'smarty' or saucy or he may have been the leader."[87] Klan groups did not harass churches or church members in Emma Turner's part of Georgia: "Dem Ku Klux—you dassent be out after dark. You better not be out on the street after dark. But Sunday night they didn't bother you when you went to church."[88]

Some attacks on church gatherings apparently were motivated by the white men's anger that blacks were no longer slaves. Josie Jordan of Tennessee, where the Klan originated, described an assault on a church meeting.

> The preacher was telling about the Bible days when the Klan rode up. They was all masked up and everybody crawled under the benches when they shouted: "We'll make you damn niggers wish you wasn't free!"
> And they just about did. The preacher got the worst whipping, blood was running from his nose and mouth and ears, and they left him laying on the floor.
> They whipped the women just like the men, but Mammy and the girls wasn't touched none and we run all the way back to the cabin. Layed down with all our clothes on and tried to sleep, but we's too scairt to close our eyes.
> Mammy reckoned old Master Lowery was a-riding with the Klan that night, else we'd got a flogging too.[89]

In a small number of cases, terrorists directed violence toward black churchgoers because they had contact with whites. All of such incidents that I have found occurred in Texas. For example, William Hamilton, who was born in 1860 near Handley, reported that, "De Klux picked on Jack Ditto's niggers mo' dan de tudders. Yous see, he am a Baptist Preachah an' preached to de cullud fo'ks, an' m'ybe de Klux don't lak fo' him to does dat."[90] It is not clear whether terrorists in these situations wanted to curb religious association per se between blacks and whites or whether they wanted only to enforce general racial boundaries as they were being defined in postwar Texas. In light of the lack of interest of Klan-type groups in separate black churches, the latter interpretation seems most likely. It is also possible that the terrorists suspected black-white political collusion under the guise of religious gatherings. Such may have been the case when a Klan spy apparently excited the eschatological expectations of a black congregation. Hardy Miller remembered that

one time we was havin' church and a Ku Klux was hid up in the scaffold. The preacher was readin' the Bible and tellin the folks there was a man sent from God and say an angel be here directly. Just then the Ku Klux fell down and the niggers all thought 'twas the angel and they got up and flew.[91]

Indeed, some Klan activity consisted essentially of practical jokes. John Crawford of Travis County, Texas, told about

how after freedom de Ku Klux Klan caused a lot of devilment roundabout de country. One day de niggers was havin' a big camp meetin' near Manor and a bunch of Ku Kluxers rode up. De preachah kept on preachin' while de flock hit it out ob there. One of de Ku Kluxers went to a barrel and drank some water. He told de preachah dat dat was de best water he had since he left H—. But de Ku Klux Klan give de preachah five dollahs fo' causin' all dat trouble.[92]

In general, Klan-type groups persecuted political activity but not religious activity—evidence that, unlike blacks, white men differentiated between religion and politics. On balance, except for possibly intensifying a black religious group's self-awareness, white terrorist activity neither accelerated nor slowed the formation of separate congregations and altered denominational affiliations by black Methodists.

As before, black Methodists acted to self-separate. There were more separate churches and congregations by 1868 and fewer black members in the MEC,S. Southern white Methodists reacted by enacting measures at the 1866 General

Conference that did not discourage the growth of the black independents and that dictated—without apparent intention that they would form a wholly separate and independent denomination—the setting up of black annual conferences to combat further conquest of people and property, especially by the northern church.

By the end of June 1868, six states of the former Confederacy had been readmitted to the Union, joining Tennessee in obtaining congressional recognition. National and regional patterns of political exclusion and participation had undergone profound changes in slightly more than three years since Appomattox.

In that same short period, the old pattern of joint worship in the same denomination was replaced by newly predominant religious patterns of exclusion and participation. Participation of blacks and whites together in religious activities now was limited to dwindling exchanges of preachers for services, to occasional black outreach for white participation in religiously related social events, to some camp meetings, and to the small number of blacks who remained members of the MEC,S. A trend of dwindling participation was characteristic not only of Methodists, but of Baptists and other denominations as well.[93] Even the few southern black Catholics began to worship separately while retaining denominational ties.[94]

By 1868, exclusion was decidedly dominant over participation in the South. Blacks worshipped separately from whites. Even within the MEC,S and the northern church, blacks increasingly worshipped in separate congregations and churches. Among the black northern independent denominations, competition and personal ambitions had bred exclusion. Leaders of both Bethel (AME) and Zion (AMEZ) still hoped for the transfer of black members remaining in the Church South and their properties.

Methodists embroiled in religious rivalries probably were unconscious of the far-reaching social and political implications of ritual exclusion. Leaders were strongly committed to various loyalties—denominational, regional, "racial," sometimes political. In some men such loyalty may have been exceeded by personal ambition. But Methodists black and white seem not to have considered that ecumenism might be better for the reconstructed South than religious exclusion.[95]

Almost all parties affected by the exodus of black Methodists allowed the waters of the Red Sea to flow back, leaving Christians separate from Christians. Even whites who first felt hurt by the early surge of blacks to separate would later agree that it was for the best. In 1868, a white Methodist

FIVE

Deserts and Definitions, 1868-1871

The exodus into separate congregations, churches, and denominations had begun spontaneously, with blacks acting as if by instinct on their distinctive appropriation of Christianity. Southerners now faced separate deserts, wildernesses of an unknown future. Whites who had believed in the perfection of southern society had lost that society and their faith in it; they struggled to redefine each person's place. Blacks who had welcomed war and emancipation as the coming of God's Kingdom now knew that the promised land was yet to be gained. They struggled to define themselves as free citizens and full participants in American society. In the churches, not participation but exclusion ruled. For example, in 1868, northern Presbyterians organized a Negro Synod of Atlantic, which included black Presbyterians from North Carolina to Florida.[1] That same year the Southern Baptist Convention declared its separation from Northern Baptists to be permanent. In 1869, the Cumberland Presbyterian Church organized the Colored Cumberland Presbyterian Church.[2]

Divisions, separations, and exclusions notwithstanding, major southern Protestant denominations continued to count the loss of their black members with regret. For example, at the 1868 Convention of the Episcopal Church, Bishop Davis of South Carolina reviewed his church's losses sadly but not without a note of resolute hope:

> The number of communicants in the diocese has been much reduced by the loss of our colored members. In 1860 we had nearly *three thousand* colored communicants reported. Not *three hundred* were reported to the last Convention. In the condition of many of our parishes it is impossible to ascertain how many of the freedmen still adhere to the Church. Many have joined the Northern Methodists. Many have followed teachers of their own color; but if our services were revived in our suspended parishes, we might hope

to rescue some of them from the fanatical and political preaching to which they are subjected. In one parish only have they adhered to the Church. Two congregations of colored worshippers have been gathered together, as in former days, to make their chapels resound with their hearty prayers and praise. But this is the only successful effort to win them back to our fold. These remarks apply to the freedmen.[3]

Some whites continued to cling to the hope that separated blacks would reform their old church affiliations. As late as 1870, the Southern Baptist Convention Sunday School Board predicted some sort of reunion

in relation to the colored children whom Providence has thrown upon our hands. . . . Violently and suddenly deprived of the patriarchal protection and care of their humane masters, and thrown upon their own resources without the necessary preparation and training, their present condition is one of deepest commiseration and sympathy. . . . We understand them better and can compassionate them more benignly than any other people. And when they shall awake from their present hallucinations, they will be sure to turn their pleading eyes and imploring hands to their former masters as their best friends and seek from them the protection and care which we are confident they will utterly fail to derive from strangers.[4]

A Presbyterian's 1867 assessment of the situation had a more sober and realistic tone; yet it also expressed regret and an optimism based on faith.

The Colored membership has melted away from our churches like snow before the rising sun. Very few have adhered to us. They have gone off into organizations of their own, under the influence and control of bodies foreign to us, and all we can do is to *wait*, until, in the Providence of God, they shall return unto the fold from which they have strayed.[5]

Episcopalian Bishop Atkinson of North Carolina gave a less hopeful report in 1871.

The efforts in this diocese for the spiritual improvement of the colored race are not as promising of good results as are desired by the friends of the freedmen. While in some few places they seem to appreciate the teachings and ministrations of the Church, in most cases they have separated themselves from the ministry of the Church, and given themselves to the guidance of ignorant teachers of their own race, who are leading them into the wildest excesses of delusion and fanaticism.[6]

Thus in a period when the exodus of blacks from their former religious homes was nearly complete, whites still were not completely reconciled to the segregation of their churches. Nevertheless, the need for new definitions was apparent, and the situation was far from simple. Among Methodists, complexities crystallized around the small remnant of blacks who remained in the MEC,S. Both northern independents, Bethel and Zion, regarded these Christians as potentially theirs. Northern Methodism was ready to receive them into the black conferences finally authorized at the 1868 General Conference and now being formed. The MEC,S, whose 1866 General Conference actions on the question of its remaining black members expressed ambivalence in ambiguous policy statements, was finding greater clarity in the practical course of events. By 1871, the self-separation and self-definition of most of the black remnant in the MEC,S would solve the problem. With the formation of the Colored Methodist Episcopal Church in America, the exodus was accomplished.

Deserts: Political, Economic, and Social Contexts

No two states presented identical backdrops for the final act in the dramatic exodus of black Methodists from the MEC,S. While several states shared similar timetables for political reconstruction, having been readmitted to the Union in Congress's Omnibus Bill, such variables as demography, local leadership, and terrorist activity by whites influenced each state differently. All the states of the former Confederacy shared certain economic problems and all struggled to construct a social order *sans* slavery. But generalizations about the South's political, economic, and social situation in these years must be made with caution.

Certain national developments affected all the states. In 1868, the Fourteenth Amendment was ratified and went into effect, defining citizenship for blacks and whites and setting forth the principles of due process and equal protection under the law. The Fifteenth Amendment, which assured all male citizens the right to vote, was not in effect until 1870; however, in the 1868 election of Grant as president, the Republicans achieved victory with the help of black voters. Republicans saw black suffrage as increasingly important. The election results led them to push for swift passage of the Fifteenth Amendment to protect the valuable black vote. Meanwhile, in 1869, the bill

151

that had established the Freedmen's Bureau expired, and Congress made no provision to continue that organization's work with the former slaves.

Congress's lack of action on behalf of ex-slaves partially reflected if not decreasing interest in the South certainly a diversion of attention from the South on the part of the northern states. These states looked increasingly to their own affairs and then to national concerns. In 1871, the scandals of the Grant administration eclipsed events in the South.

Southern Democrats were happier with less northern and Congressional scrutiny than were the Republicans—national attention had constricted some of their activity. In addition, Republican victories in 1868 brought with them consequences that, ironically, favored the Democrats. As the new state governments took office, federal troops withdrew, as early as 1869-1870 in some places. What remained of the alien influence of the U.S. Army on the authority structure of the South waned. Local white influence grew. Meanwhile, by 1869 most former Confederates had been pardoned and restored to rights as citizens. In 1870, a definite Southwide political trend to the Democrats began.

In every southern state in varying degrees, the Ku Klux Klan and other similar groups continued to influence political developments. One half million members strong in 1868, the Klan attracted more and more members from the ranks of discontented whites.[7] As before, terrorist targets were primarily political. By 1870, terrorism hobbled Reconstruction governments. Much of the activity was directed against black voters and office-holders. An investigation of Klan activity in Alabama recorded 371 cases of major violence against blacks between 1868 and 1871.[8] White terrorist groups were effective though not totally successful in driving blacks from politics.

Black men in the South struggled to gain and maintain the right to vote. Politicians strove to have schools established. For black Christians, both schools and suffrage had religious implications: they were means to the communal liberation blacks celebrated in ritual and hoped for in the new order. Several black ministers pursued second careers in politics. Some observers accused these preachers of nonreligious ambition. However, while probably not lacking in hearty political appetites, the clergyman-politician also possessed his religious tradition, including the concrete, immediate eschatological hopes characteristic of black Christianity from slavery times. Despite many frustrations, such men could point to progress toward a new order: several schools, increasing literacy, growing sophisti-cation among blacks who could vote.

In its economic life, the South continued to recover from the war. Each year crop yields more closely approached prewar levels.[9] Nevertheless, poverty was an all-too-common affliction, especially for blacks. Black labor lost a valuable ally with the 1869 end of the Freedmen's Bureau. The market for agricultural labor included a larger number of small farms than before the war. New forms of farm tenancy developed: renting outright, share tenancy, and above all, sharecropping. Many of the blacks who would make up the Colored Methodist Episcopal (CME) Church lived as agricultural workers.

Struggle accompanied social change. Whites and blacks often used conflict to decide minute matters of etiquette as well as fundamental questions of their relationship to one another. Sometimes the conflict was psychological, sometimes physical. Frequently the Klan and similar groups turned from purely political concerns to enforce preferred social practices. On occasion they punished adultery, miscegenation, and behavior they regarded as impudent.

It was in this context of social conflict, economic change, political struggles, and decreasing northern interest in the South that black southern Methodists performed the final act in their exodus.

Definitions: Black Independent Denominations

The northern independents continued to harvest members of the Church South into their own denominations. The smaller AMEZ organization had grown from approximately 42,000 members in 1860 to 164,000 in 1868;[10] by 1880 members would total approximately 250,000.[11] AMEZ growth slowed, partly because most of the black former members of the MEC,S had made their decision about denominational affiliation, partly because of internal problems such as lack of missionary workers and inadequate ministerial training.

The larger, more effectively organized AME Church gathered in self-separating southern blacks in greater numbers. Approximately 70,000 members strong at the beginning of the war, it grew to 391,044 members in 1871.[12] Its leaders endured the less than diplomatic reception of its delegation by the MEC,S 1866 General Conference and looked to the more encouraging aspects of that body's ambiguous pronouncements. Some were hopeful that the MEC,S eventually would release its black remnant to Bethel. Some talked of forming an official relationship with the MEC,S.

But Bethel also invested its energies in other strategies for winning southern blacks. The denomination actively continued to seek black congregations and churches in the South to affiliate with it. These bodies came out of the MEC,S or switched from prior allegiance to the AMEZ or Northern Methodists. The effect of this ingathering was hardly conducive to interdenominational harmony. The AME Church's sister independent and the Church South greeted its overtures of friendship and cooperation with suspicion. Besides its aggressive efforts at evangelization, AME political involvement also was threatening to other Methodist bodies. Individual members—especially preachers—were active in fighting for blacks' voting rights and for specific candidates and issues. Some even ran successfully for office. In November 1868, AME Bishop Payne praised his denomination's commitment to "constitutional government" exemplified in the political involvement of many AME men in the South. He reported that in South Carolina, twenty-eight representatives and one senator were AME members. In North Carolina there were two senators and one representative as well as four justices of the peace, a city commissioner, a supervisor of an "Insane Asylum" and "many" policemen. In Georgia's political strife, "the majority of those who were expelled from the Legislature were members of the A.M.E. Church." In Florida, thirteen of twenty-three blacks in the General Assembly were AME men, five of them ministers, one also a presiding elder. In addition, Florida had "several" AME justices of the peace and "many" county commissioners and seven preachers who also served as public school superintendents.[13] In support of such activities, the church as a whole adopted a political stance. Payne described this stance as grounded in a guiding AME conviction that

> the Lord Jesus Christ, whom they receive and obey as their Savior, is also, "The Lord of lords, and King of kings," that in His hands is placed all power in heaven and earth—that by His permission "kings rule and princes decree justice, even all the judges of the earth." This Scriptural conviction, [AME leaders] apply to politics, and teach that when a Christian approaches the poll he is morally bound to cast his vote for no one, but an open and fearless advocate of liberty, justice and all righteousness.[14]

When this communal ethic was expressed in real political representation, white and black decision makers in the MEC,S took note.

Definitions: White Methodists

The behavior of the AMEZ and—especially—the AME Church helped white leaders of the MEC,S choose their policy toward the southern church's own remaining black members.

From the first it had been clear to them that the northern church was the least desirable destination for blacks who chose to leave the Church South. Now that rival body was continuing to proselytize congregations belonging to the Church South. In 1868 it counted eight conferences with ninety thousand members in the South.[15] However, its policy of evangelizing both blacks and whites produced friction concerning race relations in some areas. In New Orleans in 1869, white members of Ames Church showed an aversion to mixed seating at worship. The pastor permitted blacks to be limited to a balcony. But six years later, the church adopted a policy of nondiscriminatory seating.[16] Once boastful of its egalitarian ways, the northern church had begun to arrange separate conferences for black congregations where demanded by whites and blacks; but this development was uneven, depending on the demography and the social climate of the various northern Methodist concentrations in the South.[17] Eventually—in 1876—the General Conference would set down the decision-making process by which majorities of black and white southern Methodists affiliated with the northern church created two separate networks of annual conferences in the South.[18] Black leaders who petitioned for such separate jurisdictions expressed the desire for fuller participation in church governance. For them, reorganization was an act of self-separation that would enhance participation rather than foster exclusion in denominational affairs.[19] Meanwhile, between 1868 and 1872, fewer new Southerners joined the northern church. Its growth slowed because there were simply fewer potential members to harvest now and because the unresolved status of racial relationships in the denomination was not likely to appeal decisively to whites or blacks with a mind to change church affiliation.

To whites the AME Church was increasingly less desirable an option for blacks who might want to separate from the MEC,S, given the independent denomination's forthright political stance. Never a secret, the church's position was only a position in the early, decisive months of separation, during "Confederate Reconstruction." It was a point of view held by a small church not yet influential in the South. Now that the denomination had grown and the MEC,S saw and felt the political activism of its members, its desirability as a potential denominational home for the black remnant faded. White

155

Methodists increasingly resolved that the northern independents represented an unsuitable solution to its own conflicts over race relations. Yet within the MEC,S the issue of what to do about the black remnant grew in urgency. Following the procedure sketched out in 1866, Colored Conferences were being organized. If they retained a connection with the MEC,S General Conference, black delegates rightfully could and would ask representation along with whites. Moreover, separate conferences posed the question of black bishops. What role would such bishops play in denominational affairs?

As the MEC,S approached its 1870 conference, it had achieved a clearer definition of its place in society vis-à-vis other Methodist bodies. But continued conflict from without as well as unresolved questions within the denomination meant that it would have to deal—literally—with its own black remnant. To achieve satisfactory, stable definition, black and white religious leaders together would have to work out a mutually acceptable arrangement.

Definitions: Church Relationships

The final act of the exodus can be fully understood only in the light of interaction between churches in the period before the final formation of the Colored Methodist Episcopal Church in America. Interaction consisted of cooperation and ecumenical outreach, denominational competition, and conflict over the decisive problem of church property.

Much of the cooperation and ecumenical outreach between Methodists of various affiliations occurred on the local level. While joint worship grew increasingly rare, some joint practices continued. Camp meetings were held. Ministers exchanged pulpits. One congregation often helped another build or repair its church building. Until a congregation of Methodists in High Point, North Carolina, could build a church, it shared a school building with a congregation of Baptists, holding services on alternate Sundays.[20] However, cooperation was sharply limited by whites' fear of social equality. Thus, even within the still "mixed" denominations, fellowship between Methodists might be ritual, as in the exchange of preachers and joint worship with continued antebellum separatist customs like seating arrangements, or educational, as in the many attempts to provide blacks with instruction, but not social outside of settings in which roles and relationships were defined clearly. Thus the Word could be shared and even, occasionally, the Lord's Supper, especially among black and white northern Methodists in the lower South; but social commensality was out of the question. Both whites and blacks attended the funeral described by Ellen Blue Jones in July 1868, but it is unlikely that they shared a meal afterward.[21]

Except for unsuccessful attempts at union, little or no interdenominational cooperation occurred between the black independents. The northern church did attempt to engineer reunion with the Church South. However, its earlier wartime and postwar strategy of absorbing or replacing the southern church had alienated southern attitudes. Formal representatives of a northern Commission on Reunion approached MEC,S bishops in 1869 and the General Conference in 1870, but the MEC,S rejected reunion despite the obvious financial benefit it would bring to the impoverished denomination. Indeed, in 1869, the MEC,S issued a formal protest against encroachment on its territory by northern missionaries and formally rejected organic union with the northern church.[22]

The most consistent program of ecumenical outreach was pursued by the black independents. As mentioned, the two African denominations seemed near union in 1868 until the AME Church apparently turned down the prospect. Zion then turned its ecumenical energies toward the northern Methodists, drawn by intimations of episcopal equality. Not surprisingly, the northern church was divided on the question of uniting with the black independent, and the merger never took place.[23] Bethel continued to focus its ecumenical attention on the MEC,S, as it had at least since 1866. Prominent in its concerns was the property of black congregations that had left the MEC,S as well as those who were likely to leave. AME leaders hoped the MEC,S would either cede properties to their church or effect a merger as the most satisfying solution to the tangled problem. However, AME leaders and members continued to engage in black sociopolitical action in the South. What AME members saw as important to communal racial improvement, MEC,S leaders viewed as meddling that would spoil society by spoiling blacks. In time, whites in the Church South came to scorn both the black independents and the northern church as "political churches."

In denominational competition, political involvement became a highly debated issue. MEC,S spokesmen charged that the black independents and the northern church had duped freedpeople into disruptive political alliances under the guise of religious affiliation. For example,

The "fiercest mischief" accomplished by the "blackcoated saints," wrote a Mississippi journalist-politician, was in "separating the . . . blacks . . . from their old masters, the white men," and then "tieing them fast . . . to Northern politicians." He called upon the Church North, as a contribution to the political and social peace of his state, to "remit the Negroes . . . back to . . . the guidance and protection of Southern white men."[24]

Georgia's Z. B. Hargrove told Congress's Joint Select Committee about a Methodist minister driven away from his home and his calling by terrorists because

he was preaching to the colored people; telling them too much; he was a republican. If he has ever done anything, I have never heard of it. . . . A great many would-be decent fellows make a great fuss about republicans being in favor of negro equality. That is one thing they do not intend to have; no negro equality about it at all.[25]

A black observer and historian argued that whites overestimated the actual use of political influence by leaders.

there are many things about the freedmen which are not known to any except those who have been closely associated with them through all these years; and one of these things is the freedmen's intuitive knowledge of the political situation. They needed no persuasion from their leaders to induce them to vote for the party of liberal ideas; they were often more radical, because less thoughtful, than their leaders.[26]

Not even the remaining black members of the MEC,S were immune from attack on political grounds. As they began to organize their own districts and conferences under the 1866 guidelines, they drew increasing fire from other Methodists. As early as December 1868, George Jackson of Kentucky, a black preacher for the southern church, reported that representatives of rival Methodist bodies were abusing him and calling him "Reb" and "Secesh."[27] Northern Methodist missionary A. S. Lakin warned a congregation that a black minister who was trying to reorganize the MEC,S in the area was a "wolf in the fold" and influenced them to tell the preacher to leave.[28]

Compounding this competition was continued strife over the issue of property. Sometimes this problem was solved locally with agreement between white trustees and preachers from the black independents. Generally the Church South followed a policy of ceding use but not possession of church properties to black congregations, especially those newly aligned with the AME Church.[29] But the property problem quickly became an interdenominational issue. Both the northern Methodists and the Church

South believed that the South was their rightful territory for evangelization. It followed that properties used by their congregations belonged to the denomination. The southern church was anxious to prevent its northern counterpart from taking over more churches than it had and eventually to expel its alien, political influence from the South. Approached by AME leaders, the Church South had experimented in transferring the use of properties to AME congregations, but that cooperative venture collapsed under a combination of the inevitable pressures of denominational competition and AME political activity. Highly political themselves, southern whites nevertheless saw AME activism as a deviation from the Gospel.[30] Further, the agreement to permit black congregations to use property whether they remained in the MEC,S or affiliated with the AME Church activated the inevitable mechanisms of competition. As Gravely remarks, "The logic of denominationalism is, as the agreement sought to recognize, voluntarism, but that implies competition as well."[31]

The AMEZ Church would not allow itself to be left out of the contest. While gravitating to the northern church in ecumenical outreach as the AME denomination gravitated to the Church South, AMEZ leaders worked hard to win southern blacks. In desire if not in practical possibility, they probably shared the sentiment of AME bishop Jabez P. Campbell: "We would like to have all the ground."[32]

Given the southern church's increasing reluctance to yield even use of property to separating black congregations, soon-to-be members of the CME Church must have seen that to separate into a competing denomination could cost them buildings and land. Would any advantage that could compensate for the loss of property be gained by affiliating with another denomination? Nor was the issue of property merely part of a cost-benefit analysis. Whatever practical considerations they took into account, the members of the black remnant within the MEC,S were grappling with religious issues bearing in a fundamental way on their distinctive heritage. As in slavery, so even more in freedom Christianity meant community and liberation—but where was the promised land? A pie-in-the-sky answer to that question was inconsistent with the traditional concreteness and immediacy of their eschatological hopes. They continued to work for and hope for a new order in the here and now. While blacks did look forward to and sing about a happiness and peace after death, that expectation did not defer their biblically based, more earthly hopes. Following a religious logic, activist southern members of the African denominations were striving to realize the promise of land in the political

159

arena. Yet they were opposed vigorously by white terrorists and by a resurgent Democratic party cheeky enough to court black votes. Would the exodus end in the desert?

Definitions: The Founding and Significance of the Colored Methodist Episcopal Church in America

The full story of the founding of the Colored Methodist Episcopal Church has yet to be told satisfactorily. The most adequate treatment is by William B. Gravely.[33] Some of the story and analysis that follows depends on Gravely's article.[34] Gravely rightly highlights the critical issues of church property and political involvement as influencing the final ecclesiastical exodus of all but a few of the black Methodists remaining in the MEC,S.

Many stories of the founding of the CME Church see its seed in the actions of the 1866 General Conference of the MEC,S. They interpret Report Number 2 of the Committee on the Religious Interests of the Colored People as a deliberate, orderly plan for separation. Some historians portray the plan as a unilateral action by white leaders. For example, Ahlstrom states that, "In 1866 the Southern Methodist church released its Negro membership so that it could form a Colored Methodist Episcopal church in 1870."[35] The 1898 account by CME historian (later bishop) C. H. Phillips has heavily influenced subsequent accounts. Phillips credited white southern Methodist missionaries with developing "the religious nature of the slave." He stated stiffly that, "It was not unnatural that the Southern Methodist Church should, after the war, have shown a disposition to do what was best for her colored contingent," quickly adding that "colored communicants . . . were toled away" by rival Methodist bodies by means of "persecution, misrepresentation, ridicule, and stratagems brought to bear against the Church, South." Pointing to the "78,000" blacks remaining in the MEC,S in 1866, Phillips claimed that, "To save this remnant was the supreme thought of the leaders of the Church, South. To organize them into an ecclesiastical body occurred to them as the only feasible thing to be done."[36] Thus, the CME historian's narrative tended to reinforce the view that the 1866 General Conference had designed a plan for the formation of a separate black denomination and that they had done so unilaterally and deliberately.

In an autobiography published in the same year as Phillips's history, Lucius Holsey, an ex-slave who became a CME bishop in 1873, depicted mutuality in the decision making process. Like Phillips, he saw the resolutions of the conference as a conscious design for a separate denomination, but he asserted that, "As far back as 1866, its organization was contemplated and desired by both classes [that is, blacks and whites] of those who composed the membership of the Methodist Episcopal Church, South." In Holsey's view, the

initiatory provisions, being agreeable to both classes of persons concerned, and being consistent with what was conceived to be the harmony and best interests of both and all, the separation was authorized—legal, formal, and productive of the best feelings and results."[37]

Holsey's version is closer to what actually happened. Initiatives by whites and blacks acting both unilaterally and together played a part in a highly complex course of events. However, due to the early interpretation of the 1866 General Conference resolutions as unilateral, deliberate, clear-sighted plans for a separate church, one question emerged from the hot denominational competition of the late 1860s and the 1870s: Was the CME Church chosen by whites as a convenient solution to the embarrassing and complicated problem presented to the MEC,S by the fact of a minority of blacks who did not join the early exodus? Those who have asked this question generally have understood the churches socially, politically, and economically. Consequently they have neglected the religious dimension.

The sequence of events began with what appeared to be the opposite side of the exodus: the decision by some black Methodists to remain in the MEC,S. These nonseparated members were not passive. As described earlier, they had been situated formerly in a variety of biracial denominational and ritual settings. They had distanced themselves enough from the predominant pattern of joint worship that the MEC,S 1866 General Conference did not doubt the feasibility of creating separate quarterly, district, and annual conferences of blacks within the denomination. Black members' own process of self-definition had made such separation a sensible alternative. They remained Methodists through and through—Methodist Episcopal, in particular. Whatever unity members of the black remnant possessed, it seems to have coalesced early around the question of leadership, especially bishops, and around the question of land, represented by their churches, old and new.

The Reports of the 1866 Committee on the Religious Interests of the Colored People must be interpreted as a response by white Methodists to pressures exerted by nonseparated blacks in the MEC,S. The reports give implicit recognition to several facts. Like their already separated coreligionists, these members wanted leaders of their own with fuller participation in denominational decision making. The 1866 Committee recommended an increase in licensed preachers and ordained deacons and elders, and it opened up the possibility of creating black presiding elders. Its proposal that separate conferences be constituted reflects a stage of organization impossible without prior formation of local groups that possessed a self-awareness and decision-making process. In other words, by the time the General Conference met in 1866, blacks still within the MEC,S had undergone the same process carried out by those who had already left. Conference recommendations provide for the retention of these members. Significantly, they specify expansion of black leadership up to—but not including—the episcopacy. Separate annual conferences were to be presided over by white bishops.

The Minutes of the Annual Conferences for 1866 list several separate "colored charges." In some cases it can be determined that black leaders—some of them newly elected or ordained—filled these charges. Thus, for some areas of the Church South, conference proceedings simply recognized practical fact.

The white Methodists who hammered out the 1866 General Conference reports were responding to reality. But they also were reflecting unrealistic antebellum dreams. The ambivalence of Report No. 2 shows that these men recognized the trend toward self-separation even among the black remnant, but that they longed to retain their historic ties in some way without relinquishing social and ecclesiastical control or falling victim to "social equality."

Following the 1866 Conference, the parallel process continued. While the northern Methodists, the AME Church, and the AMEZ Church all were organizing their new black members into new denominational structures, black annual conferences took shape within the MEC,S. By May 1870, there were five separate conferences; by the time of the December inaugural meeting of the CME General Conference, there were eight. The blacks who remained within the MEC,S in 1870 thus were distinctively organized. The general recapitulations of membership figures for 1867, which were published in 1870 in the MEC,S annual conference minutes, carry this notation: "The preachers and members of the separate Colored Connection, which the bishops are organizing, agreeably to the provisions of the General Conference, are not counted here, as they have their own Minutes."[38] The black remnant continued to show preference for its own leaders and for a role in denominational decision-making processes as full members of the Methodist connection.

Politically, fulfilling these religious aims would forge strong ties and preserve some mutual control, albeit altered. For example, once black bishops were selected, bishops would work white with black, not white over black. Socially, fulfilling these aims implied a degree of equality that probably would prove deadly to maintaining a mixed Methodist denomination in the South, notwithstanding its long tradition of joint worship in the same denomination.

Accordingly, by the time the MEC,S General Conference met in Memphis in May 1870, the ambiguous policy ambivalently articulated at the 1866 Conference had given way to a clarity worked out in everyday reality. Over time, southern Methodists, black and white, had come to understand the 1866 recommendations as a clear-cut plan for harmonious separation. The white bishops at the May 1870 Conference announced a General Conference in the winter of 1871 "for the purpose of organizing them [colored conferences] into an entirely separate Church, thus enabling them to become their own guides and governors." The black conferences did not send delegates to the May gathering, but they did send a petition of diplomatic gratitude for the leadership provided them by the bishops. In addition, they shrewdly "also thanked the white Methodists in advance for 'the provision made to transfer the property held for our use,' praising the action as 'without parallel for its magnanimity and confidence.' "[39]

Through their leaders, both black and white members of the MEC,S had made their choices. It had not been possible for both parties to accomplish everything they wanted. An analysis of what they did accomplish shows that even in this final exodus, religious concerns were decisive.

The first General Conference of the CME Church began on 15 December 1870. On 21 December, white bishops Holland N. McTyeire and Robert Paine ordained black bishops William H. Miles and Richard H. Vanderhorst. Pain, regret, and ambivalent feelings are written into accounts of the ceremony. In turning over episcopal authority to these newly ordained bishops, Bishop Paine said,

> The time has come for us to resign into your hands the presidency of this body, and the episcopal oversight of your people. . . . Your people, by their voluntary suffrages, have called you. . . . There is no strife between us—let there never be any. While our hearts are warm with love to God or man, we shall feel an interest, a peculiar interest, in your welfare. We have labored for you when they were few who cared for your souls. Our missionaries are buried on the rice, and cotton, and sugar plantations, who went preaching the gospel to your fathers and to you while slaves.

Later in the ceremony, Bishop Vanderhorst said, "Brothers, say not good bye, that is a hard word. Say it not. We love and thank you for all you have done for us. But you must not leave us—never." The intensity of the event was expressed by white Methodist minister A. L. P. Green, who declared, "This is a solemn hour. We all feel it. . . ."[40] CME historian C. H. Phillips wrote, "Those who were present and are still living will not forget the solemnity of the occasion."[41]

Genuine contemporary social, political, and economic considerations influenced the formation of the CME Church. But as early accounts show, the founding of the denomination was experienced as a religious event. Its significance must be assessed accordingly. Such an evaluation reveals that in this final act of the exodus as in prior acts by southern black Methodists, blacks were acting on their own distinctive appropriation of Christianity. One can argue the case for the CME Church on five decisive counts.

First, black actors in this phase of the exodus placed explicit stress on their religious heritage. The report of the CME Committee on Church organization made this plain.

Whereas the Methodist Episcopal Church in America was the name first given to the Methodist Church in the United States; and

Whereas we are a part of that same Church, never having seceded or separated from the Church; but in the division of the Church by the General Conference in 1844 we naturally belonged to the South, and have been in that division ever since; and now, as we belong to the colored race, we simply prefix the word "colored" to the name, and for ourselves adopt the name, as we are in fact a part of the original Church, as old as any in America; therefore be it

Resolved, 1. That our name be the "Colored Methodist Episcopal Church in America."

2. That while we thus claim for ourselves an antiquity running as far back as any branch of the Methodist family on this side of the Atlantic Ocean, and while we claim for ourselves all that we concede to others of ecclesiastical and civil rights, we shall ever hold in grateful remembrance what the Methodist Episcopal Church, South, has done for us; we shall ever cherish the kindliest feelings toward the bishops and General Conference for giving to us all that they enjoy of religious privileges, the ordination of our deacons and elders; and at this Conference our bishops will be ordained by them to the highest office known in our Church. No other church organization has thus been established in the land. We most sincerely pray, earnestly desire, and confidently believe that there will ever be the kindliest feelings cherished toward the Methodist Episcopal Church, South, and that we may ever receive their warmest sympathy and support.

3. That we request the bishops to organize our General Conference on the basis of the Discipline of the Methodist Episcopal Church, South, in its entire doctrine, discipline, and economy, making only such verbal alterations and changes as may be necessary to conform it to our name and the peculiarities of our condition.[42]

Gravely points out that the CME Church represented the vision of a "spiritual," that is, nonpolitical church in contrast to the activist African independents and the northern Methodists. Certainly this interpretation receives support from the expressions of loyalty and good will toward the MEC,S in the Report of the Committee on Church Organization. Certainly too one of the "peculiarities of our condition" faced by CME congregations was the property question. But fulfillment of the promise of land depended absolutely on adopting the nonpolitical stance agreeable to southern white Methodists and continuity of valid episcopal orders depended on the white bishops of the Church South. The "kindliest feelings" expressed by the committee report consist of gratitude for "religious privileges"—not for the preaching of missionaries now buried on plantations where these black Methodists had worked as slaves—specifically for ordination. Deeper than the debate over politics ran the question of continuity with the Methodist tradition, and the CME plan of organization stressed continuity. When one juxtaposes the committee's report with accounts of the "solemn hour" when Miles and Vanderhorst were made bishops, one recognizes that these black Christians desired continuity of religious tradition and authority as well. The "solemn hour" was highly significant for the religious legitimation it conferred on the entire leadership structure of the church. Many of the black remnant in the MEC,S and probably most of its leaders present at the December 1870 Conference had heard denominational polemicists question the validity of episcopal orders in the black northern independent denominations. The argumentation must have intensified these Methodists' concern for authenticity. The ordination by bishops of the MEC,S must have assured them of a religiously legitimate hierarchy. The ordination provided members of the CME Church with a sense of solid grounding in authoritative religious tradition, a sense analogous to that derived by Southern Baptists from Landmarkism and that derived by certain Roman Catholics from arguments based on the so-called Apostolic Succession. The CME Church constituted itself as a separate, legitimate, authoritative, Methodist religious organization.[43]

Second, the leaders of this exodus partook of the traditional characteristics of southern black Christian leaders. Miles and Vanderhorst provide instructive examples. Both men were charismatic, possessing extraordinary qualities. Both were sons of the South, both ex-slaves. Significantly, each had joined the AME Church for a time (and no doubt thereby gained ecclesiastical experience) but had returned to the parent MEC,S. The charismatic principle of identification was powerful in this case. To the typical church member, the bishops were "black like me" as well as southern and formerly slaves. Their potential for bonding members together partly explains why the CME Church survived even in the face of great hostility and sometimes of violence.

Third, indigenous charismatic leadership underscored and enhanced the characteristic southern black Christian experience of communal liberation. Born in the galleries and balconies of the joint ritual setting, this experience animated the black exodus in all its phases. In the case of the CME Church, liberation came with separation when efforts to achieve ecclesiological equality within the MEC,S failed in the face of opposition by whites. Liberation was communal to a full, almost elaborate degree. Unlike earlier black Christians who left as groups or congregations, this community moved in a fully formed Methodist organization with annual conferences, districts, and quarterly meetings. It counted fewer members than even the AMEZ denomination, but it was autonomous and indigenous to the South. Its southern base notwithstanding, its leaders designated it the CME Church in America—explicitly connected with the oldest Methodist traditions in America and pointedly distinct from the Church South whose General Conferences steadfastly refused to remove the regional term from its name.[44]

Fourth, southern black Christians understood the biblical exodus to be a liberation that led to the promised land. Their concrete application of Scripture to their own circumstances gave land unique importance in their religious hopes. Fed, then frustrated, by rumors of acres and mules, these hopes no doubt fired interdenominational struggles by southern black Methodist groups over church property. In the end, because the CME members stressed their spiritual heritage, they seemed nonpolitical enough to work out a transfer of property. One of the changes in the MEC,S Discipline adopted by the first CME General Conference specified that churches were never to be "used for political assemblages or purposes."[45] As Gravely observes, "The 'non-political' status of the C.M.E. Church, therefore, was written into its own conditions for holding property in behalf of the denomination."[46] The provision made it far less threatening as a recipient of property than its northern rivals.[47] Thus, ironically, in the matter of land, the last would be in some senses first. Moreover, I find no evidence that any political deals sweetened the exchange. The land was gained without selling black votes.

The final decisive count on which to argue that members of the CME Church acted on their own distinctive appropriation of Christianity concerns the issue of initiative. The CME remnant was the last to separate from the MEC,S, and it seemed to follow a procedure outlined by the parent church. Even in its own day, the CME Church was seen by rival Methodist groups as a subservient body that did as the masters' church bid. They called it the "Democratic" church, associating it with the political party favored by ex-Confederates. They called it a "Rebel Church," the "Slavery Church," and the "Old Kitchen Church," the last gibe an allusion to a "big house" image of heaven, where whites would occupy living rooms and drawing rooms, while blacks would be stuck in the kitchen, still servants to the whites.[48] Holsey reported that "all the colored churches had branded us as 'Democrats,' 'bootlicks,' and 'white folks' niggers,' whose only aim was ultimately to remand the freedmen back to abject bondage."[49]

In actuality, group self-consciousness and indigenous decision making followed a familiar pattern among those who constituted the CME Church. From the antebellum religious experience described earlier, they derived a distinctive appropriation of Christianity and a self-awareness of their religious distinctiveness. Local leadership developed, and after the war, the MEC,S fostered black leaders, especially after practical local developments revealed the dangers of leadership affiliated with northern bodies, black or white. Thus, Isaac Lane, who would become a CME bishop in 1873, served as a presiding elder of a Tennessee District from 1867 to 1870, when he was assigned pastor of Liberty Colored Methodist Episcopal Church in Jackson. Moreover, his style of leadership fit the charismatic pattern of southern revivalism, complete with its anti-economic stance.[50] Lucius Holsey explained:

> No salary was fixed for the circuit preachers. Each man made his living in the sweat of his face, and preached on Sunday as best he could. But at the end of the second year it was proposed by some of the members of one of the churches to give the preachers a collection, and they willingly and generously gave us both the magnanimous sum of four dollars for the two years' services. We both were present, and a wide-awake and generous brother paid us the money, and with a triumphant air on his beaming countenance, said to us, in the tone of self-congratulation, "We are glad you don't preach for money, but for souls.[51]

It is true that some members of the CME Church thought of themselves as less educated and sophisticated than those in other black Methodist bodies. In an 1891 essay, CME Bishop Holsey explained the separation of his people from the MEC,S by drawing a comparison between emancipated slave and master, who

> though divested of his slaves, yet carried with him all the notions, feelings and elements in his religious and social life that characterized his former years. On the other hand, the emancipated slave had but little in common with the former master. In fact, he had nothing but his religion, poverty and ignorance. With social elements so distinct and dissimilar, the best results of a common church relation could not be expected. . . . Social religious equality, as well as any other kind of social equality, was utterly impracticable and undesirable, and coveted by neither class of persons composing a churchship. With this state of things steadily in view, we had but one horn of the dilemma left us, and that was a free, friendly and authorized separation from the mother body.[52]

Gravely stresses that the CME denomination "was a church that literally came out of slavery. Its membership was composed exclusively of former slaves."[53] Nevertheless, they pursued the same churchly goals, acting on the same appropriation of Christianity, but working from *within* the parent church structure as long as possible. Whether sophisticated or timid, this strategy had the potential to effect an unsegregated version of southern Christianity. Moreover, even though the strategy failed, out of it emerged the only indigenous, autonomous southern black Methodist denomination of the exodus.

With the events of 1871, the exodus was accomplished. The MEC,S reported as late as 1891-1892 that it had 357 black members.[54] But by 1871, religious patterns of exclusion and participation among Methodists were set. They would last well into the next century.

SIX

Exodus Accomplished

By 1871 the pattern of joint worship that prevailed throughout the antebellum period had changed to one of virtually total racial separation. The preceding case study of black Methodists has shown that in this period they acted, spoke, sang, preached, wrote, and prayed as executors of the religious legacy earned in their forebears' and their own Christian experience. In the postwar chaos of confused whites, competing denominations, and general social flux, black initiative was decisive in the emergence of a pattern of racial separation in the rituals and denominational structures of the southern churches.

Patterns of Exclusion and Participation in the American South of the Early 1870s

In the early 1870s, black Methodists found themselves in a society still in flux. Political, economic, and social patterns of exclusion and participation continued to shift, influenced by events and by an ongoing renegotiation of their relationships by blacks and whites.

Politics continued to be the arena for fights over suffrage and office-holding. The Fifteenth Amendment guaranteed adult male suffrage, including blacks. However, as soon as Democrats (or "conservatives") wrested power from Republicans (or "radicals") in each state, they began to manipulate the franchise to their own advantage. In general, whites acted favorably toward black enfranchisement in direct proportion to how controllable the black vote appeared to be. This political reality and continued harassment by hostile whites demanded subtlety and courage of black political leaders and courage and sophistication of black voters. Indeed, by 1871 the activities of the Ku Klux Klan had elicited the federal Ku Klux Act, but President Grant elected to use it sparingly. The later trend to leave the fate of the black vote in the hands of the states was at least incipient in 1871.

Each state differed in political climate. Four either never had experienced "Radical Reconstruction" or now were in Democratic hands—Tennessee, Virginia, Georgia, and North Carolina. Seven states still were undergoing "Radical Reconstruction." These included Florida, Texas (which had joined the Union in 1870), and Mississippi (which finally had accepted the Fifteenth Amendment in 1869 and whose legislature first had met in 1870). Arkansas's Republicans faced much Klan activity. In South Carolina, Republican power had been diluted by important Democratic victories in 1870; by 1875 a Klan coalition with planters and newspapers would paralyze the government. Louisiana's Republicans, though dominant, were factionalized; there Democrats would begin to come into power in 1872. Alabama actually was run by a coalition of conservatives and Republicans; in that state much terrorist activity also influenced elections.

In this mixed political climate, some blacks held political offices and would continue to do so at least until the late 1880s. A small number of blacks served in Congress until 1901. But there was never a period of so-called Negro rule in the postwar South.

In the economic sphere, several patterns showed signs of change by 1871. Northern capital promised to play a large part in the reconstruction of the South. Indeed, many a Union soldier who had fought in the region returned, attracted by climate and economic opportunity. Some population centers began to grow into cities. New population centers (Birmingham, for example) sprouted; these too would become cities. Many black and white Southerners who had fled to urban settings during the war remained there to work. There, some flux in the kind and availability of so-called Negro jobs showed that economic boundaries for participation and exclusion still were being negotiated. Industries such as iron and textiles stood at the threshold of a historic period of growth. Transportation, too, was changing. Southern politicians struggled to strike beneficial railroad deals.

Rural economic patterns also were shifting. Landowners tended to possess smaller holdings. Lower-class whites and blacks alike were drawn increasingly into sharecropping agreements. These arrangements for agricultural labor led some to say that slavery had been abolished legally but not economically. John Hope Franklin states that,

> Contrary to the widely held view, there was no significant breakup of the plantation system during and after reconstruction. Day labor, renting, and sharecropping were innovations, to be sure, but those occupying such lowly

positions bore a relationship to the planter that, while it was not slavery, was nevertheless one of due subordination in every conceivable way.[1]

In the social sphere, flux also marked the South's "reconstruction." Some social patterns shifted with the political jostling of the period. For example, the new state constitutions might specify education in mixed schools—as in Louisiana and South Carolina—or they might be silent concerning classroom grouping—as in the case of most southern states, whose school systems then emerged as segregated. Whites debated whether blacks should be educated and what kind of education was appropriate. No consensus had developed.

Blacks continued to seek education of all kinds, the complications of sectarian rivalries notwithstanding. Blacks generally shared an understanding that education was essential to a new order, and by 1871 it was obvious that more than emancipation and Appomattox would be needed to bring about the here-and-now side of blacks' religious hopes. Black church leaders were especially active in urging and implementing programs to improve educational opportunities.

To the twentieth-century eye, social patterns in public accommodations are another measure of racial relationships. Here, too, the situation was fluid. The Black Codes had been repealed or clearly superseded by state constitutional conventions, and a federal civil rights bill guaranteeing equality in transportation, public accommodations, and education introduced in 1870 remained under consideration until 1874. On the local level, rigid boundaries like the elaborately segregated railroad waiting rooms of the 1880s and 1890s were not yet a legislative concern but rather a matter under informal social negotiation.[2]

In fact, the most pressing social concerns of the 1870s seem to have been racial self-definition and "other"-definition together with formulation of a satisfactory racial etiquette. The Klan and other white terrorist groups showed significant interest in this matter. Maggie Stenhouse reported that the Klan beat her preacher father almost to death because the service was too noisy for white neighbors.[3] A raider passed on advice to a frightened black to take off his hat when he came to a white man's house.[4]

Two particular targets of disapprobation by white males were sexual acts or relationships between black men and white women and any marriages between black and white. E. A. Hightower told the Joint Select Committee of a white man who was whipped because, while married to a white woman, he lived with a black one. According to the testimony of William H. Statlings, disguised men horribly mutilated a colored man and a white woman for cohabiting.[5] Perhaps understandably in the light of nineteenth century mores, southern women said little about such matters, so it is difficult to discover whether and to what extent they shared the sexual orthodoxy of the ruling male elite. There is some evidence that they feared rape by blacks, but it is hard to imagine that they condoned white men raping black women or consorting with black prostitutes, practices traditionally winked at by many southern white men. It does seem likely that southern white women generally would look askance at miscegenation. Whatever the case, the public voices that spoke against miscegenation were those of white males.

Blacks, on the other hand, said little but acted eloquently regarding intermarriage. Immediately after the war, they worked at both the exodus and the reconstruction of their families. By 1871, many lost family members had been found, many marriages had been solemnized, and the legal legitimacy of countless children had been secured. These actions do not point to an anti-miscegenation campaign. Rather, they were part of a profound restructuring of family. The antebellum white family in the South encompassed both blood relatives and blacks. In the case of slaveholders' families, the tie with blacks was particularly familial, even where blacks remained unrelated to the whites; but average white Southerners still regarded all blacks as children regardless of ownership. This attitude fortified the paternalism of the slave system, creating artificial families.

As Max Weber has explained, the family is one source of commensal rights and privileges, perhaps the most important source.[6] Given the quasi-familial structure of so many slaveholder-slave relationships, the predominant antebellum pattern of shared ritual commensality among black and white southern Protestants is hardly surprising. In such relationships, slaves were regarded by the slaveholder's family as part of the domestic community. They usually took ordinary meals separately, just as children customarily do in many cultures. But they took the Lord's Supper, the ritual meal, in a fashion that affirmed the religious fellowship generated by conversion and yet retained recognition of their childlike or second-class status in the domestic community. Such was the purpose of the sequential taking of Communion in joint worship and the paternalistic provision for blacks of separate services led by the whites' selected preacher, to cite the two most common ritual circumstances. In both, the domestic community of the family fostered the provision of commensality, which in turn produced religious fellowship in keeping with members' status within the family.[7]

Indeed, one notes striking parallels and enlightening dissimilarities between the status of enslaved Africans in the nineteenth-century South and the status of "sojourners," (the *gerim*) in ancient Judaism. Weber noted that the *gerim* were accorded rights and privileges as a guest tribe. In its ordinary connotations, the word guest suggests a lovely situation. However, Weber's term refers to a tribe living on the outskirts of a village and providing certain types of work not otherwise available to the community. Villagers viewed such a tribe as a group of outsiders. While benefiting economically from the guest tribe's presence, they protected themselves from social intercourse by erecting various barriers—ritual, political, legal, and so on—against the guest tribe. "The purest form of this type is found," Weber asserted, *"when the people in question have totally lost their residential anchorage and hence are completely occupied economically in meeting demands of other settled peoples."*[8] That guest tribe social status was decisive for blacks in the colonial period is evident from the fact that white colonists did not distinguish between converted and unconverted slaves; all belonged to the "other" group.[9]

Ritual, political, and legal barriers notwithstanding, a guest tribe does have some rights and privileges. For the *gerim*, these included limited access to ritual commensality. Further, from postexilic times, over a span of three generations, the *gerim* who desired inclusion could be assimilated into the Israelite "family" and accorded equal status as members with full ritual privileges.[10]

No such assimilative process existed for the black "guest tribe" in the antebellum South. Occasionally, a master might manumit one or more slaves. In these cases, a blood relationship between master and slave was often a consideration. But manumission was an exceptional occurrence, and many southern states passed laws to prevent it.[11] As a result, the slave ordinarily was accorded for life the status of second-class child at best.

The status of slaves in the churches mirrored this set pattern of partial exclusion and partial participation. There was no route—ritual or generational—by which the worshippers in the gallery or balcony or back of the church ever could approach religious services as fully assimilated, equal members of the congregation. Thus the congregation mirrored the artificial family created by paternalistic slaveholders, a family in which certain children never grew up and never were regarded as full and equal members, yet always retained somewhat restricted access to ritual commensality. As one ex-slave described it,

We had the privilege to go to church, and they would fix us up to go to services, just like we were chillen. Old McMurray was a preacher too—my father's master. We had the privilege to act like we free almost. . . . Old master built us a church, and we could have prayer meeting when we wanted to.[12]

Once emancipated from artificial antebellum families, blacks throughout the South moved to establish natural, legitimate families. They also formed religious communities in which they enjoyed full commensal rights and privileges. Some chose to do so via independent black churches such as the AME and AMEZ churches, in which full participation was facilitated by the generally race-specific composition of these denominations. Others chose separate status within a mixed denomination like the northern Methodist Church, in which the development of separate jurisdictions for blacks reduced racial friction and fostered full participation for blacks. The CME Church was yet another manifestation of the same phenomenon: the formation of religious community with full religious privilege, including the episcopacy. In antebellum times, blacks had experienced themselves as a people apart—in the churches as an *ecclesiola in ecclesia*—hence the tendency to self-separate, even under mixed denominational umbrellas.

In summary, then, most political, economic, and social patterns of exclusion and participation were still very fluid six years after Appomattox. But the fundamental restructuring of both family and ritual commensality had been accomplished, mainly due to the initiative of blacks responding to their new situation. Issues such as voting, jobs, education, and racial etiquette would be the subject of continuing controversy and change to the end of the century. In the churches, however, the period of flux was over very early.

To the hindsight of history, what happened is quite clear. Before the war, participation in joint worship and joint denominational affiliation constituted the dominant pattern and separatist customs were threads in that larger fabric. In cases of separate worship services for blacks and separate church buildings used by blacks, the parent denominations tried to hold these developments all in the family. White observers frequently kept a parental eye on the conduct of separate worship. Titles to church property, even when buildings had been constructed by blacks, were held by paternalistic white trustees. In these situations, control was a focal concern of whites; but implicit in such a concern was their notion of the quasi-familial relationship of whites and blacks. Nevertheless, under this inclusive canopy of custom and ideology, separatist customs, secret worship, and the unique socioeconomic status of blacks facilitated two developments critically important to the formation by blacks of exclusive religious associational forms. Those developments were a distinctive appropriation of Christianity by blacks and indigenous black group self-awareness.

During the war, the white male authority structure of southern society was disrupted. Many fathers—actual and symbolic—went off to war. Of these, many died, many were wounded. Even before the war's end, white Southerners were confused and demoralized to a paralyzing degree. In the same period one notes expressions of black group self-awareness and the beginning of the exodus. At least rudimentary group decision-making processes apparently preceded the choice of altered religious affiliation by each group. Often the decision to leave preceded the choice of new denominational connections. Some groups—especially those in rural areas—had few options from which to choose; other groups were courted by several competing groups. In each case, blacks acted on their own distinctive appropriation of Christianity. Indeed, even in 1871 some white Christians still were expressing ambivalence, surprise, and regret at the accomplished fact of the exodus. Later, rationalization helped reconcile whites to their altered religious relationship. In 1888, the SBC Committee on Missions to Colored People evaluated the relationship.

> Naturally enough the negroes prefer to have their own separate local churches, and for these to be presided over by ministers of their own race. They prefer also to have their own organizations for educational, missionary and other benevolent work. It is not likely that this condition of things will be changed, nor is it desirable that it should be.[13]

Too often, such rationalizations have been read as explanation for the exodus that occurred more than twenty years before. By the late 1880s and early 1890s whites did prefer racial separation in many aspects of daily life about which they had been uncertain or ambivalent in the 1860s and early 1870s. They—and many historians—projected later sentiments into earlier events, inappropriately seeing a later preference for separation as the early cause of the exodus. It is important to distinguish carefully between initiatives by blacks, reactions by whites, and long term results. With such distinctions in mind, we can summarize the altered patterns in ritual and in denominational structures.

Patterns of exclusion and participation in ritual now reflected congregational composition rather than antebellum custom. Most of the churches affiliated with the MEC,S no longer practiced separatist customs in seating and in the Lord's Supper because almost no blacks remained as members of the congregation. Those few who did remain—in 1891-1892, 357 were reported—probably continued the old ways.[14] I find no explicit discussion of the ritual practices of this minuscule remnant. It is probable that they continued separatist customs from the antebellum period.

Churches affiliated with the northern Methodist Church practiced a more varied range of customs at worship. In some areas of the South, Methodists in the early 1870s still strove for the ideal of full social equality at worship. Black and white members sat in the same areas and took the Lord's Supper together. But the northern church had relatively more success in the postwar South winning blacks. Moreover, the distribution of blacks and whites tended to favor separatism. More northern Methodist whites lived in the border states, where sentiment favoring separate conferences for blacks and whites first had surfaced.[15] As a result, in the postwar period relatively few whites had experienced joint Methodist worship with blacks. By 1884, the northern church had twenty-eight conferences in former slave states—twelve white, thirteen black, and three with both white and black ministers but predominantly white membership.[16] In the end, northern pressures favoring separation apparently prevailed. In Morrow's assessment,

> The South, although it was the laboratory for Methodist experiments in race relations, did not hold within itself the power of a definitive solution. The decision for or against segregation belonged to the General Conference which was dominated by Methodists in the Northern states. In the North, arguments for an unsegregated church had never been more than half convincing, and as the postwar pattern of custom in the South began to clarify, they rapidly spun downward in popularity. Most importantly, the advocates of segregation won strong support in the highest circles of the Methodist hierarchy.[17]

The black independents preached racial equality and Christian sharing. In ritual, however, services usually were limited de facto to blacks, and the northern independents held a separatist view of their denominations' practical mission.[18] In an 1872 report on church union, an AME committee stated the case.

> We believe the good time is coming, and ought to be now, when all the members of the great Methodistic family shall be one, forming one grand invincible army. . . . When prejudice, on account of color, shall be swept away from the Church, and shall disappear like dew before the morning sun, then, and not until then, will the grand mission of the A.M.E. Church, as a separate organization, be at an end.

Therefore we cordially welcome to our ranks the friends of Jesus every where, and of all nationalities; but especially would we say to our colored brethren: "Come thou with us and we will do thee good, for the Lord hath spoken good concerning Israel.[19]

The CME Church's unique relationship to the Church South encouraged a somewhat greater degree of sharing between blacks and whites. In his address to the General Conference of 1873, CME bishop Miles expressed gratitude to the MEC,S for "sympathy and encouragement, for brotherly counsel and material aid" and—especially—for the transfer of property and the well-remembered ordination of bishops.[20] At the same Conference, MEC,S bishop Pierce played a visible role, praying before the election of new bishops Beebe, Holsey, and Lane, and then preaching their ordination sermon.[21] However, on the local level, except for occasional exchanges of ministers, most of the sharing between MEC,S whites and CME blacks apparently took the form of financial help for the black churches from white congregations.[22] The CME Church followed the Discipline and ritual customs of the parent Church South, even adopting its hymnbook. However, the newest black independent made clear its separation from the MEC,S in order to counter the name-calling and misrepresentations that emerged in denominational competition. Moreover, the decisive differences were there as with the northern independents: the minister was "black like me" and the members participated in the liberating occurrence of conversion as remembered or as experienced communally.

Thus, the rituals of southern Methodists reinforced both the old and the new. Ritual was more important than belief for both blacks and whites in the South because almost all shared similar forms of Christianity, such as Baptist or Methodist, which ordinarily stressed experience rather than doctrine as the criterion of religious authenticity. Traditional Methodist beliefs and customs were preserved, but in the setting of God's refashioned family. Now nearly all God's children were equal when at worship; nearly all worshipped in racially separate congregations.

In denominational structures, patterns of exclusion and participation also reflected and reinforced both old and new. All Methodist groups retained their antebellum organizational design. The all-new CME Church patterned itself after the parent MEC,S. The black independents created new circuits, districts, and conferences to accommodate the influx of new groups. They elected more bishops to serve the larger numbers. The all-black denominations opened up more opportunities for blacks who felt called to Christian service, although clerical opportunities were open only to males.[23] The nearly all-white MEC,S altered its denominational structure gradually, so that when its black conferences formed the separate CME denomination, no dramatic changes were made. Like the black independents, the northern Methodist Episcopal Church created circuits, districts, and conferences to serve its newly gained southern members. It affirmed in theory the eligibility of blacks for episcopal office. In practice, participation by blacks fell far short of the episcopacy; but blacks were more visible, even if still limited in denominational decision making, than they were before the Civil War.

It is instructive to note that in 1871 as afterward, no single all-black denomination embraced all blacks who participated in the exodus. Blacks were divided within Christian traditions, such as the Baptist and Methodist ones, and across the spectrum of American Christianity from Roman Catholic to Quaker. These divisions reflected three traditional elements in blacks' distinctive appropriation of Christianity. One is their commitment to a specific strand of Christianity, usually Baptist or Methodist. Another is revivalism, which tends to foster free will theologies and works on the principle of voluntary association—hence the choice of different denominations with varying expressions of the southern Protestant creed. Third is the tradition of personal charismatic leadership characteristic of revivalistic groups and especially prominent in black religiosity as a result of near-total exclusion from official types of charisma in slavery times. Personal charisma requires recognition, and the most effective recognition comes from triumph over a charismatic foe. Thus the black religious leaders who called for Christian unity and the black denominations that made repeated overtures of friendship were bound to be frustrated. The tradition of personal charismatic leadership helped keep southern Christians, black as well as white, divided.

Significance of the Exodus for Religion in the American South

This case study promotes an awareness of how the exodus came about. Such an awareness leads in turn to an appreciation of the importance of the religious patterns it produced.

Churchgoers in the South experienced the significance of the exodus in their continued participation in now predominantly separate worship services. These services may not have seemed very different from antebellum ones, especially to the white person-in-the-pew. Certainly they have not seemed different to those historians who correctly note that the form of worship was retained by whites and blacks and who allege that separate black groups merely copied the Christianity of their white counterparts. That the forms of worship did not change is unsurprising given the conservative nature of ritual customs. The liturgical scholar Dom Gregory Dix points out that the "real basis of liturgy is custom, not law" and that custom "dies" only "by ceasing to be observed."[24] In contrast to theology, which is open to innovation by clerical elites, worship is of its nature conservative and reflects an earlier time.[25] Separated black Christians were not copying white rites, they were observing their customary celebration of community and liberation as before, albeit in an altered, separate setting.

More important than the forms of worship was the experience of separateness itself. Blacks now worshipped in congregational communities composed of natural black families. They experienced themselves both as a community and as a people apart even more intensely than in antebellum times. Whites now worshipped in congregational communities devoid of the blacks who otherwise participated in their everyday lives—for example, in work and politics. Whites experienced worship that was far less reflective of the whole society than in antebellum times. Except for those in the few remaining mixed congregations, whites experienced themselves as separate from blacks at the central rite of Christianity—the sharing of the Word and of the Lord's Supper. Ritual commensality in 1871 was predominantly—almost wholly—a de facto race-specific right and privilege.

Separation affected the style of worship somewhat. Outside observers recorded comments and complaints about the emotionalism in black services. These remarks may reflect racist alarm at what was a fundamentally lower-class or "plain folk" strain of southern revivalism exhibited by small farmers and townspeople at antebellum camp meetings.[26] However, some of the emotional intensity of these services probably came from blacks' intensified experience of themselves as a community. As Max Weber explains, "ecstasy occurs in a social form, the orgy, which is the primordial form of communal religious association."[27] Perhaps the fervor of some postwar black worship constituted an emotional orgy, a communal ecstasy.

In contrast to the possibly increased emotional fervor of blacks at worship, the style of white worship apparently showed little change in 1871, since comments about any change beyond sermon content appropriate to the times do not appear in the sources. As before, the ritual preferences of whites tended to correspond to social class, with plain folk preferring overt expression of

179

religious sentiments and upper-class whites gravitating toward rituals that were restrained in emotional expression, formal, and perhaps more cognitively oriented.

As with ritual style, so with goals of worship: the rituals of white Methodists did not change. They continued to be aimed toward conversion of individuals, which experience the service was to facilitate or call to mind. Likewise, the goals of black ritual continued to be the affirmation of community and conversion as Christian liberation. If anything, blacks now sought these goals with greater intensity for two contrasting reasons. One was that they were no longer slaves. The congregations of the exodus celebrated release from bondage. The other reason was that constitutional freedom fell far short of the liberation blacks had both celebrated and longed for. Thus the worship service helped the community deal with the failure of the new order to fulfill completely blacks' characteristically concrete and immediate religious hopes. It preserved and nurtured these hopes for another day.

Especially significant for its long-term consequences was the effect of the exodus on the experience of the sermon. The sermon functioned in Christianity in general and specifically in southern Protestantism as a commensal element. Like the Lord's Supper, the shared sermon frequently bonded antebellum blacks and whites both religiously and in a quasi-familial, political way. Accordingly, segregated reception of the Word accentuated the segregation of the Lord's Table. (Indeed, the only opportunities for shared reception of spoken religious ideas and values now would be civil-religious occasions.)

Besides completing the severance of ritual commensality, the separate sermon provided separate access to the Christian story. This had profound impact on the Christian traditions of blacks and whites. Moreover, the effects of this divided access would be accentuated by the passing of generations and the fading of a memory of joint religious experience and shared Christian heritage.

Separate denominational structures also significantly affected religious life. First of all, separate denominational structures meant that the elements of southern revivalism shared by blacks and whites now were retained separately. Lay egalitarianism in religion was limited to race-specific expression for most Southerners. Among blacks, this circumstance intensified the experience of the religious association as community. Among whites, it tended to eliminate blacks as co-Christians in whites' vision of the church. The familial kind of zeal for black souls formerly expressed by men like William Capers and Charles

Colcock Jones gradually gave way to a more detached concern for social welfare and uplift.[28] For example, the 1888 SBC Committee on Missions to Colored People expressed this altered attitude:

> let us encourage them to do their own work in their own way, giving them at the same time our sympathies and our prayers, and offering them, so far as they may indicate a willingness to accept the offer, our counsel, our men and money to aid them in their work, and let us do all this for Jesus' sake.[29]

Other formerly shared elements of southern revivalism now separately retained included associational forms and the tradition of charismatic leadership. Together, these elements sparked much of the period's denominational competiton. As leader vied with leader, sometimes splitting a congregation, and as denomination competed with denomination, southern Protestantism as a moral force possessed fragmented power in a period that would be remembered for nationwide corruption.

Divided denominations entailed weakened or broken religious ties between blacks and whites. As with separate access to the Christian story, not only would the memory of former ties grow dim or distorted, but relationships themselves would mutate. Then later generations would assume that the relationship of black and white Christians had always been as it was. This phenomenon is especially evident in interpretations of white reactions to the exodus. Even though the early period was replete with white expressions of regret, hope for a return to antebellum biracial patterns, and ambivalence, later sentiment—which had hardened into rejection—commonly was read back in time. Needless to say, such distortion of memory was not conducive to cordiality between blacks and whites.

Although shared elements of southern revivalism were separately retained after the exodus, elements distinctive to each emergent tradition were heightened. The exodus dealt white religious tradition a one-two punch on the level of religious self-understanding. The first blow came from the experience of bereavement in the context of a traditionally strongly felt (if inadequately implemented) commitment to the spiritual welfare of Afro-Southerners. At first whites tended to mourn the departure of black Christians and unrealistically predict that they would return. But among Methodists, the formation of the CME Church with the help of MEC,S leaders signaled a rethinking of whites' Christian commitment to blacks. Re-rationalized and retheologized, the commitment evolved into a less than familial concern by whites for the "other." Southern white Methodist detachment from the evangelization and education of blacks was exacerbated by the financial shambles in which the postwar MEC,S found itself and by a traditional attitude that "theological education" was "inconsistent with the Methodist emphasis on 'heart religion.' "[30] The southern Church, then, retained neither its missions to the blacks nor an effective commitment to ministerial training, leaving both areas of endeavor to the new, struggling CME Church. In 1874, that church expressed its need for a more educated ministry, but its accompanying educational ventures failed due to lack of funds.[31] Northern Methodists were more financially able and somewhat more active in the evangelization and education of blacks. They established a Freedmen's Aid Society in 1866. However, "since the society accepted the theory that the Negro had to 'lift himself,' professional training emphasized teaching and ministry."[32] In 1868, the denomination's educational policy shifted to one of higher education of blacks as teachers of their own people.[33] White Methodists, like other white Christians, increasingly came to see the salvation of black souls as the job of black churches.

The second blow the exodus dealt white religious tradition came from the cutting off of the potential for a shared socioethical vision. Donald G. Mathews has argued persuasively that blacks played an indispensable role in the shaping of the religion of the Old South.[34] After the exodus, that shaping was rerouted to extra-church channels. As a result, the exodus cut off southern white Protestants from their most available avenue to a communal and social vision of Christian ethics. They remained fixed in their commitment to regenerating society through moral influence and individual regeneration. According to Mathews, "The logic of Evangelicalism was to elevate and discipline the self within a strong community, under the aegis of a leadership which was seen as the projection of its followers." Further, Evangelical theorists claimed that "their churches were the foundations of social order."[35] To the extent that white Methodists shared such notions, their socioethical understanding was narrowed by the narrowing of the ecclesiastical community as a consequence of the exodus.[36]

The impact of the exodus on the black religious tradition was not softened by the fact that blacks themselves acted as the driving force in self-separation. The exodus irrevocably re-formed the southern black religious tradition, which means that, on the whole, it re-formed the American black religious tradition. In 1871, eighty-five to ninety-five percent of all black Americans were southern. Of the approximately 321,000 new members acquired by the northern AME Church between 1860 and 1871 and the approximately

122,000 new members gained by the northern AMEZ Church between 1860 and 1868, an overwhelming majority were Southerners; a hefty number of new preachers and other leaders in the two black independent denominations were Southerners too. As a result, participants in the exodus infused their respective communities with the central Christian experiences of antebellum southern blacks: communal liberation and liberating community.

These central religious experiences affected the social life of blacks in a unique way. The church family became the soul of the black community in the larger, oppressive American society. It was the heart of religious hope for fuller liberation among blacks already disappointed at the new order evolving after Appomattox.

Many sociologists and historians have attributed the soul or core role of the black church in the black community to a vacuum effect created by the lack of other institutions open to blacks.[37] These scholars see the church as provider of everything from entertainment to leadership training. The black church did contribute to members' everyday lives in such ways. But one must not lose sight of the fact that the now-visible institution would not have been viable without its constitutive Christian experiences of community and liberation. Not social vacuum but rather religious experience made possible the sociological function of the black church.

To some observers in the 1870s, the constitutive religious experiences of black worshippers were not Christian but African. The distinction was false. African elements were influential along with indigeneous developments that comprised blacks' appropriation of Christianity. As for those who labeled postwar revival in which blacks participated replete with African barbarity, it is likely that racist assumptions inclined them to devalue African elements and blinded them to the parallels between ritual practices of blacks and those of lower-class whites.

The evidence shows that the exodus was a revival of religion. It featured numerous conversions and reconversions, many calls to the ministry, and an outpouring of religious fervor. It celebrated blacks' Christian experiences of liberation and community. It also strengthened the black tradition's adherence to leaders with personal charisma. Some detractors of the black Methodist denominations alleged that those churches produced a pretentious proliferation of bishops. But the black bishops created in the postwar period do not signal a shift in the tradition to charisma of office rather than personal charisma. These men passed the necessary charismatic tests, being admitted on trial and proving themselves in ministry. As late as 1879, when ex-slave and later AME Bishop William H. Heard decided to seek the role of preacher,

> I was prepared educationally to stand the examination, but in those days many questions were asked to find out if the applicant had gifts, graces, and really had been called to the ministry.
>
> I exhorted for three months. I did not preach, but exhorted; for an exhorter was not permitted to take a text, but he read a chapter, or part of a chapter, and proceeded to explain the same as he understood it.[38]

The bishops' frequent engagement in denominational competition reveals that they were charismatic leaders in search of the most effective kind of recognition. Moreover, though a revered title, "bishop" signified for Methodists jurisdictional and (except for the AMEZ Church) geographic responsibility. It did not signify the sort of office understood by Roman Catholics, for example, with the bishop as recipient of a fullness of sacramental priesthood and participant in the so-called Apostolic Succession. Finally, within the black denominations, leadership tended to be communal in keeping with its charismatic style, and members of congregations were bonded by emotional ties.[39]

The exodus affected the black tradition's appropriation of Christian myth in three especially important ways. First, blacks' traditional preference for imagery drawn from the Old Testament and the book of Revelation was accentuated in the separation from white Christians. By 1871, seldom exposed to preaching by whites, blacks continued to find the Old Testament saga of the Israelites a rich source of reflection for faith. For example, the liberation of the Israelites' Exodus corresponded to their own experience, but so did the wandering in the wilderness, when a people's failings kept them from the full promise of land. Blassingame finds that among lower-class blacks in New Orleans,

> The sermons and songs about their bondage, and the passionate prayers for Divine aid, gave their services a reality, vividness, and emotionalism which created a sense of shared suffering and hope which caused the congregations to shout, cry, and raise a joyful noise to the Lord. In spite of the emotion, there was a deep practical strain running through sermons which usually compared the Negro's lot with that of the Jews and which urged him to protect and to enlarge his freedom. These men were devout, their prayers were earnest appeals to God, and their songs were narratives of their sufferings.[40]

In addition to reflecting on the biblical Exodus, blacks now could replace the hermeneutic of bondage preached by whites with emancipating reinterpretation. Writing in 1895, AMEZ bishop and historian James Walker Hood presented an extensive rereading of the Ham story that removed any stigma from contemporary blacks.[41]

The exodus put blacks' eschatological vision and traditionally concrete and immediate religious hopes into longer perspective. Partial creation of a new order and partial fulfillment of here-and-now hopes projected further hopes into a more distant future. Ex-slave Jerry Eubanks, who was born in 1846, declared,

> I look at it dis way—"What God says had got to come, comes." Dis is written in de Bible.
> Dey says "De Yankees done it"—but colored looks cross years at every thing. God did it all.[42]

Disappointments about the new order and unfulfilled hopes also had a distancing effect.[43] Indeed, Edwin S. Redkey points out that disappointment drew blacks in increased numbers to the African Colonization movement, a new and unmistakable prospective exodus.[44]

The exodus also affected blacks' experience of Jesus as Lord. They continued to see him as a brother in the kinship of suffering. However, they came to stress Jesus as deliverer. In April 1865, a black man told white teacher Laura M. Towne, "Lincoln died for we, Christ died for we, and me believe him de same mans."[45] That same month a large congregation of Richmond blacks celebrated Jesus as apocalyptic vindicator.

With the singing of a hymn beginning "Jesus my all to heaven is gone," the congregation gave expression to their newly won freedom. After each line, they repeated with added emphasis, "I'm going to join in this army; I'm going to join in this army of my Lord."[46] To the eyes of black faith, only Jesus the conqueror could have wrought the wonder of emancipation. As Leon Litwack remarks, "Seldom had their prayers been answered so concretely."[47] As a result, the figure of the triumphant Jesus was prominent in the realized eschatology of ex-slaves like Harriet Gresham of South Carolina, who remembered singing

> T'ank ye Marster Jesus, t'ank ye,
> T'ank ye Marster Jesus, t'ank ye,
> T'ank ye Marster Jesus, t'ank ye

Da Heben gwinter be my home.
No slav'ry chains to tie me down,
And no mo' driver's ho'n to blow fer me
No mo' stocks to fasten me down
Jesus break slav'ry chain, Lord
Break slav'ry chain Lord,
Break slav'ry chain Lord,
Da Heben gwinter be my home.[48]

Of course, singing of such a Jesus was possible only in separate settings. White Southerners' biblical interpretation of the postwar period was decidedly different from that of blacks.

From today's perspective, perhaps the most significant effect of the exodus on black religious tradition was its impact on the tradition's ethical vision. In antebellum times, blacks' distinctive social approach to moral issues had coexisted with the individualistic, duty-full morality advocated by whites. Over and over preachers admonished blacks to obey and not to lie or steal. Once the exodus was accomplished, the socioethical vision of black Christians was affirmed and nourished by their own preachers, by their communal self-awareness, and by the fact that a very slightly modified version of the old morality was preached at them by whites in the press, on the job, in the marketplace. The development of economic and social relationships between the races tended to be dominated by whites. The evident moral bankruptcy of such relationships as those dictated by the Black Codes and sharecropping undercut insistence by whites that society would be saved in keeping with whites' narrower socioethical understanding. Thus, in black churches, the black tradition of socioethical concern flourished. By no means the final fruit of this vision was the twentieth-century civil rights movement as led by Martin Luther King, Jr., a son of southern black revivalism.

Some sociologists and historians claim that the black churches that came out of the exodus became the most important ingredient in black American culture. Ahlstrom says that they "became the chief bearers of Afro-American heritage."[49] I believe that it is more correct to see the family as chief bearer of the heritage as a whole. But there is no doubt that the black churches of the exodus became the chief bearers of the religious heritage of African-Americans.

Significance of the Exodus for Society in the American South

In order to assess the significance of the exodus for southern society, it is necessary to examine the relationship between religious boundaries and racial boundaries. In the antebellum period, religious boundaries came to be inclusive of all races, once whites were satisfied that baptism would not wash away slave status. Within the churches, separatist customs and the paternalistic attitude of whites protected the racial definition and social location of blacks and whites.

With emancipation and Appomattox, chaos replaced clearly understood social and racial relationships. If black laborers elected to remain with their previous owners, they nevertheless changed in status to employees instead of childlike members of an extended family. Many blacks did not remain as employees with former owners; of these, many chose to work for spouses' employers instead; some left antebellum "homes" and then returned after intervals ranging from days to years.

In a time of disorder, the churches offered both blacks and whites a sense of social location as before. But the exodus effected a swift "geographical" switch. As early as the summer of 1866, social location in a church entailed racial separation for the majority of Methodists and probably for the majority of other southern Christians as well. Because blacks chose religious self-separation on the basis of their distinctive appropriation of Christianity, their social location in racially separate churches by 1871 had religious meaning. In the churches, racial separation was religiously legitimate.

In addition, the commensal boundaries that now surrounded the Table of the Lord corresponded to those ordinary sources of ritual commensality, the family and the community. As blacks worked at reconstructing their families, many even changed their names. For example, Rebecca Brown Hill, born a slave in northeast Mississippi, explained, "My folks belong to C. B. Baldwin. After 'mancipation papa stop calling himself Jacob Baldwin and called himself Jacob Brown in his own pa's name."[50] Such name changes represented to some whites "the collapse of an entire social and moral order." To some slaveholders, the shared surname represented what they believed to be intimate ties, especially with house servants. They believed that slaves did not have lasting family relationships. As Gutman remarks, "Ex-slaves who took surnames or revealed old surnames that had connections to a distant forebear, not a former owner, made choices that cut deeply into the belief system of sensitive owners."[51] A name change was only one action blacks took to re-form and stabilize families after the war. The strengthening of the black family as an institution reinforced racially separate ritual commensality in the churches. Together the black church and the black family defined racial boundaries important to all Southerners. In so doing, they helped Southerners cope with stressful social, political, and economic changes.

Did the exodus in any way bring about the stressful changes of the postwar period? It probably had little effect in the case of economic changes. However, the separate churches did affect the political ferment of the period. Some black ministers sought political office; some were elected, no doubt with some support from their congregations. Some black churches gave hospitality to political meetings. Some of the sophistication demonstrated by blacks once they were enfranchised probably was learned at church gatherings. Finally, the political views of black Christians were no doubt informed by their traditional, now strengthened, socioethical vision. The influence of the exodus on postwar southern politics is definite but impossible to quantify due to the lack of data resulting from the secrecy imposed by the prevalent threat of white terrorism.

It is also impossible to pin down the precise effect of the exodus on social change. Social patterns of racial exclusion and participation were in flux in 1871. Yet it would be naive to argue that the exodus was an isolated phenomenon devoid of social consequences. The expressions of self-reliant, independent black Christians and of their bereaved, ambivalent co-Christians show that one social consequence was to raise the status of blacks in their own eyes and in the view of white people. Black Christians were no longer second-class children in their masters' churches but families in their own religious communities.

The exodus severed the ties Christianity provided in slavery times. It cut the religious controls used by black and white Christians to manipulate one another's behavior; but it replaced the definition of racial relationships provided by slavery with at least part of a new one: separation. The exodus cut off the natural potential of commensality to foster religious and political ties between people. It changed the way the political game was played and eliminated for most blacks and whites the opportunities for sharing religious experiences so unabashedly enjoyed in the antebellum period. The exodus cut off opportunities for direct communication in religious affairs between blacks and whites at the person-in-the-pew level. Hereafter, communication would be limited to black and white religious elites, with especially unfortunate consequences for black pastors. Later they would be accused—some justly, others unjustly—of being mediators in and of an unjust social system, manipulating their congregations by preaching a submissive word, living comfortably off the combined contributions of black churchgoers and powerful, self-interested whites.[52]

Black Methodists could not have foreseen such outcomes when they separated from the MEC,S. Indeed, to them as to all blacks in the postwar South, segregation was a value-neutral term.[53] Their prior experience of society had been predominantly not one of exclusion but of participation—much of it unpleasant.[54] It was not difficult for most blacks to choose separate religious independence instead of a struggle for equality in the old joint setting. Even Methodists who chose the northern church gravitated into separate congregations. Members of the CME movement followed a parallel course. First they strove for both equality and separation within the old denomination. Then, in 1870-1871, they too chose value-neutral segregation to obtain the highly valued symbol of equality—valid episcopal orders. They also obtained a symbolic fulfillment of the biblical promise of land.[55]

The exodus must have set a precedent in the minds of Southerners for later separate institutions and accommodations. In the changes that occurred in religious commensality lay the seeds of later relationships. In antebellum times, the churches had reflected the larger hierarchical society and its peculiar institution of race-specific chattel slavery. This fact tempts one to reach beyond the 1870s and ask whether segregation at the Lord's Table in any way led to Jim Crow's lunch counter. But in 1871, the churches did not mirror a racially segregated society.

These considerations of the relationship of the exodus to social patterns of exclusion and participation would be incomplete without a discussion of the difficult question of caste. In the literature on race relations in the American South, *caste* is ordinarily a pejorative term, in the same category with words like *prejudice, discrimination*, and *injustice*. I wish explicitly to extricate the term from those emotionally provocative associations by making the following distinction. *Caste* in the pejorative sense means "out-caste." It implies rejection—a literal casting-out. *Caste* in a nonpejorative, technical sense refers to a group within a social system of one or more other groups. Each of these groups (castes) is self-separating. Some kind of religious legitimation plays a part in its self-understanding. The group observes some barriers to eating with persons outside the group and to intermarriage (that is, barriers to commensality and connubium). Such a group is (or becomes over time) a distinctive hereditary group.

189

In the American South of 1871, at least two groups fit this non-pejorative, technical description of *caste*.[56] That they were distinctive hereditary groups was evident in the fact that one group was white—that is, usually lighter in skin color—and the other group was black—that is, usually darker. The groups ordinarily observed barriers to intermarriage. Deviants were punished by means ranging from ostracism to lynching. The only patterned deviation from this norm was sexual intercourse that white males were permitted to initiate with black females, especially (but not exclusively) prostitutes. Offspring of white-black liaisons were considered members of the black caste. Before the Civil War, blacks and whites had practiced ritual commensality in joint Christian worship services. Beginning during the Civil War, the black group had withdrawn from its former religious affiliations, and by 1871, little commensality occurred.

We have seen that in this self-separation, blacks were acting on their distinctive appropriation of Christianity. They regarded their churches as religious in the strictest sense of the word and as religiously legitimated. Black churches were God-made congregations led by God-made preachers with power independent of any pre- or postwar authority structure.

Both self-separation and religious legitimation are essential to the creation of a caste system. Each group must accept its separation from the other group(s) and affirm a common religious context that legitimates the caste system.[57] In India, the religious hopes inspired by belief in concepts of *karma*, *dharma*, and *samsara* legitimated the worldly inequities of its caste system. Throughout Indian history, new groups became part of the caste system by a process Max Weber called the "Hinduization of guest tribes." Guest tribes existed truly outside of the caste system as distinctive hereditary groups that ordinarily performed a specific and valued kind of work. They were resident aliens—in biblical language, "sojourners" (*gerim*). But that status changed when a guest tribe sought religious legitimation from the social system it served with its labor. The process consisted of accepting degraded status in exchange for recognition by the Brahmins, the ruling elite. In time, the degraded status of the caste would improve due to the assimilation of newer (therefore relatively more degraded) groups and to the creative manipulation of legitimating myths by Brahmins employed by the caste's leaders.[58]

As explained earlier, a comparable process of assimilation was available to *gerim* who wished inclusion in and legitimation by ancient Judaism. The exodus exhibited rough parallels to both of these processes. Southern black Christians possessed a group self-awareness, as did guest tribes in India and the *gerim*. Their act of self-separation affirmed both their religious legitimacy as a group and their desire for inclusion in a postwar social system (the hoped-for new order) religiously grounded in Christianity. For them, religious hope was decisive.[59] The exodus was not driven predominantly by a prophetic rejection of the white person's religion but by blacks' distinctive appropriation of Christianity, with its emphasis on Jesus as both Moses and the apocalyptic vindicator who would bring about God's Kingdom on earth. Moreover, the exodus did fulfill some of the immediate religious hopes of blacks. It bestowed Christian legitimation on their communities, their marriages and families, and their leaders. Among black Methodists in separate churches, every leader from exhorter to bishop had unquestioned, undiluted, legitimate religious authority. The case of the CME Church makes clear that to gain this, the leaders accepted status that was degraded in the sense that their ministry was legitimate in their own denomination, but was not likely to be exercised in Methodism at large. Northern Methodism too offered limited scope and possibilities for its black leaders.

Insofar as the exodus paralleled the Hinduization of guest tribes and the assimilation of the *gerim* in ancient Judaism, it represented a move by blacks, accepted by whites, toward greater participation—not exclusion—in society and in Christianity. It was a move in complete harmony with African-Americans' distinctive experience of Christian liberation and Christian community. Whatever the negative consequences of racially separate worship and regardless of injustices of white denominations or any failures of the black church, the exodus stands as a historic affirmation of Christian experiences and values that are the centerpiece of African-American religiosity. Black Christians in our own day continue to strive for a new order, a community, liberation.

Notes

CHAPTER ONE

1. Eugene D. Genovese, *Roll, Jordan, Roll* (New York: Vintage Books, 1974); Donald G. Mathews, *Religion in the Old South* (Chicago: University of Chicago Press, 1977); Milton C. Sernett, *Black Religion and American Evangelicalism* (Metuchen, N.J.: The Scarecrow Press, Inc., 1975); Albert J. Raboteau, *Slave Religion* (New York: Oxford University Press, 1978).
2. Rufus B. Spain, *At Ease in Zion* (Nashville: Vanderbilt University Press, 1961); John Lee Eighmy, *Churches in Cultural Captivity* (Knoxville: The University of Tennessee Press, 1972); H. Shelton Smith, *In His Image, But . . .* (Durham, N.C.: Duke University Press, 1972); David M. Reimers, *White Protestantism and the Negro* (New York: Oxford University Press, 1965).
3. Max Weber, *Ancient Judaism* (New York: The Free Press, 1952); *The Religion of India* (New York: The Free Press, 1958); see also Weber, *The Sociology of Religion* (Boston: Beacon Press, 1963).
4. Weber, *Religion of India*, pp. 37-38; *Sociology of Religion*, pp. 40-41.
5. Sydney E. Ahlstrom, *A Religious History of the American People* (New York: Image Books, 1975), 2:169-170.
6. Jerald C. Brauer's definition; HC 440 Revivalism and American Culture, Divinity School, University of Chicago, Autumn 1978.
7. Clifton H. Johnson, ed., *God Struck Me Dead* (Philadelphia: Pilgrim Press, 1969), pp. 15-17.
8. W.P. Harrison, ed., *The Gospel Among the Slaves* (Nashville: Publishing House of the M.E. Church, South, 1893), p. 382.
9. Peter Cartwright, *Autobiography of Peter Cartwright*, ed. W.P. Strickland (Freeport, N.Y.: Books for Libraries Press, [1856] 1972), pp. 37-38.
10. Bishop Daniel Alexander Payne, *Recollections of Seventy Years* (New York: Arno Press, [1888] 1968), p. 17. For another account of a prominent black converted in a group setting, compare Lucius H. Holsey, *Autobiography, Sermons, Addresses, and Essays of Bishop L.H. Holsey, D.D.* (Atlanta, Ga.: The Franklin Printing and Publishing Co., 1898), p. 18, and Harrison, *Gospel Among the Slaves*, pp. 386-387.
11. John W. Blassingame, ed., *Slave Testimony* (Baton Rouge: Louisiana State University Press, 1977), p. 76.
12. Cartwright, *Autobiography*, pp. 48-49.

13. Quoted in John B. Boles, *The Great Revival 1787-1805*, (Lexington: University of Kentucky Press, 1972), p. 7.

14. Quoted in Boles, *The Great Revival*, p. 7.

15. Cartwright, *Autobiography*, pp. 169-170, 221, 212-214, 225-227.

16. David Benedict, *A General History of the Baptist Denomination in America and Other Parts of the World* (New York: Lewis Colby and Company, 1850). See, for example, p. 739.

17. According to Walter Brownlow Posey, the antimission movement (mainly a Baptist phenomenon) was based on fear of centralized authority, suspicion that missions were money-getting schemes, and unpaid preachers' jealousy of salaried missionaries rather than on purely theological considerations. *Religious Strife on the Southern Frontier* (Baton Rouge: Louisiana State University Press, 1965), p. 24.

18. Harrison, *Gospel Among the Slaves*, pp. 307-308.

19. Luther P. Jackson, "Religious Development of the Negro in Virginia from 1760 to 1860," *The Journal of Negro History*, Vol. 16, No. 2, April 1931, p. 186.

20. William E. Hatcher, *John Jasper: The Unmatched Negro Philosopher and Preacher* (New York: Fleming H. Revell Company, 1908), p. 36.

21. Blassingame, *Slave Testimony*, pp. 621-622.

22. Ibid., pp. 416-417, 24-25.

23. Jackson, "Religious Development of the Negro in Virginia," p. 186.

24. Blassingame, *Slave Testimony*, pp. 494-495.

25. Ibid., p. 643.

26. Harrison, *Gospel Among the Slaves*, p. 357.

27. Ibid., pp. 178-179.

28. A.C. Ramsey, "Life and Times of A.C. Ramsey," MS (uncataloged), rare book room, Birmingham Southern University Library, Birmingham, Alabama.

29. Miles Mark Fisher, *A Short History of the Baptist Denomination* (Nashville: Sunday School Publishing Board, 1933), p. 35; Harrison, *Gospel Among the Slaves*, p. 281; Blassingame, *Slave Testimony*, pp. 53-55.

30. Brauer, HC 440 Revivalism and American Culture. Of the Second Great Awakening, John B. Boles remarks, "Paradoxically, unity and schism were two results of the revival." *The Great Revival*, p. 137.

31. Charles A. Johnson, *The Frontier Camp Meeting* (Dallas: Southern Methodist University Press, 1955), pp. 114, 46.

32. Harrison, *Gospel Among the Slaves*, p. 204.

33. In Posey's view, "So strong were the tendency and the inclination toward schism that between 1790 and 1830 all major denominations in the West experienced one or more divisions because the main body of each church had not been able or did not choose to keep abreast of the radical spirit of the region." *Religious Strife on the Southern Frontier*, p. 12.

34. Class Book, Pea Ridge Class, M.E. Church Valley Creek Circuit, Alabama Conference; MS I Cab. VI E 1-31, Alabama State Archives, Montgomery, Alabama.

35. Harrison, *Gospel Among the Slaves*, p. 292. Compare a Baptist historian's account: "Religious revivals have been frequent and extensive in this community, especially among the colored population. In 1812, they received by baptism about fifteen hundred members." Benedict, *General History of the Baptist Denomination*, p. 739.

36. *Journals of the General Conference of the Methodist Episcopal Church, South* (Eastern District of Virginia: John Early, [1859?]), pp. 390, 401.

37. Max Weber points out that, in Christianity, faith is "the specific charisma of an extraordinary and purely personal reliance upon god's providence, such as the shepherds of souls and the heroes of faith must possess. By virtue of this charismatic confidence in god's support, the spiritual representative and leader of the congregation, as a virtuoso of faith, may act differently from the layman in practical situations and bring about different results, far surpassing normal human capacity. In the context of practical action, faith can provide a substitute for magical powers." *Sociology of Religion*, p. 195.

38. Max Weber, *The Theory of Social and Economic Organization* (New York: The Free Press, 1964), pp. 358-359.

39. Johnson, *God Struck Me Dead*, pp. 68, 70.

40. Weber, *Religion of India*, pp. 37-38; see also Weber, *Sociology of Religion*, pp. 84-85.

41. See, for example, Jordan, *White Over Black* (Chapel Hill: University of North Carolina Press, 1968), pp. 214-215; Genovese, *Roll, Jordan, Roll*, pp. 183-184; Mathews, *Religion in the Old South*, pp. 70-71, 79-80, 147; Raboteau, *Slave Religion*, pp. 301-302, 314-317.

42. Weber, *Religion of India*, p. 43.

43. Boles, *The Great Revival*, p. 81.

44. Jordan, *White Over Black*, pp. 131-132.

45. Boles, *The Great Revival*, p. 99; see also Posey, *Religious Strife on the Southern Frontier*, p. 27. For an explanation of Presbyterian practice, see William Warren Sweet, *Revivalism in America* (New York: Charles Scribner's Sons, 1944), pp. 132-133.

46. Blassingame, *Slave Testimony*, p. 656.

47. Quoted in Harrison, *Gospel Among the Slaves*, pp. 312-313.

48. Jordan, *White Over Black*, pp. 3-43. Compare Simone de Beauvoir, *The Second Sex* (New York: Vintage Books, [1952] 1974), pp. xv-xxxiv.

49. Mary Douglas, *Purity and Danger: An Analysis of the Concepts of Pollution and Taboo* (London: Routledge & Kegan Paul, 1966), pp. 2-6.

50. Dom Gregory Dix, *The Shape of the Liturgy* (London: Dacre Press, 1945). Dix shows that active lay participation in Christianity's sacred meal diminished over the centuries. By the eleventh century, lay people had no vocal participation in the Mass; toward the end of that century, after the investiture struggle,

there were no more prayers for the laity in the canon of the Mass, the most sacred part of the meal, the rite of consecration and Communion. Meanwhile in mid-century, Communion wine, which had been taken along with the bread by lay and nonlay alike, was reserved for priests. At the same time, however, in an effort to discipline married priests, Rome forbade laypersons to attend the Masses of such priests. I argue that placing the laity in what was, in effect, a police role while blocking their fuller, more active participation in the sacred meal gave impetus to the rise of "heretical" vernacular preachers who addressed the spiritual hungers of the liturgically disadvantaged laity. In the twelfth century, mendicant orders were founded to combat heretics, primarily by preaching. The mendicants increased the importance of the sermon at Mass. By the fifteenth century, the prayers for the faithful, which were once a part of the consecration and Communion in the Mass, now were added after the sermon. These developments suggest that the sermon had come to satisfy the commensal spiritual hungers of the laity as much as if not more than did the rite of consecration and Communion.

51. Southern Baptist Convention, *Proceedings*, 1859 (Nashville, 1845-1897), pp. 60-61.

52. See, for example, diagrams in Johnson, *Frontier Camp Meeting*, pp. 43, 47. For one report that such seats were provided, see Harrison, *Gospel Among the Slaves*, p. 340.

53. Johnson, *Frontier Camp Meeting*, p. 46.

54. Jordan explains: "The pattern of seating in most colonial churches was partly governed (whether formally or not) by accepted social distinctions; the town drunk did not occupy a prominent pew even when sober. The meaner sort of people accepted seats at the back or in the gallery; and Negroes, even Negroes who owned some property, were patently of the meaner sort." *White Over Black*, pp. 131-132. Samuel S. Hill, Jr., finds that from 1607 to the mid-twentieth century, Southerners' minds "operated with hierarchical images of order." *Religion and the Solid South* (Nashville, Tenn.: Abingdon Press, 1972), p. 14. For an example of hierarchical attitudes among whites, see Blassingame, *Slave Testimony*, p. 171.

55. According to Thomas L. Webber, stratification and class feeling in the black community may have been encouraged by whites; see *Deep Like the Rivers: Education in the Slave Quarter Community, 1831-1865* (New York: W.W. Norton and Company, Inc., 1978), pp. 38, 260. For a discussion of class distinctions among slaves, see E. Franklin Frazier, "The Negro Slave Family," *Journal of Negro History*, Vol. XV, No. 2, April 1930, pp. 208-211.

56. Harrison, *Gospel Among the Slaves*, pp. 211, 249; see also pp. 151-152 and Donald G. Mathews, "Charles Colcock Jones and the Southern Evangelical Crusade to Form a Biracial Community," *The Journal of Southern History*, Vol. 41, No. 3, August 1975, p. 311.

57. Bettis used to denounce the "excitement, shouting, hallelujahs" of Negro worship as brought on by the " 'whangdoodle' preacher who, by the cadence of a tuneful voice, strove to produce such demonstrations." George Brown

Tindall, *South Carolina Negroes 1877-1900* (Baton Rouge: Louisiana State University Press, 1966), p. 207; Alfred W. Nicholson, *Brief Sketch of the Life and Labors of Rev. Alexander Bettis* (Trenton, S.C.: published by the author, 1913), p. 32.

58. For example, see Cartwright, *Autobiography*, pp. 149-151.

59. Regarding the distinctive characteristics of black American religion, Sydney E. Ahlstrom declares that he finds them "more parsimoniously explained as an adaptation of evangelical Christianity shaped by the special needs and conditions of black people in white America." *Religious History of the American People*, 2:158.

60. I find no evidence of female preachers, black or white, in the Methodist Episcopal Church, South, before the Civil War. However, Thomas L. Webber asserts that "Even women preachers appear often enough, though admittedly less frequently than male preachers, to suggest that there was no community prohibition against their filling this crucial role." Elsewhere he states that the religious leader in the slave-quarter community on a plantation was "sometimes a woman." *Deep Like the Rivers*, pp. 149, 192. Priscilla Baltimore, a Kentucky-born slave who purchased her freedom, assisted William Paul Quinn as an A.M.E. missionary in Missouri. George A. Singleton, *The Romance of African Methodism* (New York: Exposition Press, 1952), pp. 72-73.

61. Quoted in Alwyn Barr, *Black Texans* (Austin, Tex.: Jenkins Publishing Co., 1973), p. 22.

62. John Hope Franklin, *From Slavery to Freedom*, 4th ed. (New York Alfred A. Knopf, 1974), p. 139.

63. Johnson, *God Struck Me Dead*, pp. 61, 67, 92.

64. Webber, *Deep Like the Rivers*, p. 144.

65. John W. Blassingame, *The Slave Community* (New York: Oxford University Press, 1972), p. 207.

66. Gilbert Osofsky, ed., *Puttin' On Old Massa* (New York: Harper & Row, 1969), pp. 40-41.

67. B.A. Botkin, ed., *Lay My Burden Down* (Chicago: University of Chicago Press, 1945), p. 86. Regarding the Bible as a fetish, see Newbell Niles Puckett, *Folk Beliefs of the Southern Negro* (New York: Negro Universities Press, [1926] 1968), pp. 560-561.

68. Blassingame, *Slave Community*, pp. 49-50.

69. Newman I. White, *American Negro Folk-Songs* (Hatboro, Pa.: Folklore Associates, Inc., [1928] 1965), p. 26.

70. Ibid., p. xi.

71. Ibid., p. 45. On blacks' use of biblical materials, see Sernett, *Black Religion and American Evangelicalism*, p. 107.

72. Thomas Wentworth Higginson, *Black Rebellion* (New York: Arno Press, [1889] 1969), pp. 188-189, 226-227. Regarding Prosser, see Michael Mullin, ed., *American Negro Slavery: A Documentary History* (Columbia, S.C.: University of South Carolina Press, 1976), pp. 125-126.

73. Newman I. White argued that the connection between, for example, the exodus narrative and blacks' longing for "physical" freedom was an interpretation taught to them and not a part of the original "religious" meaning of the narrative as used in religious songs. *American Negro Folk-Songs*, pp. 11-12.
74. Blassingame, *Slave Testimony*, p. 136.
75. Quoted in Webber, *Deep Like the Rivers*, p. 205. See also Osofsky, *Puttin' On Ole Massa*, p. 72, and Blassingame, *Slave Testimony*, p. 745.
76. Arna Bontemps and Langston Hughes, *The Book of Negro Folklore* (New York: Dodd, Mead & Company, 1958), p. 292. Versions of this song abound. For two early published versions, see Dena J. Epstein, *Sinful Tunes and Spirituals: Black Folk Music to the Civil War* (Urbana, Ill.: University of Illinois Press, 1977), pp. 363-365, 372-373.
77. William Francis Allen, Charles Pickard Ware, and Lucy McKim Garrison, eds., *Slave Songs of the United States* (New York: Peter Smith, [1867] 1929), pp. 76, 38, 104.
78. Bontemps and Hughes, *Book of Negro Folklore*, pp. 299-300, 303; J. Mason Brewer, *American Negro Folklore* (Chicago: Quadrangle Books, 1968), pp. 154-156.
79. Allen, *Slave Songs of the United States*, p. 94.
80. White, *American Negro Folk-Songs*, p. 463.
81. Many scholars have discussed this phenomenon. See, for example, John Lovell, Jr., *Black Song: The Forge and the Flame* (New York: The Macmillan Company, 1972), pp. 228-229, 329, and Webber, *Deep Like the Rivers*, pp. 217-218. Sterling A. Brown finds that, "Analysis of the body of white camp-meeting 'spirituals' reveals fairly perfunctory references to heaven as freedom; but in Negro spirituals references to trouble here below are far more numerous, and are poignant rather than perfunctory, springing from a deep need, not from an article of faith." "The Spirituals," in Bontemps and Hughes, *Book of Negro Folklore*, p. 287.
82. See, for example, Nehemiah Adams, *A South-Side View of Slavery* (Boston: T.R. Marvin and B.B. Mussey & Co., 1854), pp. 190-202.
83. Osofsky, *Puttin' On Ole Massa*, p. 69. See also Botkin, *Lay My Burden Down*, p. 25.
84. Botkin, *Lay My Burden Down*, p. 118.
85. Lewis Clarke, *Narrative of the Sufferings of Lewis Clarke, during a Captivity of More than Twenty-five Years, Among the Algerines of Kentucky, One of the So-Called Christian States of North America* (Boston, 1845), p. 70, quoted in Webber, *Deep Like the Rivers*, pp. 81-82.
86. Charles Emery Stevens, *Anthony Burns; A History* (Boston, 1856), pp. 174-175, quoted in Webber, *Deep Like the Rivers*, p. 82.
87. John G. Williams, *"De Ole Plantation"* (Charleston: Walker, Evans & Cogswell, Co., Printers, 1895), p. 11.

88. Genovese, *Roll, Jordan, Roll*, pp. 265-266; compare Webber, *Deep Like the Rivers*, p. 94. The story of the sheep and the goats at Judgment Day was the subject of black religious song. See Allen, *Slave Songs of the United States*, p. 53.

89. One of many songs in which Mary and Martha appear is "Who Is on the Lord's Side"; Allen, *Slave Songs of the United States*, p. 56. For an example of Paul and Silas, see Miles Mark Fisher, *Negro Slave Songs in the United States* (Ithaca, N.Y.: Cornell University Press, 1953), p. 116. For some other references to New Testament events, arguments, and figures, see Bontemps and Hughes, *The Book of Negro Folklore*, pp. 293, 308, and Blassingame, *Slave Testimony*, p. 50.

90. Allen, *Slave Songs of the United States*, pp. 54, 56; Brewer, *American Negro Folklore*, pp. 160-161.

91. Quoted in Webber, *Deep Like the Rivers*, pp. 48-49.

92. Mathews, *Religion in the Old South*, pp. 235-236.

93. Botkin, *Lay My Burden Down*, pp. 189-190.

94. Jehovah's Witnesses, for example. Ahlstrom, *Religious History of the American People*, 2:276-277.

95. Quoted in Bontemps and Hughes, *The Book of Negro Folklore*, pp. 58-59.

96. Botkin, *Lay My Burden Down*, pp. 121-122; Stroyer quoted in Blassingame, *Slave Community*, pp. 100-102.

97. Moses Grandy, *Narrative of the Life of Moses Grandy, Late a Slave in the United States of America* (Boston, 1844), p. 41.

98. Austen Steward, *Twenty-two Years a Slave and Forty Years a Freeman, Embracing a Correspondence of Several Years While President of the Wilberforce Colony* (New York: Negro Universities Press, [1856] 1968), p. 95.

99. Lovell, *Black Song*, p. 227.

100. Sterling Brown, *Negro Poetry and Drama* (New York: Atheneum, [1937] 1978), p. 17.

101. Bontemps and Hughes, *The Book of Negro Folklore*, p. 297.

102. James Russell Johnson, "The Usefulness of Religious Training on the Southern Plantation as a Means of Inculcating Servility and a Deep Sense of Inferiority in Black Folks During the Thirty Years Preceding the American Civil War" (unpublished paper, Teachers College, Columbia University, 1970), pp. 53-54; quoted in Webber, *Deep Like the Rivers*, p. 54.

103. Webber, *Deep Like the Rivers*, p. 128.

104. Ibid., p. 130.

105. Howard W. Odum and Guy B. Johnson, *The Negro and His Songs* (New York: Negro Universities Press, [1925] 1968), p. 42.

106. Bontemps and Hughes, *Book of Negro Folklore*, p. 115; Blassingame, *Slave Testimony*, p. 278.

107. Brewer, *American Negro Folklore*, p. 149.

108. Quoted in Webber, *Deep Like the Rivers*, p. 198.

109. Allen, *Slave Songs of the United States*, pp. xviii-xix.

110. Lovell, *Black Song*, p. 234.
111. Dickson D. Bruce, Jr., *And They All Sang Hallelujah* (Knoxville: The University of Tennessee Press, 1974), pp. 110, 109, 113.
112. Ibid., pp. 126-127.
113. Blassingame, *Slave Testimony*, p. 135; see also Osofsky, *Puttin' On Ole Massa*, pp. 18, 309. I find no reports of women engaging in this practice; it may have been an exclusively male prerogative.
114. Blassingame, *Slave Testimony*, p. 433.
115. Osofsky, *Puttin' On Ole Massa*, p. 211.
116. Blassingame, *Slave Testimony*, p. 659.
117. *National Anti-Slavery Standard* 25 (15 October 1864), p. 1, col. 5; quoted in Epstein, *Sinful Tunes and Spirituals*, p. 232.
118. Genovese, *Roll, Jordan, Roll*, pp. 183-184, 190; see also Mathews, *Religion in the Old South*, p. 225. For an example of the probable exercise of this power by an African-born Christian slave, see Harrison, *Gospel Among the Slaves*, pp. 366-367.
119. Blassingame, *Slave Testimony*, p. 402.
120. Ibid., p. 420.
121. John Dixon Long, *Pictures of Slavery in Church and State* (Philadelphia: published by the author, 1857), p. 92.
122. Mullin, *American Negro Slavery*, p. 21.
123. Hatcher, *John Jasper*, p. 23.
124. Quoted in Harrison, *Gospel Among the Slaves*, p. 383.
125. Mathews, *Religion in the Old South*, pp. 145, 216.
126. E. Franklin Frazier, *The Negro Church in America* (New York: Schocken Books, [1963] 1974), p. 24. See also Hart M. Nelsen, Raytha L. Yokley, and Anne K. Nelsen, eds., *The Black Church in America* (New York: Basic Books, Inc., 1971), p. 71.
127. Harrison, *Gospel Among the Slaves*, p. 311.
128. Johnson, *God Struck Me Dead*, p. 85.
129. A few black preachers and exhorters functioned as members of quarterly conferences but almost certainly none was a delegate to annual conferences or general conferences. Kenneth K. Bailey, "Protestantism and Afro-Americans in the Old South: Another Look," *The Journal of Southern History*, Vol. 41, No. 4 (November 1975): 459. For a comparison of the gifts of Cartwright and Winans, see Cartwright, *Autobiography*, pp. 56-60 and Ray Holder, *William Winans: Methodist Leader in Antebellum Mississippi* (Jackson: University Press of Mississippi, 1977), pp. 8-9.
130. Webber, *Deep Like the Rivers*, pp. 63-66, 191-192, 224-225.
131. Boles, *The Great Revival*, p. 124.
132. Mathews, *Religion in the Old South*, p. 144.
133. Anson West, *A History of Methodism in Alabama* (Nashville, Tenn.: Publishing House of the Methodist Episcopal Church, South, 1893), p. 333.

134. Blassingame, *Slave Testimony*, pp. 647-648. See also Harrison, *Gospel Among the Slaves*, p. 103; Genovese, *Roll, Jordan, Roll*, p. 602; Kenneth Stampp, *The Peculiar Institution* (New York: Vintage Books, 1956), pp. 125-127.
135. Blassingame, *Slave Community*, p. 49.
136. Harrison, *Gospel Among the Slaves*, p. 102; Webber, *Deep Like the Rivers*, p. 63.
137. Osofsky, *Puttin' On Ole Massa*, pp. 132, 216.
138. Quoted in Blassingame, *Slave Testimony*, pp. 744-745.
139. Stampp, *Peculiar Institution*, p. 87; Blassingame, *Slave Community*, pp. 207-208.
140. Cecil Wayne Cone, *The Identity Crisis in Black Theology*, (Nashville: AMEC, 1975), p. 49.
141. Higginson, *Black Rebellion*, pp. 188-189. According to Higginson, the only denomination of anyone connected with the conspiracy was rumored to be Methodist (p. 196).
142. Quoted in ibid., pp. 223-224, 241.
143. Ibid., p. 284.
144. Eighmy, *Churches in Cultural Captivity*, p. 27.
145. For example, in the case of antebellum insurrection scares, "The persistent insistence that whites or free black 'degenerates' initiated such plots allowed slaveowners the luxury of continuing to insist that their bondsmen were docile and submissive unless misled and deceived." Dan T. Carter, "The Anatomy of Fear: The Christmas Day Insurrection Scare of 1865," *The Journal of Southern History*, Vol. 42, No. 3 (August 1976): 350.
146. Epstein, *Sinful Tunes and Spirituals*, p. 127.
147. Peter Kolchin, *First Freedom* (Westport, Conn.: Greenwood Press, Publishers, 1972), p. 20. Kolchin's figures are from Florida, Texas, Georgia, Tennessee, Arkansas, Alabama, North Carolina, Louisiana, Mississippi, South Carolina, and Virginia.
148. *MEC,S Annual Conference Minutes 1846-1858*, (General Recapitulation 1857-1858), p. 818; *Methodist Episcopal Church Almanac 1861*, p. 21; based on listed total members, not including probationers.
149. See, for example, Charles F. Deems, *Annals of Southern Methodism for 1856* (Nashville, Tenn.: Stevenson and Olsen, 1857), pp. 219, 236; Marion Elias Lazenby, *History of Methodism in Alabama and West Florida* (North Alabama Conference and Alabama-West Florida Conference of the Methodist Church, 1960), pp. 303-304, and Macum Phelan, *A History of Early Methodism in Texas, 1817-1866* (Nashville: Cokesbury Press, 1924), pp. 367-369, 414-421, 461.
150. On the demography of the South's slave population, see Blassingame, *Slave Testimony*, p. li. For Alabama only, see Donald B. Dodd, *Historical Atlas of Alabama* (University of Alabama Press, 1974), pp. 37, 41-61.
151. Mathews, *Religion in the Old South*, pp. 36-37.

152. For helpful descriptions of Methodist organization, see Bernard A. Weisberger, *They Gathered at the River* (Boston: Little, Brown and Company, 1958), p. 45 and Ralph E. Morrow, *Northern Methodism and Reconstruction*, (East Lansing, Mich.: Michigan State University Press, 1956), pp. 7-9.

153. *Journal of the Methodist Episcopal Church, South, 1846*, p. 110.

154. D. Sullins, *Recollections of an Old Man: Seventy Years in Dixie, 1827-1897* (Bristol, Tenn.: The King Printing Company, 1910), p. 65.

155. Linda Brent, *Incidents in the Life of a Slave Girl*, ed. L. Maria Child (New York: Harcourt Brace Jovanovich, [1861] 1973), pp. 72-73; *Proceedings of the Meeting in Charleston, S.C., May 13-14, 1845, on the Religious Instruction of the Negroes* (Charleston, S.C.: Published by order of the Meeting, 1845), p. 34.

156. W.P. Strickland, ed., *The Genius and Mission of Methodism* (Boston: Charles H. Peirce and Company, 1851), pp. 84-85.

157. George G. Smith, *Life and Times of George Foster Pierce* (Sparta, Ga.: Hancock Publishing Company, 1888), pp. 579-580.

158. For an example of the traveling preacher's varied activities, see Harrison, *Gospel Among the Slaves*, pp. 206-207, 209-210.

159. Johnson, *God Struck Me Dead*, pp. 19-21.

160. Cartwright, *Autobiography*, p. 54.

161. Bailey, "Protestantism and Afro-Americans in the Old South," pp. 459, 461, 463.

162. Mathews, *Religion in the Old South*, p. 217.

163. Franklin, *The Free Negro in North Carolina*, pp. 178-179.

164. Horace C. Savage, *Life and Times of Bishop Isaac Lane* (Nashville: National Publication Company, 1958), pp. 26-27.

165. Harrison, *Gospel Among the Slaves*, pp. 310-311.

166. L.H. Holsey, *Autobiography, Sermons, Addresses, and Essays*, p. 14.

CHAPTER TWO

1. See, for example, B.F. Riley, *A Memorial History of the Baptists of Alabama* (Philadelphia: The Judson Press, 1923), p. 146.

2. H.E. Sterkx, *Partners in Rebellion: Alabama Women in the Civil War* (Rutherford, N.J.: Farleigh Dickinson University Press, 1970), pp. 130-131. See also Riley, *Memorial History of the Baptists of Alabama*, pp. 161-165.

3. Sterkx, *Partners in Rebellion*, p. 133.

4. Quoted in ibid., pp. 131-132. For a summary of slave discipline problems faced by southern whites, see Franklin, *From Slavery to Freedom*, pp. 226-227.

5. Sullins, *Recollections of an Old Man*, p. 262.

6. William M. Green, *Life and Papers of A.L.P. Green, D.D.*, edited by T.O. Summers (Nashville, Tenn.: Southern Methodist Publishing House, 1877), p. 232.

7. Quoted in Howard N. Rabinowitz, *Race Relations in the Urban South, 1865-1890* (New York: Oxford University Press, 1978), p. 21.
8. Ibid., p. 97.
9. Ibid., p. 21.
10. John W. Blassingame, *Black New Orleans, 1860-1880* (Chicago: The University of Chicago Press, 1973), pp. 25-26.
11. Elizabeth Allen Coxe, *Memories of a South Carolina Plantation During the War* (privately printed, 1912), p. 48.
12. George P. Rawick, ed., *The American Slave: A Composite Autobiography*, 19 vols. (Westport, Conn.: Greenwood Publishing Company, 1972), *Arkansas Narratives*, 8 Pt. 1:13.
13. Ibid., 10 Pt. 5:47.
14. C. Peter Ripley, "The Black Family in Transition: Louisiana, 1860-1865," *The Journal of Southern History*, Vol. 41, No. 3 (August 1975): 372-373.
15. Ibid., p. 373.
16. Richard C. Wade, *Slavery in the Cities: The South 1820-1860* (New York: Oxford University Press, 1964), pp. 243-244; compare Rabinowitz, *Race Relations in the Urban South*, pp. 18-19.
17. Emory S. Bucke *et al.*, *The History of American Methodism*, 3 vols. (New York: Abingdon Press, 1964), 2:244.
18. George G. Smith, *The History of Methodism in Georgia and Florida From 1785-1865* (Macon, Ga.: Jno. W. Burke & Co., 1877), p. 408.
19. Ibid.
20. Smith, *History of Georgia Methodism*, p. 322.
21. Record Book, Socopatoy Circuit, Alabama Conference, M.E. Church South, Socopatoy Church Records, Auburn University Archives, Auburn, Alabama.
22. "Church Book Containing a Record of the Proceedings of Quarterly Meeting Conferences, and Stewards' Meetings," MS I VI (C) 3-82, Alabama State Archives, Montgomery, Alabama.
23. Methodist Episcopal Church South—Alabama Conference—Quarterly Conference Reports, Denson and Dowdell Papers, MS I Cab VIE 2-97, Alabama State Archives.
24. Green, *Life and Papers of A.L.P. Green*, p. 215.
25. Rawick, *Texas Narratives*, 4, Pt. 2:131.
26. Smith, *History of Georgia Methodism*, p. 321.
27. Phelan, *History of Early Methodism in Texas*, p. 469.
28. *Minutes of the Montgomery Conference of the MEC,S, held in Tuskegee, Alabama, December 7th-13th, 1864* (Montgomery: Montgomery Advertiser Book and Job Office, 1864), p. 14.
29. Eliza Frances Andrews, *The War-Time Journal of a Georgia Girl 1864-1865* (New York: D. Appleton and Company, 1908), p. 69; see also pp. 222-223.
30. Coxe, *Memories of a South Carolina Plantation During the War*, p. 23.
31. Harrison, *Gospel Among the Slaves*, pp. 323-324.
32. Sernett, *Black Religion and American Evangelicalism*, p. 290.

33. Rawick, *Georgia Narratives*, 12, Pt. 1:247-248.
34. Sterkx, *Partners in Rebellion*, pp. 133-134.
35. Ibid., pp. 132-133.
36. For a summary of black participation in the Civil War, see Franklin, *From Slavery to Freedom*, chap. 13, esp. pp. 230-235.
37. Sterkx, *Partners in Rebellion*, p. 184.
38. Senate Doc. 307, 60th Cong., Bankhead Papers, Alabama State Archives.
39. Ibid., Doc. 269 and 59th Cong., 2d sess., Doc. 131.
40. Sterkx, *Partners in Rebellion*, p. 132. For a brief description of damages to southern Methodist institutions, see Bucke, *History of American Methodism*, p. 244-245.
41. Morrow, *Northern Methodism and Reconstruction*, p. 20.
42. Ibid., p. 33.
43. Ibid., p. 34. Other churches—Northern Baptists, United Presbyterians, Old and New School Presbyterians, and United Brethren in Christ—received similar government authorization. Ibid., (p. 58, n. 15). According to Ahlstrom, Northern Methodist attempts to encourage other northern churches to follow the Methodist example were unsuccessful. *Religious History of the American People*, 2:172.
44. Morrow, *Northern Methodism and Reconstruction*, p. 34. Regarding Lincoln's view of Stanton's decrees and Northern Methodist efforts, see pp. 37 and 15.
45. *The Methodist Almanac for the Year of Our Lord 1865* (New York: Carlton and Porter, 1864), p. 49.
46. Quoted in Morrow, *Northern Methodism and Reconstruction*, p. 125.
47. Franklin, *From Slavery to Freedom*, p. 225.
48. Quoted in Albert M. Shipp, *A History of Methodism in South Carolina* (Nashville: Southern Methodist Publishing House, 1884), p. 426. See also Wade, *Slavery in the Cities*, p. 271.
49. H.N. McTyeire, *et al.*, *Duties of Masters to Servants: Three Premium Essays* (Charleston, S.C.: Southern Baptist Publication Society, 1851), pp. 38-39.
50. Franklin, *From Slavery to Freedom*, p. 417.
51. *Journal*, Alabama Conference M.E.C. South, MS I Cab VI H I, Alabama State Archives.
52. Record Book, Socopatoy Circuit, V.A.1.ee. 3-2.
53. *Minutes of the Mobile Conference of the MEC,S, held in Tuskaloosa, Alabama, November 23-28, 1864* (Mobile: Printed at the office of "The Army Argus and Crisis," 1864), p. 19.
54. Rawick, *South Carolina Narratives*, 3, Pt. 3:3.
55. Botkin, *Lay My Burden Down*, p. 233.
56. "Church Book Containing a Record of the Proceedings of Quarterly Meeting Conferences."
57. Smith, *History of Georgia Methodism*, p. 321.
58. Ahlstrom, *Religious History of the American People*, 2:159.

59. "Church Book Containing a Record of the Proceedings of Quarterly Meeting Conferences."
60. Blassingame, *Slave Testimony*, pp. 615-616.
61. A.J.H. Duganne, *Camps and Prisons: Twenty Months in the Department of the Gulf*, 3rd ed. (New York: J.P. Robens, Publisher, 1865), p. 349.
62. Rawick, *Texas Narratives*, 4, Pt. 1:11.
63. George H. Hepworth, *The Whip, Hoe, and Sword; or, the Gulf-Department in '63* (Boston: Walker, Wise, and Company, 1864), p. 141.
64. Quoted in Hunter Dickinson Farish, *The Circuit Rider Dismounts: A Social History of Southern Methodism, 1865-1900* (Richmond, Va.: The Dietz Press, 1938), p. 22.
65. Harry V. Richardson, *Dark Salvation: The Story of Methodism as It Developed Among Blacks in America* (Garden City, New York: Anchor Press/Doubleday, 1976), pp. 194-195; Singleton, *Romance of African Methodism*, pp. 100-101, 106-107; Charles Spencer Smith, *A History of the African Methodist Episcopal Church* (Philadelphia, Pa.: Book Concern of the A.M.E. Church, 1922), pp. 53-54; Daniel A. Payne, *History of the African Methodist Episcopal Church* (Nashville, Tenn.: Publishing House of the A.M.E. Sunday School Union, 1891), pp. 469-472.
66. These minutes are printed as an appendix in Smith, *History of the African Methodist Episcopal Church*, pp. 464-502.
67. Singleton, *Romance of African Methodism*, p. 104.
68. Ahlstrom, *Religious History of the American People*, 2:162.
69. David Henry Bradley, Sr., *A History of the A.M.E. Zion Church* (Nashville, Tenn.: The Parthenon Press, 1956), pp. 160-161.
70. Rawick, *Texas Narratives* 5, Pt. 3:70.
71. Ibid., Suppl. Ser. 2, 7, Pt. 6:2683-2684.
72. Richardson, *Dark Salvation*, p. 205.
73. Morrow, *Northern Methodism and Reconstruction*, pp. 189-190.

CHAPTER THREE

1. Richardson, *Dark Salvation*, p. 224. Compare Spain, *At Ease in Zion*, p. 51.
2. Quoted in Walter L. Fleming, *Civil War and Reconstruction in Alabama* (New York: The Columbia University Press, 1905), p. 644.
3. Quoted in Richardson, *Dark Salvation*, p. 197.
4. Wesley J. Gaines, *African Methodism in the South—or—Twenty-Five Years of Freedom* (Chicago: Afro-Am Press, [1890] 1969), p. 5.
5. Frederick Douglass, *Narrative of the Life of Frederick Douglass, an American Slave* (Boston: Anti-Slavery Office, 1849), pp. 119-120.
6. Quoted in Rev. Charles B. Williams, *A History of the Baptists in North Carolina* (Raleigh: Edwards & Broughton, 1901), pp. 161-162.

7. William R. Ferris, "The Collection of Racial Lore: Approaches and Problems," *New York Folklore Quarterly*, 27 (September 1971): 261-262, quoted in Blassingame, *Slave Testimony*, p. xliv. On the methodological problem of access to the true sentiments of blacks, see Webber, *Deep Like the Rivers*, p. 221. See also Andrew E. Murray, *Presbyterians and the Negro—a History* (Philadelphia: Presbyterian Historical Society, 1966), p. 190.

8. Botkin, *Lay My Burden Down*, pp. 267-268.

9. Sullins, *Recollections of an Old Man*, p. 327.

10. Riley, *A Memorial History of the Baptists of Alabama*, pp. 166-167.

11. Ibid., p. 167.

12. Murray, *Presbyterians and the Negro*, p. 146.

13. William Warren Sweet, *The Story of Religion in America* (New York: Harper & Brothers, 1930), p. 475.

14. Clifton E. Olmstead, *History of Religion in the United States* (Englewood Cliffs, N.J.: Prentice-Hall, Inc., 1960), p. 407.

15. Ahlstrom, *Religious History of the American People*, 2:175.

16. Farish, *The Circuit Rider Dismounts*, p. 170.

17. Robert T. Handy, *A History of the Churches in the United States and Canada* (New York: Oxford University Press, 1977), pp. 271-272.

18. Jordan, *White Over Black*, p. 425.

19. August Meier, *Negro Thought in America, 1880-1915* (Ann Arbor: The University of Michigan Press, 1963), p. 13.

20. Joseph R. Washington, Jr., *Black Religion: The Negro and Christianity in the United States* (Boston: Beacon Press, 1964), pp. 200-221.

21. Nelsen, Yokley, and Nelsen, *The Black Church in America*, p. 345.

22. Spain, *At Ease in Zion*, p. 52.

23. Winthrop S. Hudson, *Religion in America* (New York: Charles Scribner's Sons, 1965), p. 224.

24. Ahlstrom, *Religious History of the American People*, 2:160.

25. See Kenneth Scott Latourette, *Christianity in a Revolutionary Age*, 4 vols. (New York: Harper & Bros., 1961), 3:80 and Spain, *At Ease in Zion*, p. 45. See also Washington, *Black Religion*, p. 197.

26. Henry Kalloch Rowe, *The History of Religion in the United States* (New York: The Macmillan Company, [1924] 1928), pp. 188-189.

27. Nicholson, *Life and Labors of Rev. Alexander Bettis*, pp. 22-23.

28. Blassingame, *Slave Testimony*, p. 660.

29. Rawick, *Florida Narratives*, 17:187.

30. Botkin, *Lay My Burden Down*, pp. 108, 321.

31. Louis Hughes, *Thirty Years a Slave* (Milwaukee: South Side Printing Company, 1897), pp. 172, 177-187.

32. Botkin, *Lay My Burden Down*, pp. 225, 227.

33. Barr, *Black Texans*, pp. 39-40.

34. Botkin, *Lay My Burden Down*, p. 282.

35. Ibid., p. 233.

36. Ibid., pp. 246-247.
37. Blassingame, *Slave Testimony*, p. 661.
38. Rawick, *Arkansas Narratives*, 11, Pt. 7:137.
39. Rawick, *Texas Narratives*, 4, Pt. 2:92.
40. Rabinowitz, *Race Relations in the Urban South*, pp. 18-20.
41. Bishop Paine to Bishop Andrew, 2 July 1865; I am grateful to William B. Gravely for sending me a copy of this letter. For a description of Freedmen's Bureau Commissioner Oliver Howard's assessment of the population shifts, see George R. Bentley, *A History of the Freedmen's Bureau* (Philadelphia: University of Pennsylvania Press, 1955), pp. 62-63.
42. Rawick, *Mississippi Narratives*, Pt 2, Suppl., Ser. 1, 12 vols. 7, Pt. 2:334.
43. Andrews, *War-Time Journal of a Georgia Girl*, p. 171.
44. Caroline E. Merrick, *Old Times in Dixie-Land: A Southern Matron's Memories* (New York: The Crafton Press, 1901), p. 78.
45. Coxe, *Memories of a South Carolina Plantation*, pp. 70-71.
46. Franklin, *From Slavery to Freedom*, pp. 241-242.
47. Allen W. Trelease judges that "too many troops were mustered out of service too quickly amid the euphoric celebration of victory in 1865. Only 20,000 troops remained on duty in the South by the fall of 1867, and this number gradually fell to 6,000 by the fall of 1876; moreover, one-quarter to half of these were stationed in Texas, chiefly on frontier duty. A much larger occupation force would have had trouble in maintaining order throughout the South." *White Terror: The Ku Klux Klan Conspiracy and Southern Reconstruction* (New York: Harper & Row, Publishers, 1971), p. xxxiv.
48. Ahlstrom, *Religious History of the American People*, 2:164. Rufus Spain considers it likely that all Baptists, black and white, lived in small towns or the open country, at least in some states. *At Ease in Zion*, p. 10.
49. See Trelease, *White Terror*; John Hope Franklin, *The Militant South, 1800-1860* (Cambridge: Harvard University Press, 1956).
50. See, for example, Trelease, *White Terror*, pp. 21, 64, 185.
51. Richardson, *Dark Salvation*, p. 197.
52. Weber, *Sociology of Religion*, pp. 40, 109, 254-255; *Ancient Judaism*, pp. 339, 417; *Religion of India*, pp. 32, 43.
53. Herbert G. Gutman, *The Black Family in Slavery and Freedom, 1750-1925* (New York: Vintage Books, 1976), pp. 204-207, 363-431.
54. Carter, "The Anatomy of Fear," pp. 358-359.
55. Trelease, *White Terror*, p. xxii.
56. See, for example, Rawick, *Mississippi Narratives*, Suppl., Ser. 1, 6, Pt. 1:16; Fleming, *Civil War and Reconstruction in Alabama*, p. 460; Robert C. Morris, "Reading, 'Riting and Reconstruction: Freedmen's Education in the South, 1865-1870" (unpublished Ph.D. dissertation, University of Chicago, 1976), pp. 154-155.
57. Quoted in W.E.B. DuBois, *Black Reconstruction in America, 1860-1880* (New York: Atheneum, [1938] 1973), pp. 641-642.

58. Rawick, Supplement, Series 2, *Alabama, Arizona, Arkansas, District of Columbia, Florida, Georgia, Indiana, Kansas, Maryland, Nebraska, New York, North Carolina, Oklahoma, Rhode Island, South Carolina, Washington Narratives*, 1:4.

59. Rawick, *Arkansas Narratives*, 11, Pt. 7:149.

60. Sweet, *Story of Religion in America*, p. 473, compare pp. 474-475; Clarence E. Walker, *A Rock in a Weary Land: The African Methodist Episcopal Church During the Civil War and Reconstruction* (Baton Rouge: Louisiana State University Press, 1982), p. 63.

61. *Minutes of the Annual Conferences of the Methodist Episcopal Church, South, for the year 1866* (Nashville, Tenn.: Southern Methodist Publishing House, 1870), p. 94; Bucke, *History of American Methodism*, 2:246.

62. MS II 26 No.13 folder 19, Methodist Conference, Alabama State Archives.

63. Record Book, Socopatoy Circuit, Auburn University Archives.

64. *Minutes of the Annual Conferences, 1866*, pp. 26-27, 14-15, 20-21, 9, 12-13. "There are great defects in the Minutes consequent upon the derangement occasioned by the late war, which the editor could not supply." Ibid., p. 94.

65. Mathews, *Religion in the Old South*, pp. 47, 98-101.

66. James Walker Hood, *One Hundred Years of the African Methodist Episcopal Church* (New York: A.M.E. Zion Book Concern, 1895), pp. 307-308.

67. Ibid., pp. 572-573.

68. M.H. Moore, *Sketches of the Pioneers of Methodism in North Carolina and Virginia* (Nashville, Tenn.: Southern Methodist Publishing House, 1884), p. 271. The incident is mentioned in a sketch of a white "pioneer"; Moore supplies no additional details concerning the fortunes of the blacks who wanted to claim their chapel.

69. *Freedmen's Record* 2 (June 1866):115-116; National Freedman II (April 1866), pp. 120-121; quoted in John T. O'Brien, "Factory, Church, and Community: Blacks in Antebellum Richmond," *The Journal of Southern History*, 44, No.4 (November 1978):535.

70. Rawick, *North Carolina Narratives* 15, Pt. 2:295. Compare *South Carolina Narratives* 2, Pt. 2:72-73; *South Carolina Narratives* 3, Pt. 4:167; *Arkansas Narratives*, 8, Pt. 2:16; *Florida Narratives*, 17:50.

71. Rawick, *South Carolina Narratives* 3, Pt. 3:173. Compare *South Carolina Narratives* 2, Pt. 1:27, 152, 170-171, 329 and 2, Pt. 2:100; *Georgia Narratives* 12, Pt. 1:197-198.

72. Rawick, *Mississippi Narratives* Suppl., Ser. 1, 6, Pt. 1:64. Compare *Texas Narratives,* Suppl. Ser. 2, 10, Pt. 9:3917.

73. Rawick, *South Carolina Narratives*, 3, Pt. 4:178.

74. Rawick, *Georgia Narratives* 13, Pt. 3:29, partially cited also in Botkin, *Lay My Burden Down*, p. 82. For other accounts of black initiative, see Rawick, *Arkansas Narratives,* Pt. 7 and *Missouri Narratives*, 11, Pt. 7:132-133.

75. Bucke, *History of American Methodism*, p. 246.

76. MS I VI (C) 3-82, Alabama State Archives.

77. *Minutes of the Annual Conferences, 1866*, pp. 20-21.
78. Andrews, *War-Time Journal of a Georgia Girl*, p. 227.
79. *Minutes of the Annual Conferences, 1866*, p. 20.
80. Arney R. Childs, ed., *Rice Planter and Sportsman: The Recollections of J. Motte Alston, 1821-1909* (Columbia, S.C.: University of South Carolina Press, 1953), p. 60.
81. Rawick, *North Carolina Narratives* 15 Pt. 2:119.
82. Quoted in Sernett, *Black Religion and American Evangelicalism*, p. 295.
83. Hood, *One Hundred Years*, pp. 339, 341.
84. Ibid., pp. 341-342.
85, *Minutes of the Annual Conferences, 1866*, pp. 23-24, 28-30.
86. Matthew Simpson, ed., *Cyclopedia of Methodism*, 5th rev. ed. (Philadelphia: Louis H. Evers, 1882), p. 169.
87. For example, see Benedict, *General History of the Baptist Denomination*, p. 698.
88. Henry L. Swint, ed., *Dear Ones at Home: Letters from Contraband Camps* (Nashville: Vanderbilt University Press, 1966), pp. 21-22.
89. Andrews, *War-Time Journal of a Georgia Girl*, p. 89.
90. Childs, *Rice Planter and Sportsman*, p. 48.
91. Green, *Life and Papers of A.L.P. Green*, pp. 520-521.
92. Ibid., p. 521.
93. McTyeire, *A History of Methodism*, p. 671.
94. Rawick, *South Carolina Narratives* 2, Pt. 1:28.
95. Rawick, *Alabama and Indiana Narratives*, 6, Pt. 2:209.
96. Rawick, *South Carolina Narratives* 3 Pt. 3:248.
97. Blassingame, *Slave Testimony*, p. 610.
98. Rawick, *Georgia Narratives* 12, Pt. 1:295.
99. Cone, *Identity Crisis in Black Theology*, p. 63.
100. *Christian Advocate*, 31 March 1864; quoted in Morrow, *Northern Methodism and Reconstruction*, p. 146.
101. Morrow, *Northern Methodism and Reconstruction*, pp. 44-45.
102. McTyeire, *History of Methodism*, p. 670.
103. Morrow, *Northern Methodism and Reconstruction*, pp. 145, 146.
104. Ibid., pp. 244, 131.
105. Ibid., p. 245.
106. Ibid., pp. 126, 181.
107. Ibid., p. 187. Concerning Lewis, see *Missionary Advocate* 21 (June 1865), p. 22.
108. Morrow, *Northern Methodism and Reconstruction*, p. 190. In areas of mixed conferences, a process of racial separation without actual division would gradually take place (p. 192).
109. Ibid., pp. 71-72.
110. Regarding Methodist teachers, see, Rawick, *Arkansas Narratives* 11, Pt. 7:115; *Florida Narratives*, 17:352-353; regarding the Freedmen's Aid Society, see *The*

Methodist Almanac for the Year of Our Lord 1870 (Cincinnati, Chicago, & St. Louis: Hitchcock & Walden, [1869]), p. 15.

111. Robert L. Hall, "Tallahassee's Black Churches, 1865-1885," *Florida Historical Quarterly*, October 1979, p. 185.
112. Singleton, *Romance of African Methodism*, p. 104.
113. *The Christian Recorder*, 9 June 1866, as presented in Walker, *Rock in a Weary Land*, p. 74.
114. Long, *Pictures of Slavery*, pp. 376-377.
115. Walker, *Rock in a Weary Land*, p. 64.
116. For a brief summary of this complex situation, see Morrow, *Northern Methodism and Reconstruction*, pp. 138-139.
117. For a thorough demonstration of postwar AME emphasis on uplift, see Walker, *Rock in a Weary Land*.
118. Quoted in Gaines, *African Methodism in the South*, p. 19.
119. Walker, *Rock in a Weary Land*, p. 91. AME missionaries were not hostile to all local custom. In 1863 Rev. J.D.S. Hall reported baptizing eleven adults by immersion rather than sprinkling at their request (p. 64).
120. Harrison, ed., *Gospel Among the Slaves*, pp. 355-356, 282.
121. [David Smith], *Biography of Rev. David Smith of the A.M.E. Church* (Freeport, N.Y.: Books for Libraries Press, [1881] 1971), pp. 93-94.
122. Hood, *One Hundred Years*, pp. 72-85.
123. Ibid., pp. 312, 327.
124. William J. Walls, *The African Methodist Episcopal Zion Church: Reality of the Black Church* (Charlotte, N.C.: A.M.E. Zion Publishing House, 1974), pp. 194-195. The organizationally poor conference was further weakened when W.H. Miles left the AMEZ connection for the CME Church and a schism followed. Hood, *One Hundred Years*, pp. 327-329; Walls, *AMEZ Church*, p. 196.
125. Hood, *One Hundred Years*, p. 353; Walls, *AMEZ Church*, p. 194.
126. Hood, *One Hundred Years*, pp. 298, 207-209, 192.
127. *Minutes of the Montgomery Conference, 1865*, p. 1.
128. Quoted in Farish, *The Circuit Rider Dismounts*, pp. 165-166.
129. Quoted ibid., pp. 166-167.
130. *Mobile News*, reprinted in *New Orleans Tribune*, 9 September 1865; quoted in Leon F. Litwack, *Been in the Storm So Long: The Aftermath of Slavery* (New York: Alfred A. Knopf, 1979), p. 469.
131. *Christian Recorder*, 21 October 1865, 30 December 1865; quoted in Walker, *Rock in a Weary Land*, p. 96.
132. A number of Southerners advocated importing Chinese coolies to take the place of lost black labor. See, for example, Spain, *At Ease in Zion*, p. 94.
133. "Minutes of Concord Presbytery," 16 September 1865, p. 223; quoted in Murray, *Presbyterians and the Negro*, p. 146.
134. Southern Baptist Convention, *Annual*, 1914, p. 298.

135. *The Episcopal Methodist* (Baltimore), 2 August 1865; quoted in Farish, *The Circuit Rider Dismounts*, pp. 164-165.
136. See, for example, Spain, *At Ease in Zion*, pp. 44, 48, 97.
137. Morrow, *Northern Methodism and Reconstruction*, p. 133, emphasis added.
138. *Journal of the General Conference of the Methodist Episcopal Church, South, Held in New Orleans, 1866* (Nashville: A.H. Redford, 1866), p. 17.
139. *Southern Christian Advocate*, Macon, Ga., 31 August 1865.
140. Ibid.
141. Ibid.
142. Farish, *The Circuit Rider Dismounts*, p. 172.
143. Morrow, *Northern Methodism and Reconstruction*, p. 130; see also William H. Lawrence, *The Centenary Souvenir, Containing a History of the Centenary Church, Charleston* (Charleston, S.C., 1885), p. ix and *Western Advocate*, 12 April 1865.
144. Richardson, *Dark Salvation*, p. 197.
145. L.M. Hagood, *The Colored Man in the Methodist Episcopal Church* (Cincinnati: Cranston & Stowe, 1890), p. 73.
146. Morrow, *Northern Methodism and Reconstruction*, p. 140.
147. Rawick, *Texas Narratives* Pt. 5, Suppl. Ser. 2, 6, Pt. 5:2413.
148. Morris, "Reading, 'Riting and Reconstruction," pp. 154-155.
149. Walker, *Rock in a Weary Land*, p. 52.
150. Morrow, *Northern Methodism and Reconstruction*, pp. 158, 171.
151. Spain, *At Ease in Zion*, pp. 85-86; Southern Baptist Convention, *Proceedings, 1866*, p. 32.
152. Fleming, *Civil War and Reconstruction in Alabama*, p. 460.
153. "COLORED SUNDAY SCHOOL," *Union Springs Times*, 18 April 1866, typescript, MS II 26 No. 13, folder 19, Alabama State Archives.
154. Quoted in Nashville *Christian Advocate*, 15 March 1866.
155. Most of the northern church's white recruits came from regions and levels of population that were nonslaveholding. Morrow, *Northern Methodism and Reconstruction*, p. 98.
156. Genovese, *Roll, Jordan, Roll*, p. 156.
157. *Proceedings of the Freedmen's Convention of Georgia Assembled at Augusta, January 10th, 1866. Containing the Speeches of Gen'l Tilson, Capt. J.E. Bryant, and Others* (Augusta, 1866), p. 30; quoted in Edmund L. Drago, *Black Politicians and Reconstruction in Georgia: A Splendid Failure* (Baton Rouge: Louisiana State University Press, 1982), p. 18.
158. Rawick, *Alabama, Arizona, Arkansas, District of Columbia, Florida, Georgia, Indiana, Kansas, Maryland, Nebraska, New York, North Carolina, Oklahoma, Rhode Island, South Carolina, Washington Narratives*, Suppl. Ser. 2, 1:8; *Arkansas Narratives* 9, Pt. 3:246.
159. Rawick, *Mississippi Narratives*, Suppl. Ser. 1, 6, Pt. 1:134.
160. Nelsen, Yokley, and Nelsen, *The Black Church in America*, p. 34.

161. Anna Julia Cooper, *A Voice From the South* (New York: Negro Universities Press, [1892] 1969), p. 34.
162. Nicholson, *Brief Sketch of the Life and Labors of Rev. Alexander Bettis*, p. 32.
163. Litwack, *Been in the Storm So Long*, p. 458.
164. *Christian Recorder*, 14 July 1866; quoted in ibid., p. 459.
165. Hodding Carter, *The Angry Scar* (Garden City, New York: Doubleday & Company, Inc., 1959), p. 89.
166. Morrow, *Northern Methodism and Reconstruction*, p. 141.
167. Harvey Wish, ed., *Reconstruction in the South 1865-1877: First-Hand Accounts of the American Southland After the Civil War, by Northerners and Southerners* (New York: Farrar, Straus and Giroux, 1965), p. 288.
168. Hans Dieter Betz, *Galatians: A Commentary on Paul's Letter to the Churches in Galatia* (Philadelphia: Fortress Press, 1979), pp. 2-3.
169. Robert M. Grant, *Augustus to Constantine* (New York: Harper & Row, 1970), pp. 55-56.

CHAPTER FOUR

1. *Minutes of the Annual Conferences of the Methodist Episcopal Church, South, 1866*, p. 94; see also Bucke, *History of American Methodism*, 2:280.
2. Weber, *The Religion of India*, pp. 12-15.
3. See John Hope Franklin, *Reconstruction After the Civil War* (Chicago: The University of Chicago Press, 1961), pp. 70-73.
4. It is probable that blacks used arson as an occasional economic weapon, but evidence indicates that whites' fear of it was more widespread than actual incidents. Ellen Blue Jones may have heard a sermon on the subject; the preacher's text "was Ex 22.6 & suits the times exactly." In the King James Version, the text reads: "If fire break out, and catch in thorns, so that the stacks of corn, or the standing corn, or the field, be consumed *therewith*; he that kindled the fire shall surely make restitution." Diary, 9 August 1868, Alabama State Archives. See also Trelease, *White Terror*, p. 213.
5. Kolchin, *First Freedom*, pp. 154-155.
6. Trelease finds that, "The Klan was accepted widely as an extralegal defense against the Union League, which Conservatives mistook for a Negro terrorist organization." *White Terror*, p. xlvi.
7. U.S. Congress, Senate, *Report of the Joint Select Committee to Inquire into the Condition of Affairs in the Late Insurrectionary States* S. Rept. 41, Pt. 1, 42nd Cong., 2d sess., (Washington: Government Printing Office, 1872), 1:21.
8. Trelease, *White Terror*, p. 131.
9. Rawick, *Texas Narratives* 5, Pt. 3:186-187, suppl., Ser. 2, 8, Pt. 7:3094-3095.
10. *Report of the Joint Select Committee*, 2:13-14. One witness testified that the building was a schoolhouse, not a church (p. 72 and compare p. 84).
11. Ibid., 2:235-236.

12. Franklin, *Reconstruction After the Civil War*, pp. 154-162.
13. Linda D. Addo and James H. McCallum, *To Be Faithful to Our Heritage: A History of Black United Methodism in North Carolina* (Commissions on Archives and History, North Carolina Annual Conference, 1980), p. 29.
14. Kolchin, *First Freedom*, p. 111; see also Singleton, *Romance of African Methodism*, p. 29, and Alexander W. Wayman, *Cyclopaedia of African Methodism* (Baltimore: Methodist Episcopal Book Depository, 1882), p. 159.
15. Theophilus Gould Steward, *Fifty Years in the Gospel Ministry* (Philadelphia: n.p., n.d.); cited in Drago, *Black Politicians and Reconstruction in Georgia*, pp. 21-22. For some examples of Baptist separations in this period, see Kolchin, *First Freedom*, p. 110, Charles Hays Rankin, "The Rise of Negro Baptist Churches in the South Through the Reconstruction Period," (unpublished masters essay, New Orleans Baptist Theological Seminary, 1955), p. 56, and J.M. Carroll, *A History of Texas Baptists* (Dallas: Baptist Standard Publishing Co., 1923), p. 347.
16. Weber, *Theory of Social and Economic Organization*, p. 369 and *From Max Weber: Essays in Sociology*, H.H. Gerth and C. Wright Mills, eds. (New York: Oxford University Press, 1946), p. 297.
17. Walker, *Rock in a Weary Land*, pp. 21, 77.
18. Ibid., p. 75.
19. Hood, *One Hundred Years*, pp. 332-333.
20. Rawick, *Texas Narratives*, Suppl., Ser. 2 3, Pt. 2:931.
21. Simpson, *Cyclopedia of Methodism*, p. 100.
22. Edwin S. Redkey, *Black Exodus: Black Nationalist and Back-to-Africa Movements 1890-1910* (New Haven, Conn.: Yale University Press, 1969), pp. 24-25; see also Walker, *Rock in a Weary Land*, pp. 122-124.
23. For an excellent example of Turner expressing the communal black Christian ethic, see Franklin, *Reconstruction After the Civil War*, pp. 131-132.
24. Ibid., p. 91.
25. Walker, *Rock in a Weary Land*, p. 122, 130-131.
26. William H. Heard, *From Slavery to the Bishopric in the A.M.E. Church* (New York: Arno Press, [1924] 1969), p. 89.
27. *Report of the Joint Select Committee*, 1:47.
28. Hood, *One Hundred Years*, p. 143.
29. *Journal of the General Conference*, pp. 486-487; see also Bucke, *History of American Methodism*, 2:253.
30. Farish, *The Circuit Rider Dismounts*, pp. 210-212.
31. Quoted in ibid., pp. 212-213.
32. Morrow, *Northern Methodism and Reconstruction*, p. 190.
33. Dwight W. Culver, *Negro Segregation in the Methodist Church* (New Haven: Yale University Press, 1953), p. 54.
34. Bucke, *History of American Methodism*, p. 537; compare Walker, *Rock in a Weary Land*, pp. 74-75.
35. Bucke, *History of American Methodism*, p. 538.

36. Hood, *One Hundred Years*, pp. 359, 365; Walls, *AMEZ Church*, p. 198; Bucke, *History of American Methodism*, pp. 560-561, 562.

37. Hood, *One Hundred Years*, p. 100.

38. Ibid., pp. 97-99; Bucke, *History of American Methodism*, p. 662; see also *Journal of the General Conference of the Methodist Episcopal Church, 1868*, p. 264.

39. Morrow, *Northern Methodism and Reconstruction*, p. 47.

40. Holsey, *Autobiography, Sermons, Addresses, and Essays*, p. 12.

41. *Annual Conference Minutes, 1860-1866*.

42. Record Book, Socopatoy Circuit, microfilm V.A.1.ee. 3-2.

43. Ellen Blue Jones Diary, No. 1 (1868).

44. *Church Book Containing a Record of the Proceedings of Quarterly Meeting Conferences, and Stewards Meetings*, MS I VI(C) 3-82, Alabama State Archives.

45. Quoted in Shipp, *The History of Methodism in South Carolina*, p. 466.

46. *Nationalist*, 12 July 1866, quoted in Kolchin, *First Freedom*, p. 112.

47. Ibid.

48. See, for example, Lazenby, *History of Methodism in Alabama and West Florida*, pp. 348, 350.

49. *Montgomery Conference Minutes, 1866*, p. 24; *Mobile Conference Minutes, 1867*, p. 2; *Montgomery Conference Minutes, 1867*, pp. 22-23. Considerations based on congregational polity may have led Baptists more urgently to control black members and sometimes to encourage secession. See, for example, Kolchin, *First Freedom*, pp. 109-110, and the 1868 action of the Red River Baptist Association dealing with the black congregation of Mount Olive Church, Rankin, "Rise of Negro Baptist Churches," and John T. Christian, *A History of the Baptists of Louisiana* (Nashville: Southern Baptist Convention, 1923), p. 141. Compare Carroll, *History of Texas Baptists*, pp. 348-349.

50. *Report of the Joint Select Committee*, North Carolina, 2:76.

51. Rabinowitz, *Race Relations in the Urban South*, p. 201.

52. Ibid., pp. 205-206.

53. *Southern Christian Advocate*, 23 November 1865; quoted in William B. Gravely, "The Social, Political and Religious Significance of the Formation of the Colored Methodist Episcopal Church (1870)," *Methodist History*, Vol. 18, No. 1 (October 1979): 8.

54. Ibid., 21 December 1865, quoted in ibid., p. 7.

55. Ibid., 31 August 1865, quoted in ibid., p. 6.

56. Ibid., 16 November 1865, quoted in ibid.

57. *Journal of the General Conference, 1866*, pp. 58-59.

58. *Southern Christian Advocate*, 4 May 1866; quoted in Gravely, "Formation of the Colored Methodist Episcopal Church," p. 11.

59. Ibid., pp. 11-12.

60. *Journal of the General Conference, 1866*, p. 39.

61. Ibid., p. 65.

62. *Southern Christian Advocate*, 20 July 1866, as paraphrased and quoted in Gravely, "Formation of the Colored Methodist Episcopal Church," p. 14.
63. Ibid., pp. 15-16.
64. Gravely reports formation of a black annual conference in Tennessee in 1867, with four more created in the next two years. Bucke dates the first Negro Annual Conference in 1870 in Texas. *History of American Methodism*, p. 284.
65. Smith, *Life and Times of George Foster Pierce*, p. 492.
66. Posey, *Religious Strife on the Southern Frontier*, p. 100.
67. Walker, *Rock in a Weary Land*, pp. 83-84.
68. Holsey, *Autobiography*, p. 24.
69. Quoted in Walker, *Rock in a Weary Land*, p. 89.
70. Ibid., pp. 102, 101.
71. Ibid., pp. 100-101.
72. See, for example, ibid., p. 90.
73. In June 1866, Congress enacted the Southern Homestead Act to give land to freedmen and loyalists. The law had little effect on blacks due to problems of getting information about it to the people and then getting the people to the designated lands. John Hope Franklin, HIST 349 Reconstruction and the New South.
74. *Christian Recorder*, 21 December 1865; quoted in Walker, *Rock in a Weary Land*, p. 97.
75. Ibid., p. 101.
76. Hagood, *The Colored Man in the Methodist Episcopal Church*, p. 73.
77. Tindall, *South Carolina Negroes 1877-1900*, p. 188.
78. Hood, *One Hundred Years*, pp. 99-100.
79. Bentley, *History of the Freedmen's Bureau*, pp. 183, 210-211.
80. See, for example, Southern Baptist Convention, *Proceedings*, 1867, p. 79; Robert A. Baker, *A Baptist Source Book* (Nashville: Broadman Press, 1966), p. 157; Fisher, *A Short History of the Baptist Denomination*, p. 111.
81. Trelease, *White Terror*, p. xlvii.
82. Ex-slave stories about Klan violence must be read very carefully; frequently the stories actually describe the behavior of antebellum "pattyrollers," (patrols of white men that enforced customary restrictions on slave mobility) which was similar but far more often directed against separate worship by blacks. For an example of the close association between "pattyroller" and Klan in ex-slave memories, see Rawick, *Alabama Narratives*, Suppl., Ser. 1, 1, Pt. 1:298.
83. Rawick, *South Carolina Narratives* 3 Pt. 4:216; Trelease, *White Terror*, p. 254.
84. Joint Select Committee, Report No. 41, Pt. 1, 1:70.
85. Rawick, *Mississippi Narratives*, Suppl., Ser. 1, 9, Pt. 4:1493.
86. Rawick, *Alabama and Indiana Narratives* 6, Pt. 1:298.
87. Rawick, *Arkansas Narratives* 8, Pt. 2:263.
88. Ibid. 10, Pt. 6:361.
89. Rawick, *Oklahoma and Mississippi Narratives* 7 Pt. 1:163; see also *Arkansas Narratives* 10 Pt. 6:77 and *Texas Narratives*, Suppl., Ser. 2, 4, Pt. 3:1267.

90. Rawick, *Texas Narratives*, Suppl., Ser. 2, 5, Pt. 4:1640; see also *Oklahoma and Mississippi Narratives* 7, Pt. 1:205 and *Texas Narratives*, Suppl., Ser. 2, 3, Pt. 2:582.
91. Rawick, *Arkansas Narratives* 10 Pt. 5:76.
92. Rawick, *Texas Narratives*, Suppl., Ser. 2, 4, Pt. 3:1000.
93. See, for example, Vernon Lane Wharton, *The Negro in Mississippi, 1865-1890* (New York: Harper & Row, [1947] 1965), pp. 257-258.
94. See, for example, John T. Gillard, *The Catholic Church and the Negro* (Baltimore: St. Joseph's Society Press, 1929), p. 39.
95. Black religious leader James Lynch was an exception, but on this subject his was a solitary and unheeded voice.
96. Morrow, *Northern Methodism and Reconstruction*, p. 185.

CHAPTER FIVE

1. Murray, *Presbyterians and the Negro*, p. 179.
2. Ibid., pp. 152-153.
3. Quoted in George Freeman Bragg, Jr., *History of the Afro-American Group of the Episcopal Church* (Baltimore: Church Advocate Press, 1922), p. 128.
4. Southern Baptist Convention, *Proceedings*, 1870, p. 32.
5. Murray, *Presbyterians and the Negro*, p. 146.
6. Bragg, *History of the Afro-American Group of the Episcopal Church*, p. 129.
7. Franklin, *Reconstruction After the Civil War*, pp. 152-173; see also Trelease, *White Terror*, p. 49.
8. Franklin, *Reconstruction After the Civil War*, pp. 152-173. The Klan was formally disbanded in 1871; however, acts of physical intimidation continued.
9. For example, in 1860 the South's cotton harvest consisted of 3,800,000 bales. In 1866 it produced only 2,000,000. But by 1869, in an economy more diversified than before the war, the harvest was 3,000,000 bales, and by 1878 cotton production reached its prewar level amid new kinds of agricultural and other economic endeavor. Franklin, HIST 349 Reconstruction and the New South.
10. Bucke, *History of American Methodism*, 2:280.
11. Richardson, *Dark Salvation*, p. 253; Winthrop S. Hudson sets the figure at approximately 300,000. *Religion in America*, p. 225.
12. Bucke, *History of American Methodism*, 2:280.
13. Payne, *Address Before the College Aid Society*, p. 6.
14. Ibid., p. 5.
15. Morrow, *Northern Methodism and Reconstruction*, p. 52.
16. Blassingame, *Black New Orleans*, p. 199; compare Morrow, *Northern Methodism and Reconstruction*, p. 188 for a somewhat different reading of this episode.

17. For two 1868 expressions of opposition to black-white commensality in Tennessee, see Morrow, *Northern Methodism and Reconstruction*, pp. 112, 188.

18. Ibid., pp. 196-197; compare Farish, *The Circuit Rider Dismounts*, pp. 214-215.

19. See, for example, the arguments of some Georgia clergy in the Atlanta *Methodist Advocate*, 1 May 1872, quoted in Drago, *Black Politicians and Reconstruction in Georgia*, p. 19.

20. Addo and McCallum, *To Be Faithful to Our Heritage*, p. 31.

21. Ellen Blue Jones Diary, Vol. 1, 5 July 1868.

22. For a summary of denominational maneuvering in the matter of their relationship see Bucke, *History of American Methodism*, 2:299-303, 660-664.

23. Hood, *One Hundred Years*, pp. 97-99.

24. Morrow, *Northern Methodism and Reconstruction*, p. 225, citing Knoxville *Whig*, 11 August 1869, Nashville *Advocate*, 19 December 1874, and *Methodist Advocate*, 2 February 1875, which quotes Meridian Mississippi *Daily Mercury*.

25. Joint Select Committee, Georgia, 1:81-82. Compare Kolchin, *First Freedom*, p. 121.

26. Hood, *One Hundred Years*, p. 18.

27. *Southern Christian Advocate*, 4 December 1868, cited in Gravely, "Significance of the Formation of the Colored Methodist Episcopal Church," pp. 20-21.

28. Joint Select Committee, Senate Report No. 41, p. 495.

29. Gravely, "Formation of the Colored Methodist Episcopal Church," pp. 10, 13.

30. Ibid., pp. 17-18.

31. Ibid., p. 15.

32. Quoted in Walker, *Rock in a Weary Land*, p. 82.

33. Gravely, "Social, Political, and Religious Significance of the Colored Methodist Episcopal Church."

34. In addition, I am indebted to this scholar for help in locating additional sources pertaining to black Methodists.

35. Ahlstrom, *Religious History of the American People*, 2:161. For expressions of the unilateral interpretation, see Sweet, *Story of Religion in America*, p. 473; Olmstead, *History of Religion in the United States*, p. 407; Latourette, *Christianity in a Revolutionary Age*, 3:79.

36. C.H. Phillips, *The History of the Colored Methodist Episcopal Church in America: Comprising Its Organization, Subsequent Development, and Present Status* (Jackson, Tenn.: Publishing House C.M.E. Church, [1898] 1925), p. 25.

37. Holsey, *Autobiography, Sermons, Addresses, and Essays*, p. 214.

38. *Minutes of the Annual Conferences of the Methodist Episcopal Church, South, for the Year 1867* (Nashville, Tenn.: Southern Methodist Publishing House, 1870), p. 196; see also 1868 *Minutes*, p. 295, and 1869 *Minutes*, p. 393. The 1870 *Minutes*, published in 1871, carry the same notation, p. 521.

39. Gravely, "Formation of the Colored Methodist Episcopal Church," p. 21; Thomas O. Summers, ed., *Journal of the General Conference of the Methodist Episcopal Church, South, Held in Memphis, 1870* (Nashville: Publishing House

of the Methodist Episcopal Church, South, 1870), pp. 167-168. See also Phillips, *History of the Colored Methodist Episcopal Church*, p. 26, and Bucke, *History of American Methodism*, 2:284.

40. *Nashville Christian Advocate*, 7 January 1871, quoted in Gravely, "Formation of the Colored Methodist Episcopal Church," pp. 24-25.

41. Phillips, *History of the Colored Methodist Episcopal Church*, p. 44.

42. Ibid., p. 35. Contrast the stress on religious heritage in the CME plan of organization with this excerpt from the AMEZ Founders' Address: "such was the relation in which we stood to the white bishops and Conference relative to the ecclesiastical government of the African Methodist Church or Society in America, that so long as we remained in that situation our preachers would never be able to enjoy those privileges which the Discipline of the white Church holds out to all its members that are called of God to preach, in consequence of the difference of color. We have been led also to conclude that the usefulness of our preachers has been very much hindered, and our brethren in general have been deprived of those blessings which Almighty God may have designed to grant them through the means of those preachers whom he has from time to time raised up from among them, because there have been no means adopted by the said bishops and Conference for our preachers to travel through the connection and promulgate the Gospel of our Lord Jesus Christ; and they have had no access to the only source from whence they might have obtained a support, at least, while they traveled." Hood, *One Hundred Years*, pp. 8-9.

43. For an example of CME reverence for orders and sacramental tradition, see Rawick, *Arkansas Narratives* 9 Pt. 3:322-324.

44. The name Episcopal Methodist Church had been approved by the MEC,S General Conference in 1866, but was voted down afterward by the Annual Conferences. Bucke, 2:276.

45. *Nashville Christian Advocate*, 7 January 1871, quoted in Gravely, "Formation of the Colored Methodist Episcopal Church," p. 23.

46. Ibid.

47. On the granting of land to the CME Church, see Savage, *Life and Times of Bishop Isaac Lane*, p. 67.

48. Phillips, *History of the Colored Methodist Episcopal Church*, pp. 71-72; Farish, *The Circuit Rider Dismounts*, p. 173.

49. Holsey, *Autobiography, Sermons, Addresses, and Essays*, p. 25.

50. Savage, *Life and Times of Bishop Isaac Lane*, p. 59. For two examples of less well-known CME leaders who had characteristic careers in southern Methodism, see Harrison, *Gospel Among the Slaves*, pp. 391-394.

51. Holsey, *Autobiography, Sermons, Addresses, and Essays*, p. 14.

52. Ibid., pp. 215-216.

53. Gravely, "Formation of the Colored Methodist Episcopal Church," p. 23.

54. An ex-slave explained, "We all went to the white folks church, but we had a place in back of the church where we would set. Some of the slaves kept their

membership in the white church till several years after the War. Some kept it as long as they lived." Rawick, *Unwritten History of Slavery*, 18:131.

CHAPTER SIX

1. Franklin, *Reconstruction After the Civil War*, pp. 219-220.
2. See Rabinowitz, *Race Relations in the Urban South*, pp. 188, 388.
3. Rawick, *Arkansas Narratives* 10, Pt. 6:224 and Botkin, *Lay My Burden Down*, pp. 258-259.
4. Trelease, *White Terror*, p. 360.
5. Joint Select Committee, Georgia, 7:1204, 1120.
6. Weber, *Sociology of Religion*, pp. 40-41.
7. Ibid.
8. Weber, *Religion of India*, pp. 12-15, emphasis added.
9. Jordan, *White Over Black*, p. 93.
10. Weber, *Ancient Judaism*, p. 363.
11. The rate of increase in the free black population declined sharply after 1810 due to such laws and to white apprehensions concerning the presence of free blacks in society. Franklin, *From Slavery to Freedom*, pp. 165-166.
12. Rawick, *Unwritten History of Slavery*, 18:239.
13. SBC, *Proceedings*, 1870, p. 19.
14. Culver, *Negro Segregation in the Methodist Church* (New Haven: Yale University Press, 1953), p. 52.
15. See Morrow, *Northern Methodism and Reconstruction*, p. 120, nn. 7, 8, and compare p. 127.
16. Culver, *Negro Segregation in the Methodist Church*, p. 59.
17. Morrow, *Northern Methodism and Reconstruction*, p. 194.
18. Theoretically whites could be members of the AME Church but not part of the clergy. Walker, *Rock in a Weary Land*, pp. 24-25.
19. James E. Handy, *Scraps of African Methodist Episcopal History* (Philadelphia: A.M.E. Book Concern, [1900?]), pp. 251-252.
20. Phillips, *History of the Colored Methodist Episcopal Church*, p. 58.
21. Ibid., pp. 60-61.
22. William Hawes of Atchison, Kentucky, reported that around 1877, "The colored fo'ks down there wanted a bigger church so they got out and got subscriptions, the white fo'ks helped us too. Before I left Atchison we had a two story brick church an' a membership of one thousand." Rawick, *Alabama, Arizona, Arkansas, District of Columbia, Florida, Georgia, Indiana, Kansas, Maryland, Nebraska, New York, North Carolina, Oklahoma, Rhode Island, South Carolina, Washington Narratives*, Suppl., Ser. 2, 1:326.
23. In the 1840s, a movement to license women as AME preachers failed; Walker, *Rock in a Weary Land*, pp. 25-26. In 1868, the AMEZ Church deleted "male"

as a requirement for ordination, but no woman was ordained before the 1890s; Bucke, *History of American Methodism*, 2:566.

24. Dix, *Shape of the Liturgy*, pp. 619, 716-717.
25. Ibid., pp. 523, 740.
26. Bruce, *And They All Sang Hallelujah*, pp. 6-7.
27. Weber, *Sociology of Religion*, p. 3, and compare p. 101.
28. See Mathews, "Charles Colcock Jones and the Southern Evangelical Crusade to Form a Biracial Community," pp. 299-320.
29. SBC, *Proceedings*, 1888, p. 19.
30. Bucke, *History of American Methodism*, 2:305, 288.
31. Ibid., p. 286.
32. Ibid., p. 366.
33. Ibid., p. 364.
34. Mathews, *Religion in the Old South*, pp. 249-250.
35. Ibid., pp. 247, 249.
36. See also Hill, *Religion and the Solid South*, p. 21.
37. Examples abound. See, for instance, Benjamin E. Mays and Joseph W. Nicholson, *The Negro's Church* (New York: Russell & Russell, 1933); Hudson, *Religion in America*, p. 225.
38. Heard, *From Slavery to the Bishopric*, p. 68. The denomination ascertained, then tested, Heard's personal charisma. "Only the proved novice is allowed to exercise authority." Weber, *Theory of Social and Economic Organization*, p. 367.
39. Weber, *Theory of Social and Economic Organization*, pp. 360-361.
40. Blassingame, *Black New Orleans*, p. 151.
41. Hood, *One Hundred Years*, pp. 27-55.
42. Rawick, *Mississippi Narratives* 7, Pt. 2:700.
43. Weber points out that in ethical religion, the disprivileged have a "hope for and expectation of just compensation." *Sociology of Religion*, p. 108.
44. Redkey, *Black Exodus*, p. 21.
45. Rupert Sargent Holland, ed., *Letters and Diary of Laura M. Towne* (Cambridge: The Riverside Press, 1912), p. 162.
46. Litwack, *Been in the Storm So Long*, p. 170.
47. Ibid., p. 122.
48. Rawick, *Florida Narratives* 17:160-161.
49. Ahlstrom, *Religious History of the American People*, 2:148.
50. Rawick, *Arkansas Narratives* 9 Pt. 3:267. See also *Oklahoma Narratives*, Suppl., Ser. 1, 12:130-131, which concerns the family name change made by the grandfather of John Hope Franklin.
51. Gutman, *Black Family in Slavery and Freedom*, p. 255.
52. Black theologian James H. Cone charges that with the rise of segregation and discrimination, "The black minister thus became a most devoted 'Uncle Tom,' the transmitter of white wishes, the admonisher of obedience to the caste system. He was the liaison man between the white power structure and the

oppressed blacks, serving the dual function of assuring whites that all is well in the black community, dampening the spirit of freedom among his people. More than any other one person in the black community, the black minister perpetuated the white system of black dehumanization." Nelsen, *Black Church in America*, p. 346.

53. John Hope Franklin, HIST 349 Reconstruction and the New South.
54. Franklin asserts that slavery as a system offered slaves no positive reinforcement. Ibid.
55. Regarding the persistent hope of postwar blacks for promised land, see Peter Randolph, *From Slave Cabin to the Pulpit* (Boston: James H. Earle, Publisher, 1893), pp. 69-70; Kolchin, *First Freedom*, p. 185; Meier, *Negro Thought in America*, p. 11.
56. Max Weber implicitly recognizes this point in his refutation of explanations of caste order based on "race psychology" or on "blood." *Religion of India*, p. 124.
57. See ibid., pp. 16-18.
58. Ibid., pp. 9-20.
59. In contrast, Weber found that "the strongest motive for the assimilation of Hinduism was undoubtedly the desire for legitimation," not religious hope. Ibid., p. 16.

Bibliography

ARCHIVAL MATERIAL

Allen, William Francis. William F. Allen Diary, Beaufort, South Carolina, 5 November 1863-12 February 1864. State Historical Society of Wisconsin, Madison, Wisconsin.

_____. Correspondence—Outgoing January 1854-December 1866. State Historical Society of Wisconsin, Madison, Wisconsin.

Bankhead, John Hollis, Sr. Bankhead Papers. Alabama State Archives, Montgomery, Ala.

"Coulered Members of the Methodist E Church South, Jas W Brown Pastor" 1854-1857. Alabama State Archives, Montgomery, Ala.

"Court St. M E Montgomery Quarterly Conference" 1830-1847. Alabama State Archives, Montgomery, Ala.

Dayton Church Register, Dayton, Alabama, 1851-1879. Alabama State Archives, Montgomery, Ala.

Denson and Dowdell Papers (Methodist Episcopal Church, South—Alabama Conference—Quarterly Conference Reports, including Oak Bowerey Circuit Records). Alabama State Archives, Montgomery, Ala.

"Hayneville Circuit, M.E. Church, South, 1836-1855." Alabama State Archives, Montgomery, Ala.

Jones, Ellen Blue. Ellen Blue Jones Diaries. 7 vols. Alabama State Archives, Montgomery, Ala.

Methodist Church Register, Auburn, Alabama. Auburn University Archives, Auburn, Ala.

Methodist Conference Miscellaneous Notes. Alabama State Archives, Montgomery, Ala.

Methodist Conference, Sunday School and Orphanage Records. Alabama State Archives, Montgomery, Ala.

Methodist Episcopal Church, Tuskegee, Alabama. Membership list, 1843-1855. Alabama State Archives, Montgomery, Ala.

Methodist Episcopal Church, South. Journal, Alabama Conference M.E.C. South, 1856-1857, 1859. Alabama State Archives, Montgomery, Ala.

Pea Ridge Class, M E Church Valley Creek Circuit, Alabama Conference. Class Book, 1845-1847. Alabama State Archives, Montgomery, Ala.

Ramsey, A.C. "Life and Times of A.C. Ramsey." Rare Book Room, Birmingham Southern University, Birmingham, Ala.

"Register of Members and Probationers in Sumterville Church, 1858-1882," Sumterville, Sumter County, Alabama. Alabama State Archives, Montgomery, Ala.

Rehoboth Methodist Church, Hale County, Alabama. List of Members 1851-1875. Alabama State Archives, Montgomery, Ala.

_____. Sunday School Cash Book, 1873-1879.

Socopatoy Church Records (Alabama Conference, M.E. Church South). Auburn University Archives, Auburn, Ala.

Woodville Station and Union Town Station. Church Book Containing a Record of the Proceedings of Quarterly Meeting Conferences, and Stewards' Meetings. Alabama State Archives, Montgomery, Ala.

CONTEMPORARY MATERIAL

Adams, Nehemiah. *A South-Side View of Slavery; or, Three Months at the South*. Boston: T.R. Marvin, and B.B. Mussey & Co., 1854.

Alexander, Gross. *History of the Methodist Episcopal Church, South*. New York, 1893-1897.

Allen, William Francis, Charles Pickard Ware, and Lucy McKim Garrison. *Slave Songs of the United States*. New York: Peter Smith, [1867] 1929.

Ames, Mary. *From a New England Woman's Diary in Dixie in 1865*. Norwood, Mass.: The Plimpton Press, 1906.

Andrews, Eliza Frances. *The War-Time Journal of a Georgia Girl 1864-1865*. New York: D. Appleton and Company, 1908.

Armistead, Wilson. *A Tribute for the Negro: Being a Vindication of the Moral, Intellectual, and Religious Capabilities of The Coloured Portion of Mankind; with Particular Reference to the African Race*. Westport, Conn.: Negro Universities Press, [1848] 1970.

Avary, Myrta Lockett. *Dixie After the War: An Exposition of Social Conditions Existing in the South, During the Twelve Years Succeeding the Fall of Richmond*. New York: Doubleday, Page & Company, 1906.

Baker, Robert A. *A Baptist Source Book*. Nashville, Tenn.: Broadman Press, 1966.

Ball, Charles. *Fifty Years in Chains*. New York: Dover Publications, Inc., 1970. Republication of *Slavery in the United States: A Narrative of the Life* and *Adventures of Charles Ball, A Black Man*. New York: John S. Taylor, 1837.

Bangs, Nathan. *An Authentic History of the Missions Under the Care of the Missionary Society of the Methodist Episcopal Church*. New York: J. Emory and B. Waugh, 1832.

Benedict, David. *A General History of the Baptist Denomination in America and Other Parts of the World*. New York: Lewis Colby and Company, 1850.

Blassingame, John W., ed. *Slave Testimony: Two Centuries of Letters, Speeches, Interviews, and Autobiographies*. Baton Rouge: Louisiana State University Press, 1977.

Boothe, Charles Octavius. *The Cyclopedia of the Colored Baptists of Alabama: Their Leaders and Their Work*. Birmingham: Alabama Publishing Company, 1895.

Bremer, Fredrika. *The Homes of the New World; Impressions of America*. 2 vols. New York: Harper & Brothers, Publishers, 1854.

Brent, Linda. *Incidents in the Life of a Slave Girl*. Edited by L. Maria Child. New York: Harcourt Brace Jovanovich, [1861] 1973.

Bruce, H. C. *The New Man. Twenty-Nine Years a Slave. Twenty-Nine Years a Free Man*. New York: Negro Universities Press, [1895] 1969.

Burkhead, L.S. *Centennial of Methodism in North-Carolina*. Raleigh: John Nichols, Book and Job Printer, 1876.

[Cartwright, Peter.] *Autobiography of Peter Cartwright*. Edited by W. P. Strickland. Freeport, N.Y.: Books for Libraries Press, [1856] 1972.

Childs, Arney R., ed. *Rice Planter and Sportsman: The Recollections of J. Motte Alston, 1821-1909*. Columbia, S.C.: University of South Carolina Press, 1953.

Chreitzburg, A. M. *Early Methodism in the Carolinas*. Nashville, Tenn.: Publishing House of the Methodist Episcopal Church, South, 1897.

Christian Advocate. Nashville, Tenn., 15 March 1866 and 12 April 1866.

Clark, Elmer T., ed. *The Journal and Letters of Francis Asbury*. 3 vols. Nashville: Abingdon Press, 1958.

"Colloquy with Colored Ministers, A Civil War Document." *The Journal of Negro History*, Vol. 16, No.1 (January 1931): 88-94.

Cooper, Anna Julia. *A Voice From the South*. New York: Negro Universities Press, [1892] 1969.

Coxe, Elizabeth Allen. *Memories of a South Carolina Plantation During the War*. Privately printed, 1912.

Curry, Daniel. *Life-Story of Rev. Davis Wasgatt Clark, D.D., Bishop of the Methodist Episcopal Church*. New York: Nelson & Phillips, 1874.

Davis, Noah. *A Narrative of the Life of Rev. Noah Davis, A Colored Man*. Philadelphia, Pa.: Rhistoric Publications, [1859] n.d.

Deems, Charles F., ed. *Annals of Southern Methodism for 1856*. Nashville, Tenn.: Stevenson & Owen, 1857.

Douglass, Frederick. *Narrative of the Life of Frederick Douglass, an American Slave*. Boston: Anti-Slavery Office, 1849.

Drew, Benjamin. *The Refugee: A North-Side View of Slavery*. Reading, Mass.: Addison-Wesley Publishing Company, [1856] 1969.

Duganne, A.J.H. *Camps and Prisons: Twenty Months in the Department of the Gulf*. 3rd. ed. New York: J.P. Robens, Publisher, 1865.

Flint, Timothy. *Recollections of the Last Ten Years in the Valley of the Mississippi*. Edited by George R. Brooks. Carbondale, Ill.: Southern Illinois University Press, [1826] 1968.

Foote, William Henry. *Sketches of North Carolina, Historical and Biographical, Illustrative of the Principles of a Portion of Her Early Settlers*. New York: Robert Carter, 1846.

Gaines, Wesley J. *African Methodism in the South—or—Twenty-Five Years of Freedom*. Chicago: Afro-Am Press, [1890] 1969.

Goss, C.C. *Statistical History of the First Century of American Methodism: With a Summary of the Origin and Present Operations of Other Denominations*. New York: Carlton & Porter, 1866.

Grandy, Moses. *Narrative of the Life of Moses Grandy, Late a Slave in the United States of America*, Boston, 1844.

Grayson, William J. *The Hireling and the Slave, Chicora, and Other Poems*. Miami, Fla.: Mnemosyne Publishing Co., Inc., [1856] 1969.

Green, William M. *Life and Papers of A.L.P. Green, D.D.* Edited by T.O. Summers. Nashville, Tenn.: Southern Methodist Publishing House, 1877.

Hagood, L.M. *The Colored Man in the Methodist Episcopal Church*. Cincinnati: Cranston & Stowe, 1890.

Harrison, W.P., comp. and ed. *The Gospel Among the Slaves: A Short Account of Missionary Operations Among the African Slaves of the Southern States*. Nashville, Tenn.: Publishing House of the M.E. Church, South, 1893.

Hepworth, George H. *The Whip, Hoe, and Sword; or, the Gulf-Department in '63*. Boston: Walker, Wise, and Company, 1864.

Higginson, Thomas Wentworth. *Black Rebellion*. New York: Arno Press, [1889] 1969.

Holland, Rupert Sargent, ed. *Letters and Diary of Laura M. Towne*. Cambridge: The Riverside Press, 1912.

Holsey, L. H. *Autobiography, Sermons, Addresses, and Essays of Bishop L.H. Holsey, D.D.* Atlanta, Georgia: The Franklin Printing and Publishing Co., 1898.

Hood, J. W. *One Hundred Years of the African Methodist Episcopal Church; or, The Centennial of African Methodism.* New York: A.M.E. Zion Book Concern, 1895.

Hughes, Louis. *Thirty Years a Slave.* Milwaukee: South Side Printing Co., 1897.

Jones, Thomas H. *The Experience of Thomas H. Jones, Who Was a Slave for Forty-Three Years.* New York: AMS Press, [1871] 1975.

Katz, William Loren, ed. *Five Slave Narratives.* New York: Arno Press, 1969. The narratives are those of Lunsford Lane, William Wells Brown, Moses Grandy, J.W.C. Pennington, and Jacob Stroyer.

Kealing, H.T. *History of African Methodism in Texas.* Waco, Texas: C.F. Blanks, Printer and Stationer, 1885.

Kemble, Frances Anne. *Further Records 1848-1883: A Series of Letters by Frances Anne Kemble Forming a Sequel to Records of a Girlhood and Records of Later Life.* New York: Henry Holt and Company, 1891.

_____. *Journal of a Residence on a Georgian Plantation in 1838-1839.* New York: Harper & Brothers, Publishers, 1863.

_____. *Records of a Girlhood.* New York: Henry Holt and Company, 1879.

_____. *Records of Later Life.* New York: Henry Holt and Company, 1882.

Lanman, Charles. *Haw-ho-noo; or, Records of a Tourist.* Philadelphia: Lippincott, Grambo and Co., 1850.

Lawrence, William H. *The Centenary Souvenir, Containing a History of the Centenary Church, Charleston.* Charleston, S.C., 1885

Leftwich, W.M. *Martyrdom in Missouri: A History of Religious Proscription, the Seizure of Churches, and the Persecution of Ministers of the Gospel, in the State of Missouri During the Late Civil War and under the "Test Oath" of the New Constitution.* St. Louis: Southwestern Book and Publishing Company, 1870.

Lewis, G. *Impressions of America and the American Churches: From the Journal of the Rev. G. Lewis.* New York: Negro Universities Press, [1848] 1968.

Lewis, W.H. *The History of Methodism in Missouri for a Decade of Years from 1860 to 1870.* Nashville, Tenn.: Publishing House of the M.E. Church, South, 1890.

Livermore, Mary A. *My Story of the War: A Woman's Narrative of Four Years Personal Experience in the Union Army.* Hartford, Conn.: A.D. Worthington and Company, 1889.

Long, John Dixon. *Pictures of Slavery in Church and State*. Philadelphia: published by the author, 1857.

Mallard, R.Q. *Plantation Life Before Emancipation*. Detroit, Mich.: Negro History Press, [1892] n.d.

McLean, John H. *Reminiscences of Rev. Jno. H. McLean, A.M., D.D.* Nashville, Tenn.: Smith & Lamar, Publishing House M.E. Church, South, 1918.

McTyeire, Holland N. *A History of Methodism*. Nashville, Tenn.: Publishing House of the Methodist Episcopal Church, South, 1898.

McTyeire, H. N., C. F. Sturgis, and A. T. Holmes. *Duties of Masters to Servants: Three Premium Essays*. Charleston, S.C.: Southern Baptist Publication Society, 1851.

Meacham, James. "A Journal and Travel of James Meacham" Pt. I: 19 May-31 August 1789. *Historical Papers*. Series IX. Trinity College Historical Society and North Carolina Conference Historical Society, 1912, pp. 66-95.

Meade, William. *Sermons, Dialogues and Narratives for Servants, To Be Read to Them in Families; Abridged, Altered, and Adapted to Their Condition*. Richmond, Va.: Office of the Southern Churchman, 1836.

Merrick, Caroline E. *Old Times in Dixie Land: A Southern Matron's Memories*. New York: The Grafton Press, 1901.

Methodist Episcopal Church. *The Methodist Almanac for the Year of Our Lord 1861*. New York: Carlton & Porter, 1860.

_____. *The Methodist Almanac for the Year of Our Lord 1862*. New York: Carlton & Porter, 1861.

_____. *The Methodist Almanac for the Year of Our Lord 1863*. New York: Carlton & Porter, 1862.

_____. *The Methodist Almanac for the Year of Our Lord 1864*. New York: Carlton & Porter, 1863.

_____. *The Methodist Almanac for the Year of Our Lord 1864*. New York: Carlton & Porter, 1863.

_____. *The Methodist Almanac for the Year of Our Lord 1865*. New York: Carlton & Porter, 1864.

_____. *The Methodist Almanac for the Year of Our Lord 1866*. New York: Carlton & Porter, 1865.

_____. *The Methodist Almanac for the Year of Our Lord 1867*. New York: Carlton & Porter, 1866.

_____. *The Methodist Almanac for the Year of Our Lord 1868*. New York: Carlton & Porter, 1867.

_____. *The Methodist Almanac for the Year of Our Lord 1869*. New York: Carlton & Lanahan, 1868.

_____. *The Methodist Almanac for the Year of Our Lord 1870*. Cincinnati: Hitchcock & Walden, [1869].

Methodist Episcopal Church, South. *Catechisms of the Methodist Episcopal Church, South*. Nashville, Tenn.: Southern Methodist Publishing House, 1861. This volume includes William Capers, *Catechism for the Use of Methodist Missions*, 3rd. ed., 1847.

_____. *A Collection of Hymns for Public, Social, and Domestic Worship*. Nashville, Tenn.: Southern Methodist Publishing House, 1860.

_____. *The Doctrines and Discipline of the Methodist Episcopal Church, South*. Nashville, Tenn.: E. Stevenson and F.A. Owen, Agents, for the Methodist Episcopal Church, South, 1855.

_____. *The Doctrines and Discipline of the Methodist Episcopal Church, South*. Nashville, Tenn.: Southern Methodist Publishing House, 1859.

_____. *The Doctrines and Discipline of the Methodist Episcopal Church, South*. Nashville, Tenn.: A.H. Redford [for the] Methodist Episcopal Church, South, 1866.

_____. *The Doctrines and Discipline of the Methodist Episcopal Church, South*. Nashville, Tenn.: Publishing House of the Methodist Episcopal Church, South, 1870.

_____. *The Doctrines and Discipline of the Methodist Episcopal Church, South*. Nashville, Tenn.: Publishing House of the Methodist Episcopal Church, South, 1874.

_____. *The Ritual, the General Rules, and Articles of Religion of the Methodist Episcopal Church, South*. Nashville, Tenn.: Southern Methodist Publishing House, 1860.

_____. *Journals of the General Conference of the Methodist Episcopal Church, South*. Nashville, Tenn.: A.H. Redford, 1866. Volume contains Journals of Conferences held in 1846, 1850, 1854, 1858, 1866.

_____. *Minutes of the Annual Conferences of the Methodist Episcopal Church, South, for the Years 1845-1846*. Richmond: John Early for the Methodist Episcopal Church, South, 1846.

_____. *Minutes of the Annual Conferences of the Methodist Episcopal Church, South, for the Years 1846-1847*. Richmond: John Early for the Methodist Episcopal Church, South, 1847.

_____. *Minutes of the Annual Conferences of the Methodist Episcopal Church, South, for the Years 1847-1848*. Richmond: John Early for the Methodist Episcopal Church, South, 1848.

_____. *Minutes of the Annual Conferences of the Methodist Episcopal Church, South, for the Years 1848-1849*. Richmond: Richmond Christian Advocate Office, 1849.

_____. *Minutes of the Annual Conferences of the Methodist Episcopal Church, South.* Volume contains Minutes for the years 1849-1850, 1850-1851(Chas. H. Wynne, Printer), 1851-1852 (Colin & Nowlan, Printers), 1852-1853, 1853-1854.

_____. *Minutes of the Annual Conferences of the Methodist Episcopal Church, South.* Volume contains Minutes for the years 1854-1855, 1855-1856,1856-1857, 1857-1858, all published in Nashville, Tenn., by E. Stevenson & F.A. Owen, Agents, for the Methodist Episcopal Church, South, in the years 1855, 1856, 1857, 1858, respectively.

_____. *Minutes of the Annual Conferences of the Methodist Episcopal Church, South.* Volume contains Minutes for the years 1861, 1862, 1863, 1864, 1865, all published in Nashville, Tenn., by Southern Methodist Publishing House, 1870.

_____. *Minutes of the Annual Conferences of the Methodist Episcopal Church, South.* Volume contains Minutes for the years 1866, 1867, 1868, 1869, 1870, 1871, 1872, all published in Nashville, Tenn., by Southern Methodist Publishing House, in the years 1870 (for Minutes 1866-1869), 1871, 1872, 1873, respectively.

_____. Mobile Conference. *Minutes of the Mobile Conference of the Methodist Episcopal Church, South, held in Tuskaloosa, Alabama, November 23-28, 1864.* Mobile: Printed at the Office of "The Army Argus and Crisis," 1864.

_____. *Minutes of the Mobile Conference of the Methodist Episcopal Church, South, held in Mobile, Alabama, November 29-December 5, 1865.* Mobile: Thompson & Powers, Printers, 1865.

_____. *Minutes of the Mobile Conference of the Methodist Episcopal Church, South, held in Marion, Alabama, December 11-16,1867.* Nashville, Tenn.: Printed at the Southern Methodist Publishing House, 1868.

_____. *Minutes of the Mobile Conference of the Methodist Episcopal Church, South, held in Meridian, Mississippi, December 2-8, 1868.* Nashville, Tenn.: Printed at the Southern Methodist Publishing House, 1869.

Methodist Episcopal Church, South, Montgomery Conference. *Minutes of the Montgomery Conference of the Methodist Episcopal Church, South, held in Tuskegee, Alabama, December 7th-13th, 1864.* Montgomery: Montgomery Advertiser Book and Job Office, 1864.

_____. *Minutes of the Montgomery Conference of the Methodist Episcopal Church, South (Second Session) held in Lowndesboro, Alabama, 1865.* n.p., n.d.

_____. *Minutes of the Montgomery Conference of the Methodist Episcopal Church, South, at Jacksonville Alabama, Commencing Wednesday, December*

5th, 1866. Montgomery, Ala.: Barrett & Brown, Book and Job Printers, 1866.

_____. *Minutes of the Montgomery Conference of the Methodist Episcopal Church, South, at Opelika, Alabama, commencing Wednesday December 4, 1867.* Montgomery, Ala.: Barrett & Brown, Book and Job Printers, 1868.

_____. *Minutes of the Montgomery Conference of the Methodist Episcopal Church, South, at Greenville, Alabama, Thursday December 9th, 1868.* Montgomery, Ala.: Barrett & Brown, Printers and Binders, 1869.

Moore, John Jamison. *History of the A.M.E. Zion Church, in America.* York, Pa.: Teachers' Journal Office, 1884.

Moore, M. H. *Sketches of the Pioneers of Methodism in North Carolina and Virginia.* Nashville, Tenn.: Southern Methodist Publishing House, 1884.

Mott, A. *Biographical Sketches and Interesting Anecdotes of Persons of Color.* New York: M. Day, Printer, 1839.

Mullin, Michael, ed. *American Negro Slavery: A Documentary History.* Columbia, S.C.: University of South Carolina Press, 1976.

[Offley, G.W.] *A Narrative of the Life and Labors of the Rev. G.W. Offley, A Colored Man, and Local Preacher.* Hartford, Conn., 1860.

Osofsky, Gilbert, ed. *Puttin' On Ole Massa: The Slave Narratives of Henry Bibb, William Wells Brown, and Solomon Northrup.* New York: Harper & Row, 1969.

Payne, Daniel A. *History of the African Methodist Episcopal Church.* Nashville, Tenn.: Publishing House of the A.M.E. Sunday-School Union, 1891.

_____. *Recollections of Seventy Years.* New York: Arno Press, [1888] 1968.

Pearson, Elizabeth Ware, ed. *Letters From Port Royal: Written at the Time of the Civil War.* Boston: W.B. Clarke, Company, 1906.

Peterson, P.A. *History of the Revisions of the Discipline of the Methodist Episcopal Church, South.* Nashville, Tenn.: Publishing House of the M.E. Church, South, 1889.

Proceedings of the Meeting in Charleston, S.C., May 13-15, 1845 on the Religious Instruction of the Negroes, Together with the Report of the Committee, and the Address to the Public. Charleston, S.C.: Published by order of the Meeting, 1845.

Pulszky, Francis and Theresa. *White, Red, Black: Sketches of American Society in the United States During the Visit of Their Guests.* New York: Johnson Reprint Corporation, [1853] 1970.

Randolph, Peter. *From Slave Cabin to the Pulpit: The Autobiography of Rev. Peter Randolph: The Southern Question Illustrated and Sketches of Slave Life.* Boston: James H. Earle, Publisher, 1893.

Reid, Whitelaw. *After the War: A Tour of the Southern States 1865-1866.* Edited by C. Vann Woodward. New York: Harper Torchbooks, 1965.

Report of the Joint Select Committee to Inquire into the Condition of Affairs in the Late Insurrectionary States. 13 vols. Washington, D.C.: Govern-ment Printing Office, 1872.

Shipp, Albert M. *The History of Methodism in South Carolina.* Nashville: Southern Methodist Publishing House, 1884.

Simms, James M. *The First Colored Baptist Church in North America.* Philadelphia: J.B. Lippincott Company, 1888.

Simpson, Matthew, ed. *Cyclopedia of Methodism.* 5th rev. ed. Philadelphia: Louis H. Evers, 1882.

Smith, Daniel E. Huger, Alice R. Huger Smith, and Arney R. Childs, eds. *Mason Smith Family Letters 1860-1868.* Columbia, S.C.: University of South Carolina Press, 1950.

[Smith, David.] *Biography of Rev. David Smith of the A.M.E. Church.* Freeport, New York: Books for Libraries Press, [1881] 1971.

Smith, George G. *The History of Georgia Methodism From 1786 to 1866.* Atlanta, Ga.: A.B. Caldwell, Publishers, 1913.

_____. *The History of Methodism in Georgia and Florida, From 1785-1865.* Macon, Ga.: Jno. W. Burke & Co., 1877.

_____. *The Life and Times of George Foster Pierce, D.D., L.L.D.* Sparta, Ga.: Hancock Publishing Company, 1888.

Smith, James L. *Autobiography of James L. Smith.* Norwich: The Bulletin Company, 1881.

Southern Baptist Convention. *Proceedings of the Southern Baptist Convention.* Nashville, Tenn.: 1845-1897.

Southern Christian Advocate. 14 August 1862-20 November 1867.

Steward, Austin. *Twenty-two Years a Slave, and Forty Years a Freeman.* New York: Negro Universities Press, [1856] 1968.

Steward, Theophilus Gould. *Fifty Years in the Gospel Ministry.* Philadelphia: n.p., n.d.

Strickland, W.P., ed. *The Genius and Mission of Methodism.* Boston: Charles H. Peirce and Company, 1851.

Sullins, D. *Recollections of an Old Man: Seventy Years in Dixie 1827-1897.* Bristol, Tenn.: The King Printing Co., 1910.

Swint, Henry L., ed. *Dear Ones at Home: Letters from Contraband Camps.* Nashville, Tenn.: Vanderbilt University Press, 1966.

Thompson, Patrick H. *The History of the Negro Baptists in Mississippi.* Jackson, Miss.: The R.W. Bailey Printing Co., 1898.

Tong, H.F. *Historical Sketches of the Baptists of Southeast Missouri.* St. Louis: National Baptist Publishing Co., 1888.

Wayman, Alexander W. *Cyclopaedia of African Methodism*. Baltimore: Methodist Episcopal Book Depository, 1882.

Wayman, A.W. *My Recollections of African M.E. Ministers, or Forty Years' Experience in the African Methodist Episcopal Church*. Philadelphia: A.M.E. Book Rooms, 1881.

West, Anson. *A History of Methodism in Alabama*. Nashville, Tenn.: Publishing House Methodist Episcopal Church, South, 1893.

Wightman, William M. *Life of William Capers, D.D., One of the Bishops of the Methodist Episcopal Church, South; Including an Autobiography*. Nashville, Tenn.: Southern Methodist Publishing House, 1859.

Wiley, Bell Irvin, ed. *Letters of Warren Akin Confederate Congressman*. Athens: University of Georgia Press, 1959.

Williams, Charles B. *A History of the Baptists in North Carolina*. Raleigh: Edwards & Broughton, 1901.

Williams, John G. *"De Ole Plantation."* Charleston, S.C.: Walker, Evans & Cogswell Co., 1895.

Wish, Harvey, ed. *Reconstruction in the South 1865-1877: First-Hand Accounts of the American Southland After the Civil War, by Northerners & Southerners*. New York: Farrar, Straus and Giroux, 1965.

Zamba. *The Life and Adventures of Zamba, an African Negro King; and His Experience of Slavery in South Carolina*. Corrected and arranged by Peter Neilson. London: Smith, Elder and Co., 1847.

LATER SPECIAL MATERIAL

Armstrong, Orland Kay. *Old Massa's People: The Old Slaves Tell Their Story*. Indianapolis: The Bobbs-Merrill Company, 1931.

Botkin, B.A., ed. *Lay My Burden Down: A Folk History of Slavery*. Chicago: University of Chicago Press, 1945.

Bragg, George Freeman, Jr. *History of the Afro-American Group of the Episcopal Church*. Baltimore: Church Advocate Press, 1922.

Carroll, J. M. *A History of Texas Baptists*. Dallas, Texas: Baptist Standard Publishing Co., 1923.

Christian, John T. *A History of the Baptists of Louisiana*. Nashville: Southern Baptist Convention, 1923.

Cooke, R.J. *History of the Ritual of the Methodist Episcopal Church With a Commentary on Its Offices*. Cincinnati: Jennings & Pye, 1900.

Coppin, L. J. *Unwritten History*. New York: Negro Universities Press, [1919] 1968.

Eppes, Mrs. Nicholas Ware. *The Negro of the Old South: A Bit of Period History*. Chicago: Joseph G. Branch Publishing Company, 1925.

Fleming, Walter L. *Civil War and Reconstruction in Alabama*. New York: The Columbia University Press, 1905.

Handy, James E. *Scraps of African Methodist Episcopal History*. Philadelphia: A.M.E. Book Concern, [1900?].

Harmon, Nolan B. *The Rites and Ritual of Episcopal Methodism: With Particular Reference to the Rituals of the Methodist Episcopal Church and the Methodist Episcopal Church, South, Respectively*. Nashville, Tenn.: Publishing House of the M.E. Church, South, 1926.

Hatcher, William E. *John Jasper: The Unmatched Negro Philosopher and Preacher*. New York: Fleming H. Revell Company, 1908.

Heard, William H. *From Slavery to the Bishopric in the A.M.E. Church*. New York: Arno Press, [1924] 1969.

Johnson, Clifton H., ed. *God Struck Me Dead: Religious Conversion Experiences and Autobiographies of Ex-Slaves*. Philadelphia: Pilgrim Press, 1969.

Leonard, Daisy Anderson. *From Slavery to Affluence: Memoirs of Robert Anderson, Ex-Slave.* Steamboat Springs, Colorado: The Steamboat Pilot, [1927] 1967.

Long, Charles Sumner. *History of The A.M.E. Church In Florida*. Philadelphia: A.M.E. Book Concern, 1939.

Macrae, David. *The Americans At Home*. New York: E.P. Dutton & Co., Inc., 1952.

Mixon, W. H. *History of the African Methodist Episcopal Church in Alabama, with Biographical Sketches*. Nashville, Tenn.: A.M.E. Church Sunday School Union, 1902.

Nicholson, Alfred W. *Brief Sketch of the Life and Labors of Rev. Alexander Bettis*. Trenton, S.C.: published by the author, 1913.

Perdue, Charles L., Jr., Thomas E. Barden, and Robert K. Phillips, eds. *Weevils in the Wheat: Interviews with Virginia Ex-Slaves*. Bloomington: Indiana University Press, 1980.

Phillips, C.H. *The History of the Colored Methodist Episcopal Church in America*. 3rd. ed. Jackson, Tenn.: Publishing House C.M.E. Church, [1898] 1925.

Plyler, A.W. *The Iron Duke of the Methodist Itinerancy: An Account of the Life and Labors of the Reverend John Tillet of North Carolina*. Nashville, Tenn.: Cokesbury Press, 1925.

Rawick, George P., ed. *The American Slave: A Composite Autobiography*. 19 vols. Westport, Conn.: Greenwood Publishing Company, 1972.

_____. *The American Slave: A Composite Autobiography*. Supplement, Series 1. 12 vols. Westport, Conn.: Greenwood Publishing Company, 1977.

_____. *The American Slave: A Composite Autobiography*. Supplement, Series 2. 10 vols. Westport, Conn.: Greenwood Publishing Company, 1979.

Riley, B.F. *A Memorial History of the Baptists of Alabama*. Philadelphia: The Judson Press, 1923.

Russell, William Howard. *My Diary North and South*. Edited by Fletcher Pratt. New York: Harper & Brothers, Publishers, 1954.

Smith, Charles Spencer. *A History of the African Methodist Episcopal Church*. Philadelphia: Book Concern of the A.M.E. Church, 1922.

Stakely, Charles A. *History of the First Baptist Church of Montgomery, Alabama*. Montgomery, Ala.: The Paragon Press, 1930.

Wallace, Jesse Thomas. *A History of the Negroes of Mississippi from 1865 to 1890*. New York: Johnson Reprint Corporation, [1927] 1970.

Washington, Booker T. *Up From Slavery*. New York: Bantam Books, [1900?] 1963.

Wright, Richard R., Jr. *Centennial Encyclopedia of the African Methodist Episcopal Church*. Philadelphia: Book Concern of the A.M.E. Church, 1916.

Yetman, Norman R. *Life Under the "Peculiar Institution": Selections from the Slave Narrative Collection*. New York: Holt, Rinehart and Winston, Inc., 1970.

SECONDARY AND ANCILLARY MATERIAL

Addo, Linda D. and James H. McCallum. *To Be Faithful to Our Heritage: A History of Black United Methodism in North Carolina*. Commissions on Archives and History, North Carolina Annual Conference, 1980.

Ahlstrom, Sydney E. *A Religious History of the American People*. 2 vols. Garden City, New York: Image Books, 1975. Vol. 2.

Alabama Historical Commission. *Alabama's Tapestry of Historic Places*. Montgomery, Ala.: Alabama Historical Commission, 1978.

Armstrong, Warren B. "Union Chaplains and the Education of the Freedmen," *The Journal of Negro History* Vol. 52, No. 2 (April 1967): 104-115.

Bacon, Leonard Woolsey. *A History of American Christianity*. New York: The Christian Literature Co., 1897.

Bailey, Kenneth K. "Protestantism and Afro-Americans in the Old South: Another Look," *The Journal of Southern History* Vol. 41, No. 4 (November 1975): 451-472.

Baptist General Convention of Texas. *Centennial Story of Texas Baptists.* Dallas: Executive Board of the Baptist General Convention of Texas, 1936.

Barclay, Wade Crawford. *Early American Methodism 1769-1844.* New York: The Board of Missions and Church Extension of the Methodist Church, 1949.

Barr, Alwyn. *Black Texans: A History of Negroes in Texas 1528-1971.* Austin, Texas: Jenkins Publishing Company, 1973.

Beauvoir, Simone de. *The Second Sex.* New York: Vintage Books, 1974.

Bentley, George R. *A History of the Freedmen's Bureau.* Philadelphia: University of Pennsylvania Press, 1955.

Bergman, Peter M. *The Chronological History of the Negro in America.* New York: Harper & Row, Publishers, 1969.

Betz, Hans Dieter. *Galatians: A Commentary on Paul's Letter to the Churches in Galatia.* Philadelphia: Fortress Press, 1979.

Blassingame, John W. *Black New Orleans, 1860-1880.* Chicago: The University of Chicago Press, 1973.

_____. *The Slave Community: Plantation Life in the Antebellum South.* New York: Oxford University Press, 1972.

_____. "Using the Testimony of Ex-Slaves: Approaches and Problems," *The Journal of Southern History* Vol. 41, No. 4 (November 1975): 473-492.

Boles, John B. *The Great Revival 1787-1805.* Lexington, Ky.: The University Press of Kentucky, 1972.

Bontemps, Arna and Hughes, Langston, eds. *The Book of Negro Folklore.* New York: Dodd, Mead & Co., 1958.

Boren, Carter E. *Religion on the Texas Frontier.* San Antonio, Texas: The Naylor Company, 1968.

Bradley, David Henry, Sr. *A History of the A.M.E. Zion Church.* Nashville, Tenn.: The Parthenon Press, 1956.

Brewer, J. Mason. *American Negro Folklore.* Chicago: Quadrangle Books, 1968.

Brown, Sterling. *Negro Poetry and Drama.* New York: Atheneum, [1937] 1978.

Bruce, Dickson D., Jr. *And They All Sang Hallelujah.* Knoxville: University of Tennessee Press, 1974.

Bucke, Emory Stevens et al. *The History of American Methodism.* 3 vols. New York: Abingdon Press, 1964.

Byrne, Donald E., Jr. *No Foot of Land: Folklore of American Methodist Itinerants*. Metuchen, N.J.: The Scarecrow Press, Inc. and The American Theological Library Association, 1975.

Carter, Dan T. "The Anatomy of Fear: The Christmas Day Insurrection Scare of 1865," *The Journal of Southern History*, Vol. 42, No. 3 (August 1976): 345-364.

Carter, Hodding. *The Angry Scar*. Garden City, New York: Doubleday & Company, Inc., 1959.

Clarke, Erskine. *Wrestlin' Jacob: A Portrait of Religion in the Old South*. Atlanta: John Knox Press, 1979.

Clinton, Catherine. *The Plantation Mistress: Women's World in the Old South*. New York: Pantheon Books, 1982.

Cone, Cecil Wayne. *The Identity Crisis in Black Theology*. Nashville: AMEC, 1975.

Culver, Dwight W. *Negro Segregation in the Methodist Church*. New Haven: Yale University Press, 1953.

Del Pino, Julius E. "Blacks in the United Methodist Church from Its Beginning to 1968," *Methodist History*, Vol. 19, No. 1 (October 1980): 3-20.

Dix, Dom Gregory. *The Shape of the Liturgy*. London: Dacre Press, 1945.

Dodd, Donald B. *Historical Atlas of Alabama*. University, Alabama: The University of Alabama Press, 1974.

Dorchester, Daniel. *Christianity in the United States from the First Settlement down to the Present Time*. New York: Phillips & Hunt, 1888.

Douglas, Mary. *Purity and Danger: An Analysis of the Concepts of Pollution and Taboo*. London: Routledge & Kegan Paul, 1966.

Drago, Edmund L. *Black Politicians and Reconstruction in Georgia: A Splendid Failure*. Baton Rouge: Louisiana State University Press, 1982.

DuBois, W.E.B. *Black Reconstruction in America, 1860-1880*. New York: Atheneum, [1935] 1973.

Eighmy, John Lee. *Churches in Cultural Captivity: A History of the Social Attitudes of Southern Baptists*. Knoxville: The University of Tennessee Press, 1972.

Epstein, Dena J. *Sinful Tunes and Spirituals: Black Folk Music to the Civil War*. Urbana, Ill.: University of Illinois Press, 1977.

Farish, Hunter Dickinson. *The Circuit Rider Dismounts: A Social History of Southern Methodism 1865-1900*. Richmond, Va.: The Dietz Press, 1938.

Feldstein, Stanley. *Once a Slave: The Slaves' View of Slavery*. New York: William Morrow and Company, Inc., 1971.

Fischer, Roger A. *The Segregation Struggle in Louisiana, 1862-77*. Urbana: University of Illinois Press, 1974.

Fisher, Miles Mark. *Negro Slave Songs in the United States*. Ithaca, N.Y.: Cornell University Press, 1953.

_____. *A Short History of the Baptist Denomination*. Nashville: Sunday School Publishing Board, 1933.

Foner, Eric, ed. *Nat Turner*. Englewood Cliffs, N.J.: Prentice-Hall, Inc., 1971.

Franklin, John Hope. *The Free Negro in North Carolina 1790-1860*. New York: W.W. Norton & Company, [1943] 1971.

_____. *From Slavery to Freedom: A History of Negro Americans*. 4th ed. New York: Alfred A. Knopf, 1974.

_____. *The Militant South, 1800-1860*. Cambridge: Belknap Press of Harvard University Press, 1956.

_____. *Reconstruction After the Civil War*. Chicago: The University of Chicago Press, 1961.

Frazier, E. Franklin. *The Negro Church in America*. New York: Schocken Books, 1974.

_____. *The Negro Family in the United States*. Chicago: The University of Chicago Press, 1966.

_____. "The Negro Slave Family," *Journal of Negro History*, Vol. 15, No. 2 (April 1930): 198-259.

Genovese, Eugene D. *Roll, Jordan, Roll*. New York: Vintage Books, 1974.

George, Carol V.R. *Segregated Sabbaths: Richard Allen and the Emergence of Independent Black Churches 1760-1840*. New York: Oxford University Press, 1973.

Gillard, John T. *The Catholic Church and the Negro*. Baltimore: St. Joseph's Society Press, 1929.

Grant, Robert M. *Augustus to Constantine*, New York: Harper & Row, 1970.

Gravely, William B. *Gilbert Haven, Methodist Abolitionist: A Study in Race, Religion, and Reform, 1850-1880*. Nashville: Abingdon Press, 1973.

_____. "The Social, Political and Religious Significance of the Formation of the Colored Methodist Episcopal Church (1870)," *Methodist History*, Vol. 18, No. 1 (October 1979): 3-25.

Gutman, Herbert G. *The Black Family in Slavery and Freedom, 1750-1925*. New York: Vintage Books, 1976.

Hall, Robert L. "Tallahassee's Black Churches, 1865-1885," *Florida Historical Quarterly*, October 1979, pp. 185-196.

Hamilton, Charles V. *The Black Preacher in America*. New York: William Morrow & Company, Inc., 1972.

Handy, Robert T. *A History of the Churches in the United States and Canada*. New York: Oxford University Press, 1977.

Harding, Vincent. *There Is a River: The Black Struggle for Freedom in America*. New York: Harcourt Brace Jovanovich, Publishers, 1981.

Hartzell, Joseph C. "Methodism and the Negro in the United States," *The Journal of Negro History*, Vol. 8, No. 3 (July 1923): 301-315.

Hatch, Roger D. "The Issue of Race and the Writing of the History of Christianity in America." Unpublished Ph.D. dissertation, University of Chicago, 1974.

Hill, Samuel S., Jr. *Southern Churches in Crisis*. New York: Holt, Rinehart and Winston, 1966.

Hill, Samuel S., Jr., Edgar T. Thompson, Anne Firor Scott, Charles Hudson, and Edwin S. Gaustad. *Religion and the Solid South*. Nashville: Abingdon Press, 1972.

Holder, Ray. *William Winans: Methodist Leader in Antebellum Mississippi*. Jackson: University Press of Mississippi, 1977.

Hudson, Winthrop S. *Religion in America*. New York: Charles Scribner's Sons, 1965.

Jackson, Luther P. "Religious Development of the Negro in Virginia from 1760 to 1860." *The Journal of Negro History*, Vol. 16, No. 2 (April 1931): 168-239.

Jackson, Margaret Young. "An Investigation of Biographies and Auto-biographies of American Slaves Published Between 1840 and 1860: Based Upon the Cornell Special Slavery Collection." Unpublished Ph.D. dissertation, Cornell University, 1954.

Johnson, Charles A. *The Frontier Camp Meeting*. Dallas: Southern Methodist University Press, 1955.

Johnson, James Weldon, and J. Rosamond Johnson. *The Books of American Negro Spirituals*. New York: The Viking Press, 1944.

Jordan, Winthrop D. *White Over Black: American Attitudes Toward the Negro 1550-1812*. Chapel Hill: The University of North Carolina Press, 1968.

Kolchin, Peter. *First Freedom: The Responses of Alabama's Blacks to Emancipation and Reconstruction*. Westport, Conn.: Greenwood Press, Publishers, 1972.

Krebs, Sylvia H. "Will the Freedmen Work? White Alabamians Adjust to Free Black Labor," *Alabama Historical Quarterly*, Vol. 36, No. 2 (Summer 1974): 151-163.

Lakey, Othal Hawthorne. *The Rise of "Colored Methodism": A Study of the Background and the Beginnings of the Christian Methodist Episcopal Church.* Dallas, Texas: Crescendo Book Publications, 1972.

Latourette, Kenneth Scott. *Christianity in a Revolutionary Age: A History of Christianity in the Nineteenth and Twentieth Centuries.* 4 vols. New York: Harper & Brothers, 1961. Vol. 3.

Lazenby, Marion Elias. *History of Methodism in Alabama and West Florida.* North Alabama Conference and Alabama-West Florida Conference of the Methodist Church, 1960.

Levine, Lawrence W. *Black Culture and Black Consciousness: Afro-American Folk Thought from Slavery to Freedom.* New York: Oxford University Press, 1977.

Litwack, Leon F. *Been in the Storm So Long: The Aftermath of Slavery.* New York: Alfred A. Knopf, 1979.

Lovell, John, Jr. *Black Song: The Forge and the Flame.* New York: The Macmillan Company, 1972.

Mathews, Donald G. "Charles Colcock Jones and the Southern Evangelical Crusade to Form a Biracial Community." *The Journal of Southern History,* Vol. 41, No. 3 (August 1975): 299-320.

_____. *Religion in the Old South.* Chicago: The University of Chicago Press, 1977.

_____. *Slavery and Methodism: A Chapter in American Morality 1780-1845.* Princeton, New Jersey: Princeton University Press, 1965.

Mays, Benjamin Elijah and Joseph William Nicholson. *The Negro's Church.* New York: Russell & Russell, 1933.

McLoughlin, William G., Jr. *Modern Revivalism.* New York: The Ronald Press Company, 1959.

Mead, Sidney E. *The Lively Experiment: The Shaping of Christianity in America.* New York: Harper & Row, 1963.

Meier, August. *Negro Thought in America, 1880-1915.* Ann Arbor: The University of Michigan Press, 1963.

Messner, William F. "Black Violence and White Response: Louisiana, 1862." *The Journal of Southern History,* Vol. 41, No. 1 (February 1975): 19-38.

Morris, Robert C. "Reading, 'Riting and Reconstruction: Freedmen's Education in the South, 1865-1870." Unpublished Ph.D. dissertation, University of Chicago, 1976.

Morrow, Ralph E. *Northern Methodism and Reconstruction.* East Lansing, Michigan: Michigan State University Press, 1956.

Murray, Andrew E. *Presbyterians and the Negro—a History.* Philadelphia: Presbyterian Historical Society, 1966.

Nelsen, Hart M., Raytha L. Yokley, and Anne K. Nelsen, eds. *The Black Church in America*. New York: Basic Books, Inc., 1971.

Niebuhr, H. Richard. *The Kingdom of God in America*. New York: Harper & Row, 1937.

O'Brien, John T. "Factory, Church, and Community: Blacks in Antebellum Richmond" *The Journal of Southern History*, Vol. 44, No. 4 (November 1978).

Odum, Howard W. and Guy B. Johnson. *The Negro and His Songs: A Study of Typical Negro Songs in the South*. New York: Negro Universities Press, [1925] 1968.

Olmstead, Clifton E. *History of Religion in the United States*. Englewood Cliffs, N.J.: Prentice-Hall, Inc., 1960.

Parris, John R. *John Wesley's Doctrine of the Sacraments*. London: The Epworth Press, 1963.

Pelt, Owen D. and Ralph Lee Smith. *The Story of the National Baptists*. New York: Vantage Press, 1960.

Phelan, Macum. *A History of Early Methodism in Texas, 1817-1866*. Nashville: Cokesbury Press, 1924.

Pipes, William H. *Say Amen, Brother! Old Time Negro Preaching: A Study in American Frustration*. Westport, Conn.: Negro Universities Press, 1970.

Posey, Walter Brownlow. *Religious Strife on the Southern Frontier*. Baton Rouge: Louisiana State University Press, 1965.

Puckett, Newbell Niles. *Folk Beliefs of the Southern Negro*. New York: Negro Universities Press, [1926] 1968.

Rabinowitz, Howard N. *Race Relations in the Urban South, 1865-1890*. New York: Oxford University Press, 1978.

Raboteau, Albert J. *Slave Religion: The "Invisible Institution" in the Antebellum South*. New York: Oxford University Press, 1978.

Rankin, Charles Hays. "The Rise of Negro Baptist Churches in the South Through the Reconstruction Period," Unpublished masters essay, New Orleans Baptist Theological Seminary, June 1955.

Redkey, Edwin S. *Black Exodus: Black Nationalist and Back-to-Africa Movements 1890-1910*. New Haven: Yale University Press, 1969.

Reimers, David M. *White Protestantism and the Negro*. New York: Oxford University Press, 1965.

Richardson, Harry V. *Dark Salvation: The Story of Methodism as It Developed Among Blacks in America*. Garden City, New York: Anchor Press/Doubleday, 1976.

Ripley, C. Peter. "The Black Family in Transition: Louisiana, 1860-1865." *The Journal of Southern History*, Vol. 41, No. 3 (August 1975): 369-380.

Rowe, Henry Kalloch. *The History of Religion in the United States*. New York: The Macmillan Company, [1924] 1928.

Rupp, Israel Daniel, ed. *History of All the Religious Denominations in the United States*. Harrisburg, Pa: John Winebrenner, V.D.M., 1849.

Savage, Horace C. *Life and Times of Bishop Isaac Lane*. Nashville: National Publication Company, 1958.

Schaff, Philip. *America: A Sketch of Its Political, Social, and Religious Character*. Cambridge, Mass.: The Belknap Press of Harvard University Press, [1855] 1961.

Schneider, A. Gregory. "Perfecting the Family of God: Religious Community and Family Values in Early American Methodism." Unpublished Ph.D. dissertation, University of Chicago, June 1981.

Sernett, Milton C. *Black Religion and American Evangelicalism: White Protestants, Plantation Missions, and the Flowering of Negro Christianity, 1787-1865*. Metuchen, N.J.: The Scarecrow Press, Inc., 1975.

Shea, John Gilmary. *A History of the Catholic Church*. New York: John G. Shea, 1890.

Shils, Edward. "Primordial, Personal, Sacred and Civil Ties." *Selected Essays by Edward Shils*. Chicago: Center for Social Organization Studies, Department of Sociology, University of Chicago, 1970.

Silvestro, Clement Mario. "None But Patriots: The Union Leagues in Civil War and Reconstruction." Unpublished Ph.D. dissertation, University of Wisconsin, January, 1959.

Singleton, George A. *The Romance of African Methodism: A Study of African Methodism: A Study of the African Methodist Episcopal Church*. New York: Exposition Press, 1952.

Smith, H. Shelton. *In His Image, But . . . : Racism in Southern Religion, 1780-1910*. Durham, N.C.: Duke University Press, 1972.

Southall, Eugene Portlette, "The Attitude of the Methodist Episcopal Church, South, toward the Negro from 1844 to 1870." *The Journal of Negro History*, Vol. 16, No. 4 (October 1931): 359-370.

Spain, Rufus B. *At Ease in Zion: A Social History of Southern Baptists, 1865-1900*. Nashville: Vanderbilt University Press, 1961.

Stampp, Kenneth M. *The Peculiar Institution*. New York: Vintage Books, 1956.

Sterkx, H.E. *Partners in Rebellion: Alabama Women in the Civil War*. Rutherford, N.J.: Fairleigh Dickinson University Press, 1970.

Sweet, William Warren. *The Methodist Episcopal Church and the Civil War*. Cincinnati: Methodist Book Concern Press, [1912].

_____. *Revivalism in America*. New York: Charles Scribner's Sons, 1944.

_____. *The Story of Religion in America*. New York: Harper & Brothers, 1930.

Thrift, Charles Tinsley. *The Trail of the Florida Circuit Rider: An Introduction to the Rise of Methodism in Middle and East Florida*. Lakeland, Fla.: The Florida Southern College Press, 1944.

Tigert, J. J., IV. *Bishop Holland Nimmons McTyeire: Ecclesiastical and Educational Architect*. Nashville: Vanderbilt University Press, 1955.

Tindall, George Brown. *South Carolina Negroes 1877-1900*. Baton Rouge: Louisiana State University Press, 1966.

Trelease, Allen W. *White Terror: The Ku Klux Klan Conspiracy and Southern Reconstruction*. New York: Harper & Row, Publishers, 1971.

Vernon, Walter N. *Methodism Moves Across North Texas*. Dallas, Texas: The Historical Society, North Texas Conference, The Methodist Church, 1967.

Wade, Richard C. *Slavery in the Cities: The South 1820-1860*. New York: Oxford University Press, 1964.

Walker, Clarence E. *A Rock in a Weary Land: The African Methodist Episcopal Church During the Civil War and Reconstruction*. Baton Rouge: Louisiana State University Press, 1982.

Walls, William J. *The African Methodist Episcopal Zion Church: Reality of the Black Church*. Charlotte, North Carolina: A.M.E. Zion Publishing House, 1974.

Washington, Joseph R. Jr, "Black Folk Religion," in David Edwin Harrell, Jr., ed., *Varieties of Southern Evangelicalism*. Macon, Ga.: Mercer University Press, 1981.

_____. *Black Religion: The Negro and Christianity in the United States*. Boston: Beacon Press, 1964.

Webber, Thomas L. *Deep Like the Rivers: Education in the Slave Quarter Community 1831-1865*. New York: W.W. Norton & Company, Inc., 1978.

Weber, Max. *Ancient Judaism*. New York: The Free Press, 1952.

_____. *From Max Weber: Essays in Sociology*. Edited by H.H. Gerth and C. Wright Mills. New York: Oxford University Press, 1946.

_____. *The Religion of India*. New York: The Free Press, 1958.

_____. *The Sociology of Religion*. Boston: Beacon Press, 1964.

_____. *The Theory of Social and Economic Organization*. New York: The Free Press, 1964.

Weisberger, Bernard A. *They Gathered at the River*. Boston: Little, Brown and Company, 1958.

Wharton, Vernon Lane. *The Negro in Mississippi 1865-1890*. New York: Harper & Row, [1947] 1965.

White, Newman I. *American Negro Folk-Songs*. Hatboro, Pa.: Folklore Associates, Inc., [1928] 1965.

Williams, Thomas Leonard. "The Methodist Mission to the Slaves." Unpublished Ph.D. dissertation, Yale University, 1943.

Wilmore, Gayraud S. *Black Religion and Black Radicalism*. Garden City, N.Y.: Anchor Press/Doubleday, 1973.

Wilson, Charles Reagan. *Baptized in Blood: The Religion of the Lost Cause, 1865-1920*. Athens, Ga.: The University of Georgia Press, 1980.

_____. "The Religion of the Lost Cause: Ritual and Organization of the Southern Civil Religion, 1865-1920." *The Journal of Southern History*, Vol. 46, No. 2 (May 1980): 219-238.

Woodward, C. Vann. *The Strange Career of Jim Crow*. 2nd rev. ed. New York: Oxford University Press, 1966.

Wright, Bishop Richard R., Jr. *The Bishops of the African Methodist Episcopal Church*. Nashville: The A.M.E. Sunday School Union, 1963.

Index

Chicago Studies in the History of American Religion

Editors

JERALD C. BRAUER & MARTIN E. MARTY

(continued, over)